T0214791

Lecture Notes in Artificial Intelligence   12462

Subseries of Lecture Notes in Computer Science

More information about this series at http://www.springer.com/series/1244

Claude Frasson · Panagiotis Bamidis ·
Panagiotis Vlamos (Eds.)

Brain Function Assessment in Learning

Second International Conference, BFAL 2020
Heraklion, Crete, Greece, October 9–11, 2020
Proceedings

Springer

Editors
Claude Frasson
Department of Computer Science
University of Montreal
Montreal, QC, Canada

Panagiotis Bamidis ⓘ
Lab of Medical Physics
Aristotle University of Thessaloniki
Thessaloniki, Greece

Panagiotis Vlamos
Department of Informatics
Ionian University
Corfu, Greece

ISSN 0302-9743   ISSN 1611-3349 (electronic)
Lecture Notes in Artificial Intelligence
ISBN 978-3-030-60734-0   ISBN 978-3-030-60735-7 (eBook)
https://doi.org/10.1007/978-3-030-60735-7

LNCS Sublibrary: SL7 – Artificial Intelligence

This Springer imprint is published by the registered company Springer Nature Switzerland AG
The registered company address is: Gewerbestrasse 11, 6330 Cham, Switzerland

Preface

This volume contains the refereed papers presented at the Second International Conference on Brain Function Assessment in Learning (BFAL 2020). The BFAL conference addresses a multidisciplinary domain which regroups specialists in neuroscience, computer science, medicine, education, human-computer interactions, and social interaction. It promotes a cross-disciplinary approach to better understanding how to use the brain's capabilities to improve cognition and learning. The convergence of cognitive studies, tools of artificial intelligence, neuroscience approaches, and health applications opens a new era of multidisciplinary research tracks. The emergence of new assessment devices allows new ways of experimentation in laboratories, with light, non-intrusive, and low-cost sensors.

The call for scientific papers focused on a variety of topics of interest, including, but not limited to:

- Alzheimer's and Related Disorders
- Bioethics
- Biofeedback Systems
- Biometric Systems
- Brain Activity and Neurocognitive Functions
- Brain-Computational Mechanisms
- Brain Control for Learning
- Brain Data Extraction
- Brain Imaging
- Brain Plasticity
- Brain Training
- Consciousness and Social Behaviors
- Data Mining
- Emotional Processes in Learning and Memory
- Internet of Things
- Human-Computer Interface
- Healthcare Applications
- Image Processing
- Intelligent Environments
- Intelligent Training
- Intelligent Agents
- Intelligent Video Games
- Memory Neural Processes
- Mental Health
- Neurocognitive Development
- Neurolinguistics

- Sleep, Plasticity, and Memory
- Social Cognition
- Virtual Reality

The conference gave the researchers the opportunity to examine multiple applications of brain function assessment in learning – mainly in the education and health fields – which are becoming more and more promising, initiating an exchange of ideas on important open questions. For example, what is the role of virtual reality in medical training, for Alzheimer treatment, or for virtual patients? How can brain assessment foster serendipitous learning, considering a set of cooperative viewpoints? How can EEG help to distinguish between writing and typing? How can gesture recognition be useful for Alzheimer behavior? How can brain function analysis and technology improve dyslexia and autism? How can mobile technology improve mild cognitive impairment? What is the influence of emotions in medical education? What are adults stress responses to unexpected tasks? How can brain-based quiz games improve cognitive functions? How can mathematical problem solving and fuzzy logic improve learning? What is the role of neuroscience to knowledge transformation and distance learning?

There were 35 submissions. Each submission was reviewed by at least 1, and on average 2.1, Program Committee (PC) members, according to a double-blind process. The PC decided to accept 11 full papers leading to an acceptance rate of 31%. 10 additional short papers were accepted, building a complete and well-balanced program structured into two main sections: Neural Assessment and Learning.

BFAL 2020 was initially scheduled to take place in Heraklion, Greece, as a side-event of the GENEDIS 2020 conference. However, due to COVID-19 related constraints, the conference was held as an online event. The hosting institution of the conference was the University of West Attica, Greece, under the auspices of the Institute of Intelligent Systems (IIS).

We would like to express our gratitude to many different contributors for the success of the BFAL 2020 conference:

- All the authors for presenting original and high-quality research work, promoting innovation in the fields of Neural Assessment and Learning.
- The keynote speakers, Dr. Themis Exarchos, Dr. Anastasios Mikropoulos, and Dr. Dimitrios Vlachakis for honoring the conference with their input to the vibrant scientific discourse of the conference.
- The members of the PC for their constructive work in making suggestions and improvements to the papers.
- The program chairs for their devoted work towards the success of the conference.
- The University of West Attica for hosting this conference virtually, with special thanks to the Vice Rector, Prof. Cleo Sgouropoulou.
- The GENEDIS conference, and in particular Dr. Panagiotis Vlamos for inviting BFAL 2020 as a side-event.
- The organization team of NEOANALYSIS, and in particular Dr. Kitty Panourgia (organization chair), Elisavet Vasileiou, Isaak Tselepis, and Aggelos Amarantos.

We would like to emphasize that the BFAL 2020 conference series opens challenging yet intriguing endeavors in the original and multidisciplinary sphere of Brain Function Assessment in Learning, and we look forward to the next BFAL conference.

August 2020

Panagiotis Bamidis
Claude Frasson
Panagiotis Vlamos

Organization

Program Committee

Program Committee Chairs

Panagiotis Bamidis	Aristotle University of Thessaloniki, Greece
Claude Frasson	University of Montreal, Canada
Panagiotis Vlamos	Ionian University, Greece

Program Committee Members

Herve Abdi	The University of Texas at Dallas, USA
Panagiotis Bamidis	Aristotle University of Thessaloniki, Greece
Sylvie Belleville	Institut universitaire de gériatrie de Montréal, Canada
Anastasios Bezerianos	National University of Singapore, Singapore
Tassos Bountis	Nazarbayev University, Kazakhstan
Stefano A. Cerri	LIRMM, University of Montpellier, CNRS, France
Sergio Cruces	University of Seville, Spain
Daniela Giordano	University of Catania, Italy
Irini Giannopoulou	Bond University, Australia
Foteini Grivokostopoulou	University of Patras, Greece
Peter Groumpos	University of Patras, Greece
Claude Frasson	University of Montreal, Canada
Ioannis Hatzilygeroudis	University of Patras, Greece
Pengyu Hong	Brandeis University, USA
Andreas Ioannides	AAI Scientific Cultural Service Ltd, Cyprus
Manousos A. Klados	The University of Sheffield, UK
Stathis Konstantinidis	University of Nottingham, UK
George Kostopoulos	University of Patras, Greece
Wentai Liu	UCLA, USA
Alessandro Micarelli	Roma Tre University, Italy
Maria Moundridou	School of Pedagogical and Technological Education (ASPETE), Greece
Phoivos Mylonas	National Technical University of Athens, Greece
Philippe Robert	Nice University Hospital Center, France
Christos Schizas	University of Cyprus, Cyprus
Cleo Sgouropoulou	University of West Attica, Greece
Andrzej Skowron	University of Warsaw, Poland
Stefan Trausan-Matu	University POLITEHNICA of Bucharest, Romania
Arjen Vanooyen	University of Utrecht, The Netherlands

Jayalakshmi Viswanathan	University of Maryland, USA
Ana Vivas	The University of Sheffield, UK
Panagiotis Vlamos	Ionian University, Greece

Organization Committee

| Kitty Panourgia | Neoanalysis Ltd, Greece |

Abstract of Invited Talks

Decision Support Systems in Neurodegenerative Diseases Diagnosis, Treatment and Management

Themis Exarchos

Department of Informatics, Ionian University, 49100, Corfu, Greece
exarchos@ionio.gr

Abstract. Neurodegenerative diseases are an heterogeneous group of disorders that are characterized by the progressive degeneration of the structure and function of the central or peripheral nervous system. The most common ones include Alzheimer's disease and Parkinson's disease. The presentation will focus on the most recent achievements and research results of decision support systems, both defined using data driven as well as knowledge based methods towards the diagnosis, treatment, and management of the most common neurodegenerative disorders. Systems, platforms, and methodologies employing typical clinical data, wearable, or ambient sensors, as well as more complex omics information will be presented, with the advantages and disadvantages of each.

Keywords: Decision support systems · Neurodegenerative diseases · Diagnosis · treatment · Management

Educational Neuroscience in General and Special Education

Anastasios Tassos Mikropoulos

The Educational Approaches to Virtual Reality Technologies Laboratory,
University of Ioannina, Ioannina, Greece

In neuroscience, learning can be described as the process of creating neural connections in response to external stimuli; accordingly, education is defined as the process of creating and controlling these external stimuli. The basis of educational neuroscience is that anything that influences learning has its foundation in the human brain. Neuroscientific methods act collaboratively with the methodology of social sciences and contribute to the field of education. Under this framework, EEG signals were used to investigate how feedback could be best incorporated in a digital educational game. Our findings showed that the auditory feedback was preferred compared to visual, because the alpha and beta brain oscillations of participants were increased. In special education, our results from a study with Auditory Evoked Potentials showed that visually impaired individuals processed auditory stimuli faster, regardless if these lacked semantic content, in comparison to their non-visually impaired counterparts, since the N400 component was presented earlier in the waveforms of visually impaired individuals. Findings like these indicate that the understanding of the way the human brain functions could affect instructional practices and provide a conceptual framework of how the human brain creates cognitive schemata.

Introducing Drugonfly; A Novel Computer-Aided Drug Repurposing Pipeline Based on Genomic, Structural and Physicochemical Profiles

Dimitrios Vlachakis[1,2,3] ⓘ

[1] Genetics and Computational Biology Group, Laboratory
of Genetics, Department of Biotechnology, School of Applied
Biology and Biotechnology, Agricultural University of Athens, era Odos 75 Str.
11855, Athens, Greece
[2] Laboratory of Molecular Endocrinology, Division of Endocrinology and
Metabolism, Center of Clinical, Experimental Surgery and Translational
Research, Biomedical Research Foundation of the Academy of Athens, Soranou
Ephessiou Str., 11527, Athens, Greece
[3] University Research Institute of Maternal and Child Health and Precision
Medicine, Medical School, National and Kapodistrian University of Athens,
hivon 1 & Papadiamantopoulou Str. 11527, Athens, Greece

Abstract. Herein, we are proposing a novel and radical pipeline that will facilitate the repurposing of approved drugs in an unprecedented way that will eventually yield invaluable insights and results that will aid the pharma-medical domain to tackle many more pathologies using weaponry that has already been approved, is safe for the public, is very rapid relative to conventional drug design, and requires no further significant investment to be made. The ultimate goal is to develop a novel clinical concept and establish a computer-aided pipeline that will facilitate and rationalize the repurposing of approved drugs, orphan drugs, and generics. The end result of the described pipeline is a competitive and reliable software that will be made available for the scientific community.

Keywords: Drug design · Drug repurposing · Bioinformatics · Metagenomics · Data mining · Data analytics

Contents

Learning

Neural Assessment

The Role of Medical Error and the Emotions it Induces in Learning – A Study Using Virtual Patients

Maria-Revekka Kyriakidou[ID], Panagiotis Antoniou[(⊠)][ID], George Arfaras[ID], and Panagiotis Bamidis[ID]

Lab of Medical Physics, School of Medicine, Faculty of Health Sciences, Aristotle University of Thessaloniki, Thessaloniki, Greece
mariareveccak@gmail.com, pantonio@otenet.gr,
georgearfaras@gmail.com, pdbamidis@gmail.com

Abstract. Virtual Patients (VPs) and Affective Learning are promising tools in the research for enhancement of educational efficacy. The purpose of this research is to explore the effect of medical error and the emotions it evokes on learning by using these tools.

A sample of four undergraduate medical students took part in the experiment. Each student managed two VPs, while connected to biosignal recording devices (heart rate, skin conductance, brain activity, pupil diameter). Before and after managing the VPs, each student filled in a sheet for each VP, containing one competence self-evaluation question and one knowledge assessment question, so that possible differences in their responses could be spotted.

The results showed that: a) medical errors with VPs can probably have slight effects on the affect state as indicated by the biosignals, b) some of the errors made by the students with virtual patients did contribute to learning – for the rest of the errors there were no control questions. This research was unable to establish a correlation between the affect state following an error and the learning outcome.

Keywords: Medical error · Medical education · Virtual patients · Biosignals · Emotion detection · Affective learning

1 Introduction

1.1 Virtual Patients in Medical Education

Medical students develop their clinical and patient management skills mainly by practice on real patients during their residency. This policy poses risks for the safety of patients [1]. Technology provides several tools for alleviating this risk [2]. To address this issue, solving medical cases with virtual patients has been proposed as complementary training for medical students [3, 4]. The term virtual patients (VP) refers to an interactive computer simulation of real clinical case scenarios aiming at medical training, education and evaluation [5]. In this environment students can safely train on real

© Springer Nature Switzerland AG 2020
C. Frasson et al. (Eds.): BFAL 2020, LNAI 12462, pp. 3–12, 2020.
https://doi.org/10.1007/978-3-030-60735-7_1

problems, examine and clinically manage virtual patients, make mistakes and learn from them (error-management training), thus allowing for active learning [6, 7]. Moreover, the immediate feedback given to the students, as they are shown the consequences of their decisions in real time, helps them realize their knowledge gaps. That gives them an opportunity to reflect upon their mistakes and adapt their learning so that they fill their knowledge gaps [8]. Such scenarios allow exploring the impact of affected states on learning as well as using modification of affected states to further develop competency [6]. VPs have become rather established in medical education after an initial acceptance period [9, 10] and have been enhanced with several "ease of use" technological provisions such as semantic annotations for machine discoverability and repurposing potential [11].

1.2 Affective Computing and Learning

Affective Computing is about designing and developing systems that can interpret and respond to human emotions. It expands Human-Computer Interaction by including tools which recognize the user's emotions [12]. So, the main goal is the accurate detection and recognition of the affect state, as this would allow computers to recognize human emotions in real time and react accordingly [13].

The relation between Affective Computing and learning is known as Affective Learning and it is demonstrated by technologies which during the learning procedure perceive affect states and respond to them in order to facilitate transfer of knowledge and skill development [14]. Affect state detection during the learning procedure can help enhance interest and participation of learners in ways formerly impossible [15].

The use of biosignal sensors, such as an EEG device, could allow educational systems to identify affect states, to better understand students' nonverbal reactions [15] and to inform students about the state they are in [14]. This way, students can reflect upon the impact of their affect state on their learning and adapt it accordingly. For instance, a computer which detects that the student makes a mistake, albeit he is focused, could let him carry on, as his mistakes might help him learn better. However, if the student is nervous and repeats his mistakes, the computer could inform him about his affect state, so that he is motivated to employ a different strategy [14].

It has been attempted in several studies to detect affect states of humans exposed to stimuli (auditory-visual stimuli, during car driving, etc.) by monitoring their physiological reactions (biosignals), using encephalography (EEG), electrocardiography etc. [16]. Generally, it seems that accuracy in emotion detection is better when more methods of recording biosignals are combined [13].

In medical training there are platforms (e.g. Open Labyrinth [11]) which provide simulations of medical cases. Students try to solve the medical cases, relying on their judgement to make each time the best possible decision, while experiencing at the same time the consequences of their mistakes. As a result, emotions are aroused, which can be identified by biosignal recording devices [6].

This aim of this paper is to explore the effect of medical error and the emotions it evokes on learning. Specifically, we set out to explore the following research questions:

1. Could a medical error within a VP scenario elicit emotions to medical students?

2. Could these emotions (if and once evoked) have an effect on students' learning (competence self-evaluation and knowledge assessment)?

The paper is structured as follows: After this brief introduction, the Methodology section describes the technological and research toolsets and procedures that were used for this work. The Results section presents the direct outcomes of this experimental work and the Discussion section explores the interpretation of the principal results as well as their impact and limitations for future research.

2   Methodology

2.1   Sample

The research was conducted in two distinct phases: the pilot phase and the main phase.

In the pilot phase there was a call for volunteer participants among students in the 5th or 6th year of study, making sure they already had been taught basic Pediatrics, since the VPs they would have to manage were all pediatric. Three students responded: two in the 10th semester (male, 23, and female, 24) and one in the 12th (male, 24).

In the main phase there was a call for volunteer participants from earlier years of study, since it was found in the pilot phase that students from later years did not make many errors. Four students responded, two in the 2nd semester (male, 28, and male, 19), one in the 4th (female, 25) and one in the 6th (female, 25). None of them had any knowledge of Pediatrics.

Having been briefed about the research purpose and the experimental procedure, all students signed a declaration of consent. Finally, data anonymization was performed.

2.2   Emotion Arousal Tools - Educational Environment

Virtual patients. The educational intervention and emotion arousal tool were 10 virtual patients, selected among the 59 created by faculty members of the Department and loaded on the OpenLabyrinth platform. The selection of VPs was based on two conditions: a) they should be pediatric cases, and b) each node should clearly and emphatically set off the right choice from the wrong, in order to trigger emotions to the participants more efficiently. OpenLabyrinth is an online activity modelling system that allows users to build interactive educational activities such as virtual patients, simulations, games, mazes and algorithms [17]. Depending on the decisions the user makes each time, the scenario takes a different path.

2.3   Data Collection Methods and Tools

Brief Description of Biosignal Recording Tools. The following biosignal recording tools were used to detect the subjects' affect state:

Emotiv EPOC+ is a portable electroencephalography device. It consists of 14 channels with gold-plated electrodes to record electrical signals produced by the brain to detect cognitive function, emotions, and user expressions [18]. Emotiv BCI is the program that analyzes the generated electroencephalogram and translates it into emotional responses (stress, engagement, excitement, attention, interest, relaxation) through its internal algorithms. These responses are displayed on the computer screen in real time as numeric values in percentage of relative intensity (0%–100%), updated every 10 s (0.1 Hz).

The Empatica E4 wristband is a portable wireless device designed for easy, continuous and real-time collection of biosignals. Heart Rate (HR) is measured via photoplethysmography with a sampling rate of 1 Hz. Electrodermal activity (EDA) is measured with a sampling rate of 4 Hz and indicates the subject's perspiration level [19].

The Gazepoint 3 eye tracker is a handy, high-performance ocular tracker. The ophthalmic detector detects two features of the eye: the corneal reflex and the pupillary light reflex (pupillometry), with a sampling rate of 60 Hz [20].

Competence Self-evaluation and Knowledge Assessment Sheets. For the evaluation of the learning outcome, competence self-evaluation questions (subjective measurement) and knowledge assessment questions were used. Both were created by a medical doctor, faculty member of the Department. A sheet was created for every VP, containing one question of competence self-evaluation and one question of knowledge assessment.

2.4   Procedure

Pilot Phase. To assess the virtual environment and the questionnaires, in order to reveal and timely deal with possible underlying problems, a pilot research involving three participants was carried out.

The experimental procedure lasted about half an hour for every student and consisted of five stages:

1. The participant randomly selects a folder containing competence self-evaluation and knowledge assessment sheets for the two VPs he/she is going to treat and fills in one batch (pre-test).
2. The three biosignal recording devices (GP3 eyetracker, EMOTIV EPOC+, Empatica E4) are installed.
3. The participant rests for 10 min, to provide a biosignal recording in relaxed state.
4. The participant treats two VPs, while his emotional reactions are being recorded by the three devices described above. Specifically, the student reads the initial screen of the VP and decides on a course of action to deal with the case, selecting from a number of given choices. His decision leads him to the next screen of the VP scenario. The treatment of the first VP is completed when the student arrives at the screen that offers no more choices. The same procedure is repeated for the second VP.
5. The procedure is completed with the student filling the second batch of the competence self-evaluation and knowledge assessment sheets (post-test).

Main Phase (4 Participants). The pilot phase proved one of the VPs as most suitable for this research (based on the large number of errors made by one participant – no errors were made with the other VPs). So, it was decided for the main phase that each participant is assigned two preselected VPs rather than left to randomly select two. Apparently, one of the preselected VPs was the one picked out from the pilot phase as the most suitable. The other was suggested by a medical doctor, an associate of the institution. Both were modified by the associate doctor so that the feedback given to the participant after each error is more intense; this way it is more likely to upset the participant and trigger detectable changes to his biosignals. Other than that, the experimental procedure ran exactly as in the pilot phase.

2.5 Data Processing

Since the size of the sample was quite small, there was no point in performing statistical analysis. Instead, descriptive statistics were used.

In order to answer the first research question, there was a check for change in biosignals immediately after the occurrence of every medical error. Changes in biosignals indicated changes in the student's affect state. One of the participants in the pilot phase was excluded from the biosignal analysis, because most of the subject's biosignals were missing (the encephalogram failed due to the subject's cochlear implant, and the Pupillometry failed due to the subject's constant wiggle).

Regarding the second research question, the students' answers on the competence self-evaluation and knowledge assessment sheets before solving the medical cases were compared with the corresponding answers after, and, where they differed, a correlation with the students' emotions when they made errors was sought.

3 Results

3.1 Biosignals

The following Figs. (1, 2, 3, 4 and 5) show node values (means of the values within each node) for the students' biosignals recorded while they treated two VPs each. Positive

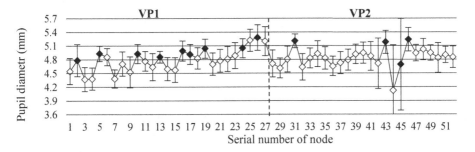

Fig. 1. Pupillometry of subject VPEL002

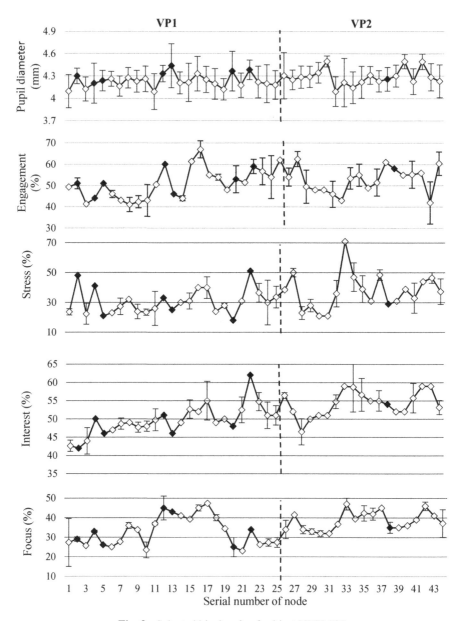

Fig. 2. Selected biosignals of subject VPEL005

nodes (those following a correct decision) are depicted in white and negative nodes (those following a wrong decision) in black. Standard deviation lines have been added. The diagrams for HR and EDA are not presented because they did not show any significant variations. For the same reason or for reasons of technical problems and unreliability some diagrams relating to components of the EEG have been omitted.

Pilot Phase. Worth noting is the Pupillometry of VPEL002 which shows pupil dilation almost after every error (Fig. 1).

Main Phase. Examination of the biosignals of VPEL005 reveals a simultaneous variation in many or all the biosignals at certain negative nodes (Fig. 2).

VPEL004 shows greater pupil dilation after a certain error (Fig. 3).

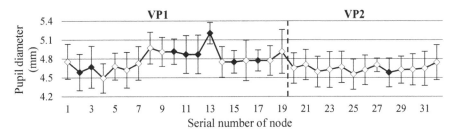

Fig. 3. Pupillometry of subject VPEL004

The Pupillometry for VPEL006 shows greater variation at two negative nodes (Fig. 4).

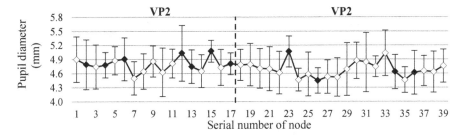

Fig. 4. Pupillometry of subject VPEL006

VPEL007 shows greater pupil dilation (Pupillometry) and, at the same time, greater drop of relaxation (Emotiv) at a certain negative node (Fig. 5).

3.2 Competence Self-evaluation

Except for VPEL007 with the first VP, all other answers claim equal (2 answers) or greater (5 answers) competence to deal with the case, after treating the relevant VP (Fig. 6).

3.3 Knowledge Assessment

All the students corrected their answers to the knowledge assessment questions after treating the VPs, except for VPEL006, who answered correctly the question for VP2 both before and after treating the VPs.

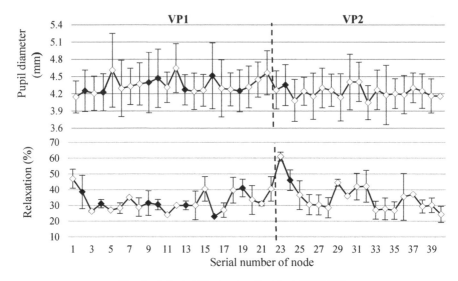

Fig. 5. Selected biosignals of subject VPEL007

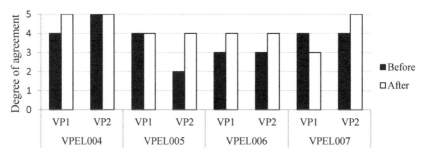

Fig. 6. Degree of agreement stated by VPEL004, VPEL005, VPEL006, VPEL007 to the statement «I feel I can deal with…» before and after treatment of the two VPs in a five-level Likert scale: 1 = strongly disagree, 2 = disagree, 3 = neither agree nor disagree, 4 = agree, 5 = strongly agree

4   Discussion

This study attempted to find correlations between three parameters: medical error, emotion during medical error occurrence, and the effect on learning outcomes. Results showed that: a) medical error with virtual patients is likely to cause mild changes in emotional state as shown by biosignals, b) some of the errors students made with virtual patients probably contributed to learning – for the rest of the errors there was no control question.

The results of the present study agree in part with those of other studies insofar as it confirms that mistakes aid learning, but do not prove the role of emotions as a mediator in learning. Previous research has indicated that mistakes cause negative emotions that affect learning [21, 22].

The absence of significant changes in the students' biosignals when informed by the system that they were wrong may indicate that, were there some changes in their emotional state, their intensity was mild, while in other cases their emotional state remained neutral. However, it is worth noting that this hypothesis is in line with the findings of Vogel & Schwabe research [23], which showed that mild and short-term stress facilitates learning, while high-intensity and chronic stress has adverse effects on learning. Similar results were obtained by Zhao [22].

A significant limitation of the study was the small sample size (n = 4), which did not allow statistical tests to be carried out and safe conclusions to be drawn. However, it must be noted that the high volume of data epochs analyzed in each specific subject provide a solid basis for the aforementioned qualitative results.

The VPs used in this study allow return to the previous node, so when students made a wrong decision they knew they could correct it by returning and making another choice. This worked unfavorably to the immersion in the educational environment. Also, some EEG measurements were considered unreliable due to poor contact of some electrodes.

Future research should provide more solid conclusions by increasing the sample of participants. In addition, the problem of immersion of learners can be addressed by using Virtual Patients in Virtual/Mixed Reality environments.

Finally, learning following VP scenarios could be monitored by repeating a VP scenario session after a reasonable time, instead of self-evaluation and knowledge assessment sheets. This way, not only the process would be simpler, but also the participant's choices would be checked one by one and not just by random sampling, as do the questionnaires.

References

1. Young, J.Q., Ranji, S.R., Wachter, R.M., Lee, C.M., Niehaus, B., Auerbach, A.D.: "July effect": impact of the academic year-end changeover on patient outcomes: a systematic review. Ann. Intern. Med. **155**, 309–315 (2011). https://doi.org/10.7326/0003-4819-155-5-201109 060-00354
2. Bamidis, P., Dimitrova, V., Treasure-Jones, T., Poulton, T., Roberts, T.: Augmented Minds: Technology's role in supporting 21st Century Doctors. Work. Eur. TEL Work. Learn. Prof. Dev. (2017)
3. Bradley, P.: The history of simulation in medical education and possible future directions. Med. Educ. **40**, 254–262 (2006). https://doi.org/10.1111/j.1365-2929.2006.02394.x
4. Bamidis, P.D., Abakassova, G., Poulton, T.: Guest editorial: medical curricula transformations – EPBLNET. Mefanet J. **5**, 4–5 (2011)
5. Ellaway, R., Candler, C., Greene, P., Smothers, V.: An architectural model for MedBiquitous virtual patients. MedBiquitous, pp. 1–15 (2006)
6. Bamidis, P.D.: Brain Function Assessment in Learning. In: Frasson, C., Kostopoulos, G. (eds.) First International Conference, Brain Function Assessment in Learning. Springer International Publishing, Patras (2017). https://doi.org/10.1007/978-3-319-67615-9
7. Eva, K.W.: Diagnostic error in medical education: where wrongs can make rights. Adv. Heal. Sci. Educ. **14**, 71–81 (2009). https://doi.org/10.1007/s10459-009-9188-9
8. Kopp, V., Stark, R., Fischer, M.R.: Fostering diagnostic knowledge through computer-supported, case-based worked examples: effects of erroneous examples and feedback. Med. Educ. **42**, 823–829 (2008). https://doi.org/10.1111/j.1365-2923.2008.03122.x

9. Poulton, T., Balasubramaniam, C.: Virtual patients: a year of change. Med. Teach. **33**, 933–937 (2011). https://doi.org/10.3109/0142159X.2011.613501

10. Dafli, E., Fountoukidis, I., Hatzisevastou, C., Bamidis, P.D.: Curricular integration of virtual patients: a unifying perspective of medical teachers and students. BMC Med. Educ. **19**, 1–11 (2019). https://doi.org/10.1186/s12909-019-1849-7

11. Dafli, E., Antoniou, P., Ioannidis, L., Dombros, N., Topps, D., Bamidis, P.D.: Virtual patients on the semantic web: a proof-of-application study. J. Med. Internet Res. **17**, e16 (2015). https://doi.org/10.2196/jmir.3933

12. Picard, R.W.: Affective Computing for HCI. In: Proceedings 8th HCI Int. Human-Computer Interact. Ergon. User Interfaces. 829–833 (1999)

13. Gouizi, K., Bereksi Reguig, F., Maaoui, C.: Emotion recognition from physiological signals. J. Med. Eng. Technol. **35**, 300–307 (2011). https://doi.org/10.3109/03091902.2011.601784

14. Picard, R.W., et al.: Affective learning - a manifesto. BT Technol. J. **22**, 253–268 (2004). https://doi.org/10.1023/B:BTTJ.0000047603.37042.33

15. Menezes, M.L.R., et al.: Towards emotion recognition for virtual environments: an evaluation of eeg features on benchmark dataset. Pers. Ubiquit. Comput. **21**(6), 1003–1013 (2017). https://doi.org/10.1007/s00779-017-1072-7

16. Kusserow, M., Amft, O., Tröster, G.: Monitoring stress arousal in the wild. IEEE Pervasive Comput. **12**, 28–37 (2013). https://doi.org/10.1109/MPRV.2012.56

17. OpenLabyrinth: User Guide version 3.2.1 (2014). http://demo.openlabyrinth.ca/documents/UserGuide.pdf

18. Emotiv web page. https://www.emotiv.com/

19. Empatica E4 product page. https://www.empatica.com/en-eu/research/e4/

20. Gazepoint GP3 product page. https://www.gazept.com/product/gazepoint-gp3-eye-tracker/

21. Edmondson, A.C.: Learning from mistakes is easier said than done: group and organizational influences on the detection and correction of human error. J. Appl. Behav. Sci. **40**, 66–90 (2004). https://doi.org/10.1177/0021886304263849

22. Zhao, B.: Learning from errors: the role of context, emotion, and personality. J. Internet Bank. Commer. **32**, 435–463 (2011). https://doi.org/10.1002/job

23. Vogel, S., Schwabe, L.: Learning and memory under stress: implications for the classroom. npj Sci. Learn. **1**, 1–10 (2016). https://doi.org/10.1038/npjscilearn.2016.11

Virtual Reality Orientation Game for Alzheimer's Disease Using Real-Time Help System

Manish Kumar Jha[1]([✉]), Hamdi Ben Abdessalem[1], Marwa Boukadida[1],
Alexie Byrns[1], Marc Cuesta[2], Marie-Andrée Bruneau[2], Sylvie Belleville[2],
and Claude Frasson[1]

[1] Département d'Informatique et de Recherche Opérationnelle, Université de Montréal,
Montréal, Canada
{manish.jha,hamdi.ben.abdessalem,marwa.boukadida,
alexie.byrns}@umontreal.ca, frasson@iro.umontreal.ca
[2] Centre de Recherche de l'Institut de Gériatrie de Montréal, Montréal, Canada
marc.cuesta@criugm.qc.ca,
{marie.andree.bruneau,sylvie.belleville}@umontreal.ca

Abstract. Studies support cognitive training as a potentially efficient method to postpone cognitive decline in persons with mild cognitive impairment (MCI). Virtual reality (VR) based serious games have found application in this field due to high level of immersion and interaction possible with the environment. We propose a fully immersive virtual reality 3D orientation game with real-time guidance system for training of elder adults. We studied the immediate after-effects of playing the orientation game on memory and attention abilities. After playing the game, participants performed better in memory exercises compared to attention exercises. The game was equipped with a real time guidance system to help the participants complete the tasks in the game. We noticed that certain hints which displayed positive messages or were easier to comprehend, helped in reducing frustration. On the other hand, hints which gave a warning message or were more difficult to follow, caused frustration to increase.

Keywords: Guidance system · Orientation · Game adaptation · Virtual reality · EEG

1 Introduction

Spatial navigation, an application of higher cognitive functions, is a key part of human life and is essential for carrying out activities every day. Allison et al. [1] showed that early-stage symptomatic Alzheimer's Disease (AD) related deficits in the aspects of spatial navigation for the use of both wayfinding and route learning strategies. According to the cognitive map theory, the formation of representations of spatial information using spatial reference frames and cues from the surroundings, in other words, the creation of a cognitive map – helps reduce cognitive load and increases recall and the encoding

© Springer Nature Switzerland AG 2020
C. Frasson et al. (Eds.): BFAL 2020, LNAI 12462, pp. 13–23, 2020.
https://doi.org/10.1007/978-3-030-60735-7_2

of novel information [2, 3]. It has been observed that decrease in the volume of the hippocampus – a structure playing a key role in memory – correlate with a decline in cognitive function. Indeed, it is speculated that increasing grey matter in the hippocampus could entail better memory [4]. Interestingly, playing 3D video games over a period, such as Super Mario 64, reportedly increases hippocampal volume [5], as well as increases performance in episodic and spatial memory quests. It is speculated that 3D games, such as Super Mario 64, lead players to create a cognitive map of the environment.

Cognitive training on older adults suggest that cognitive training may also serve to optimize the cognitive functioning of persons with noticeable cognitive decline and contribute to a slowing of the onset of the disability [6]. It has been observed that virtual environments lead to formation of cognitive maps similar as in the real environments, despite certain limitations (misperception, cyber-sickness and disorientation) [7]. There is an increasing trend of using virtual reality (VR) games and applications for cognitive training of the elderly. A VR environment offers a safe way to achieve high level of inter-action along with the possibility of performing activities, adaptable to the characteristics and needs of individual patients [8, 9]. Another key aspect of using VR for training is that it allows the collection of data in the form of biomedical signals of the participant, which can be analyzed to study and improve the effectiveness of training sessions. In terms of interaction, fully immersive VR environments using head mounted display cre-ate a more realistic sense of presence compared to non-immersive or partial-immersive environments (monitor-display) [10].

In this paper, we implemented a fully immersive 3D- VR game in which the partic-ipants use his/her navigational skills to form a cognitive map of the environment and complete the tasks within the game. The environment simulates a public garden in the form of a maze, and the tasks are to search for certain items of interest in a listed order. While the participant plays the game, the system records their EEG signals by the means of an Emotiv headset. Navigating in an unfamiliar environment can be challenging, con-sequently leading to increased negative emotions if the participant fails to locate the required item. Hence, we implemented an intelligent guidance system that assesses the emotions of the participants, tracks their movement in real-time, and pro-vide hints to complete the tasks in the game.

Our objective is to explore the effect of a fully immersive VR navigation game on the performance of attention and memory capacities of patients suffering from subjective cognitive decline (SCD), a preclinical state of Alzheimer's Disease (AD). Our re-search concentrates on understanding if **it is possible to improve memory and attention performance through a virtual maze game.** We also explore the benefits of hints in game can in terms of change in frustration of the participants on providing hints.

The rest of this paper is organized as follows. In Sect. 2, we give an overview of the related works. In Sect. 3, we describe our approach. In Sect. 4, we detail the experimental procedure, and finally, in Sect. 5 we present the obtained results.

2 Related Works

Over the years, many studies have implemented multiple VR environments for cognitive training. In one of the earlier studies, attention enhancement in young students was observed in a VR classroom compared to non-VR control group [11]. Another study done on graduate students, observed an improved ability to recall the spatial location of objects in VR environment simulating an apartment [12]. Optale et al. [13] observed that VR memory training during a period of three months presented an improvement in long term memory in elders with memory impairment. They suggested that repeated exposure of elderly to VR based cognitive training may simulate their attention owing to high degree of immersion and interaction. In a recent work, a VR environment simulating activity of daily life (e.g. cooking) and an environment focused on memory training using autobiographical memory has been proposed [14]. Gamito et al. [15] used working memory tasks (i.e. buying several items), visuo-spatial orientation tasks (i.e. finding the way to the minimarket) in a VR environment for training of stroke patients two to three sessions per week over the four to six week period of treatment. Their study revealed a general improvement in attention and memory abilities over multiple training sessions.

Research have used physiological sensing approaches like electroencephalography (EEG) to detect and analyze mental states and emotion to assist in learning, intelligent video games etc. Ghali et al. [16] used EEG signals to assess participants' mental states and focused on their engagement and frustration. Based on these two mental states they proposed help strategies in a physics game. For the elderly, continuous feed-back and guidance to complete the quests is one of the key elements, game designers need to consider. Games that have elements which encourage positive emotions and tense feelings, rather than excitement and continuous challenge are more suited to the elders [17]. Additionally, research shows that it is more beneficial for AD patients to be helped through the completion of a challenge, rather than see the challenge failed [18]. It is important to present both audio and visual cues to cater to the needs of a specific profile of patients suffering from either visual or auditory impairments [13]. Thus, real-time assistance with audio and visual feedback is one of the mandatory components in games for elders, to incorporate mechanism which achieves high-level engagement by keeping player filled with positive emotions.

3   Orientation Game

We created a fully immersive and interactive VR environment that is adaptable in real-time using Unity 3D. We aim to integrates the benefits induced by the creation of a cognitive map of the surroundings in a fully immersive 3D VR environment. Items are placed at a suitable distance from each other throughout the garden, forcing users to explore the environment. The guidance system is designed to help the users in completing the tasks without being overloaded with negative emotions.

3.1   Environment: Orientation Game

We designed a VR environment that simulates a botanical garden. The environment is in the form of 5 × 5 maze where trees make up the walls of the maze and clearings through the trees are the pathways. The user navigates on the environment using a joystick by clicking in the direction in which they wish to move. The user can see other elements in the game: a map of the garden, their position and direction in the form of a red arrow on the map, a blue circle representing the target location of the items (dis-played when the game starts or when a hint is shown), visual hints and verbal messages displayed when needed.

When the game starts, the user is introduced to a tutorial to familiarize with the environment and the controls. We explain the elements displayed in the game, we provide an example item to find and collect which allows the users to understand the movement within the environment and the different types of hints. Once the tutorial finishes and the user is ready, the game can start. The game consists of four quests. In each of the first three quests, we start by asking the user to collect an item which is in a specific location of the maze. The item's name is displayed in a list and its location is indicated by a flashing circle on the map for 5 s. The user must then reach this location and collect the requested item. Once the user has arrived at the correct location, they must search for it by looking around and click joystick button to collect it. Every time an item is collected, we display the list remove it from the list and show the next item with its location. When all the three items are collected, one at a time, the user is presented to the fourth one. For the last quest, the user needs to return to the starting point and put the three collected items in a basket. The items are lavender, coconuts, and apples. Figure 1 shows the different elements displayed in the environment at the start of the game.

Fig. 1. The list of items to collect and the map representing the environment.

3.2 Guidance System

The guidance system actively tracks participant's emotions and movement and pro-vides hints that help to complete the tasks of the game. The list of emotions used in this experiment are provided by Emotiv proprietary software: frustration, excitement, engagement, meditation, and valence. Although we do not have access to the Emotiv system proprietary algorithms to infer mental states from raw data and frequency bands, several studies have established the reliability of the output. It also keeps track of the history of the participant's movement and actions that are taken while completing the quests within the maze. The guidance system sits outside the VR environment and the emotions tracking system, and it receives emotions of the participants as well as their position every second.

There are three different types of activation of hints:

1. Emotions: At every timestamp, the mean of the change and the rate of the change of emotion values every ten seconds are used to calculate a net score for each emotion. The emotion with the maximum score is compared with an empirically defined threshold. A score higher than the threshold activates the emotion-based hints
2. Away from target: If the participant takes three steps or more, all of which are at four blocks or more from the target, the hint level 2-1 is activated.
3. No Movement: If the participant does not move for more than a given amount of time, the hint 2-1 based on no movement is activated.

Hint levels		Participant's position	Object's location	Message (Audio and Visual)	Highlighted Path in Map
Level 1		✓	✓		
Level 2	2-1	✓	✓	Please check the position of the object on the map and try to reach it.	
	2-2	✓	✓	You are too far. Try to take a few steps back.	
	2-3	✓	✓	1. Good job, you're almost there! 2. Keep up the good work! 3. You are in the right direction!	
Level 3		✓		Follow the path indicated, the object is nearby.	Path to cell nearest to target object
Level 4		✓		Follow this path, you will find the object.	Complete path to the object.

Fig. 2. Different levels of hints

Figure 2 displays the level of detail provided in different hints. The number of details provided by the guidance system increases progressively with the level of hints. Level 1 provides the least information and displays only the participant's location and the object's location on the map. Additionally, level 2 displays a text message in a prompt in the VR environment along with the verbal narration of the message. Level 3 hint highlights a path in the map, which the participant can follow to reach a location immediately next to the actual location of the object. This still leaves some scope of exploration and allows the participant to search for the object in all possible directions. Level 4 hint highlights the complete path leading to the object's location on the map. In case of activation based on participant's emotion, if the hint is triggered by a negative emotion such as frustration, the level of hint increases which subsequently provides more details to find the object. On the other hand, if the hint is triggered by positive emotions such as excitement or engagement, the level of hint decreases. In case of hint activated due to no movement of the participant, the level increases every fifteen seconds till the participant moves, at which point it resets to level 1. When the participant is away from the object as determined by the guidance system, the hint provided is always level 2-1.

Once the help is received by the VE, the latter displays it as a text/sound message or as a path displayed on the map. The way the help is displayed depends on the hint level described earlier. As an example, Fig. 3 shows the hint level 4 as a complete path to the target location on the map, where the numbers represent the steps the user must follow to reach the target position. Hint is given with a verbal message asking the user to follow the steps displayed which will lead then to the item. Every hint when dis-played, remains on the screen for a duration of four seconds.

Fig. 3. Hint level 4

4   Experiments

We analyzed the impact of our orientation game on the attention and memory perfor-mance to test the performance of our approach which is based on the cognitive map theory. Therefore, in addition to the game, we developed 3 attention exercises et 3 memory exercises to compare participants' performances before and after the therapy.

4.1   Attention Exercises

The participant starts with the first attention exercise. In this exercise, we present a sound sequence of 5 numbers then a numerical pad is displayed, and the participant must repeat the same sequence; then we hide the pad, we present another sound sequence of

3 numbers and the participant must report the sequence in the backward order. In the second attention exercise, we present a sound sequence of different letters at a rate of one per second and the participant must click the space bar each time they hear the letter "A". The third attention exercise is about naming different objects. For every object, we show an image for 4 s then we replace it by four letters and the participant is asked to select the first letter of the object's name.

4.2 Memory Exercises

The fourth exercise which is the first memory exercise is a contextual memory test. The participant is asked to memorize a series of different objects which are presented either visually or orally with their names. Once the series is over, we introduce a series of objects' images or names presented auditorily. For each object, the participant must determine whether the object showed or heard was presented in the first series of objects. They must tell if it was seen visually, auditorily or never presented in the previous series by clicking on one of the 3 buttons displayed. For instance, an image of a ship is shown in the first series, and in the second series, the participant should choose if they saw it, heard its name, or if the object was not presented in the previous sequence.

In the fifth exercise, which is a short-term memory test, we start by presenting ten white circles. Then we highlight a series of circles one by one to create a sequence and the participant is asked to memorize it. The participants are then asked to reproduce the same sequence. We present two sequences with two different levels of difficulty.

The sixth and last memory exercise is a working memory one. We present a set of 3 pictures for a short period of time that the participant must memorize. Then, this set is replaced by four sets of three pictures and the participant is asked to identify the set which was presented. They do this for two sets.

4.3 Process of the Experiment

Our approach was performed on 17 participants (13 females) with subjective cognitive decline (SCD). The mean age was 72.76 with a standard deviation SD = 5.66. Each participant must go through two sessions.

In the first session, we described the study to the participants and invited them to sign a consent form. Then, we asked them to perform clinical tests in order to confirm diagnosis and determine whether they are eligible to participate in the experiment or not. Once we make sure that a participant is eligible, they are invited to take part in the experiment. We invite the participant to fill two pre-experiment forms: the Positive and Negative Affect Schedule (PANAS) scale [19], a self-assessment of emotions, and a questionnaire on cyber-sickness [20].

Once they finish the first step, the participant is equipped with an EEG headset and is invited to resolve attention and memory exercises. After the participant finishes the exercises, they are equipped with Fove VR headset and can start the orientation therapy. Participants are encouraged to take the time they need in order to navigate in the environment. Once the orientation therapy game is finished, we remove the Fove VR headset and the participant is invited to complete the same 6 exercises with different examples than the first time.

Finally, we remove the EEG headset and the participant fills up four post-experiment forms: PANAS scale, cyber-sickness, the AttrackDiff 2 [21] and a self-report form. Figure 4 shows the different steps of the process of the experiment.

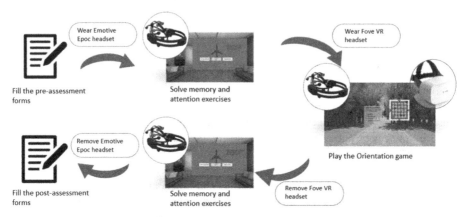

Fig. 4. Process of the experiments

5   Results and Discussion

The first objective of this research is to check whether **it is possible to improve memory and attention performance through a virtual maze game**. We started by analysing the difference between the performance before and after the orientation therapy. For the attention exercises, the performance improvement are as follows: On the exercise 1, the general mean improvement was 4.41%. For exercise 2, the performance improvement was 1.6%. On the third exercise, there was a mean improvement of 0%. We also analysed the improvement of the memory exercises. For exercise 4, the mean improvement was 0.98%. On exercise 5, there was a mean improvement of 12.94%. For exercise 6, the mean frustration was 32.35%. We note that exercise 6 has the highest percentage of improvement. We analysed then the attention exercises versus the memory exercises. Figure 5 shows a clear difference between the improvement of performance on attention exercises versus the memory exercises.

The trend obtained in our first analysis lead to our second research question which is to check whether it is possible to reduce participants' negative emotions by helping them to orient in the orientation game. To this end, we analyzed the frustration of the participants before and after the hints was given. Figure 6 shows a comparison of mean of the total frustration in ten seconds before the hint was provided and next ten seconds after the hint was provided.

For the different types of hints, we observed that except for hint level 2-2 and hint level 4, the average values of frustration for all the participants were lesser in the next ten seconds after the hints were provided. Hint level 2-2 provides a warning message: 'You're too far. Try to take few steps back.'. This led the participants to believe that they

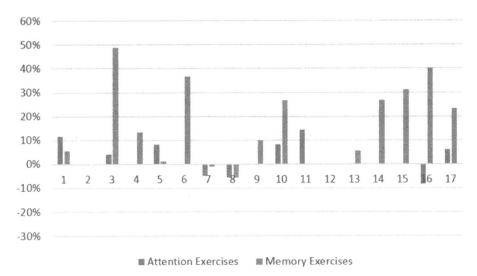

Fig. 5. Histogram of performance improvement for attention vs memory exercises

might be doing something wrong leading to higher frustration. Hint level 4 dis-plays the complete path to the item's location. But, since we configured the hint to appear for only four seconds, it was not enough for the participants to memorize the complete path to the item's location, which may have led to a higher level of frustration.

In the after-experiment survey, 78% of the participants found the hints to be helpful to solve the quests, which further supports the utility of the real-time guidance system in 3D VR orientation games.

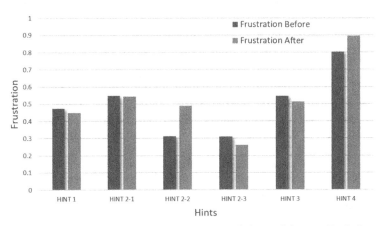

Fig. 6. Average values of frustrations for each hint over all the participants, 10 s before and after the hints were provided.

6 Conclusion

In this paper, we presented a novel approach to intelligently help patients suffering from pre-clinical states of Alzheimer's disease to orient in a fully immersive virtual reality maze game to improve their attention and memory performance. We conducted experiments involving 17 participants and results show that after the orientation game, almost all participants had an improvement in memory performance. Results show that the real-time guidance system is helpful to the participants in completing the tasks in the game. Simple and positive hints help to stabilize the frustration of participant and complete the given tasks. However, hints which have a warning tone or are more difficult to understand may have opposite effect and increases their frustration. This shows that audio-visual hints in a serious game for elderly should have positive message and be easy to comprehend.

Acknowledgments. We acknowledge NSERC-CRD and Beam Me Up for funding this work.

References

1. Allison, S.L., Fagan, A.M., Morris, J.C., Head, D.: Spatial navigation in preclinical Alzheimer's disease. J. Alzheimer's Dis. **52**, 77–90 (2016)
2. Kitchin, R.M.: Cognitive maps: what are they and why study them? J. Environ. Psychol. **14**, 1–19 (1994)
3. Tolman, E.C.: Cognitive maps in rats and men. Psychol. Rev. **55**, 189 (1948)
4. Konishi, K., Bohbot, V.D.: Spatial navigational strategies correlate with gray matter in the hippocampus of healthy older adults tested in a virtual maze. Front. Aging Neurosci. **5**, 1 (2013)
5. West, G.L., et al.: Playing Super Mario 64 increases hippocampal grey matter in older adults. PLoS One **12**, e0187779 (2017)
6. Belleville, S.: Cognitive training for persons with mild cognitive impairment. Int. Psychogeriatr. **20**, 57–66 (2008)
7. Péruch, P., Gaunet, F.: Virtual environments as a promising tool for investigating human spatial cognition. Cahiers de Psychologie Cognitive/Curr. Psychol. Cogn. **17**, 881–899 (1998)
8. Ball, K., et al.: Effects of cognitive training interventions with older adults: a randomized controlled trial. Jama **288**, 2271–2281 (2002)
9. García-Betances, R.I., Arredondo Waldmeyer, M.T., Fico, G., Cabrera-Umpiérrez, M.F.: A succinct overview of virtual reality technology use in Alzheimer's disease. Front. Aging Neurosci. **7**, 80 (2015)
10. Westwood, J.D., Haluck, R., Hoffman, H.: Medicine Meets Virtual Reality 15: In Vivo, in Vitro, in Silico: Designing the Next in Medicine. IOS Press, Amsterdam (2007)
11. Rizzo, A.A., et al.: The virtual classroom: a virtual reality environment for the assessment and rehabilitation of attention deficits. CyberPsychol. Behav. **3**, 483–499 (2000)
12. Intraraprasit, M., Phanpanya, P., Jinjakam, C.: Cognitive training using immersive virtual reality. Presented at the 2017 10th Biomedical Engineering International Conference (BMEiCON) (2017)
13. Optale, G., et al.: Controlling memory impairment in elderly adults using virtual reality memory training: a randomized controlled pilot study. Neurorehabil. Neural Repair **24**, 348–357 (2010)

14. Caggianese, G., et al.: Towards a virtual reality cognitive training system for mild cognitive impairment and Alzheimer's disease patients. Presented at the 2018 32nd International Conference on Advanced Information Networking and Applications Workshops (WAINA) (2018)
15. Gamito, P., et al.: Cognitive training on stroke patients via virtual reality-based serious games. Disabil. Rehabil. **39**, 385–388 (2017)
16. Ghali, R., Abdessalem, H.B., Frasson, C.: Improving intuitive reasoning through assistance strategies in a virtual reality game. Presented at the Thirtieth International Flairs Conference (2017)
17. Imbeault, F., Bouchard, B., Bouzouane, A.: Serious games in cognitive training for Alzheimer's patients. Presented at the 2011 IEEE 1st International Conference on Serious Games and Applications for Health (SeGAH) (2011)
18. Pigot, H., Mayers, A., Giroux, S.: The intelligent habitat and everyday life activity support. Presented at the Proceedings of the 5th International Conference on Simulations in Biomedicine, April 2003
19. Watson, D., Clark, L.A., Carey, G.: Positive and negative affectivity and their relation to anxiety and depressive disorders. J. Abnorm. Psychol. **97**, 346 (1988)
20. Kennedy, R.S., Lane, N.E., Berbaum, K.S., Lilienthal, M.G.: Simulator sickness questionnaire: an enhanced method for quantifying simulator sickness. Int. J. Aviat. Psychol. **3**, 203–220 (1993)
21. Lallemand, C., Koenig, V., Gronier, G., Martin, R.: Création et validation d'une version française du questionnaire AttrakDiff pour l'évaluation de l'expérience utilisateur des systèmes interactifs. Eur. Rev. Appl. Psychol. **65**, 239–252 (2015)

Multi-class Time Continuity Voting for EEG Classification

Xiaodong Qu[✉], Peiyan Liu, Zhaonan Li, and Timothy Hickey

Brandeis University, Waltham, MA 02453, USA
{xiqu,peiyanlilu,zli,tjhickey}@brandeis.edu

Abstract. In this study we propose a new machine learning classification method to distinguish brain activity patterns for healthy subjects. We used ElectroEncephaloGraphic (EEG) data associated with five userdefined mental tasks. We collected a data set using the Muse headband with four EEG electrodes (TP9, AF7, AF8, and TP10). Sixteen healthy subjects participated in this six-session experiment. In each session, we instructed them to conduct five different one-minute tasks, we abbreviated the tasks as think, count, recall, breathe and draw. After dealing with noise and outliers, we first fairly compared the performance of existing classifiers, including linear classifiers, non-linear Bayesian classifiers, nearest-neighbor classifiers, ensemble methods, and deep learning, with the same settings. Among these, Random Forest (RF), and Long Short-Term Memory (LSTM) outperform others. We then introduced a new ensemble classifier called Time Continuity Voting (TCV), combining these top two. The timewise cross-validation results showed that TCV could correctly classify the five tasks (20% by chance) with an accuracy of 70% which is at least 6% higher than the top individual classifiers.

Keywords: Time Continuity Voting · Machine learning · Deep learning · Classification · ElectroEncephaloGraphy · EEG

1 Introduction

Brain Computer Interfaces (BCI), have been widely used for clinical and non clinical applications, such as diagnosis of abnormal states, evaluation the effect of the treatments, helping patients with motor disabilities to move a mouse or to control a motorized wheelchair, mental workload, seizure detection, motor imagery tasks (left hand, right hand, foot and tongue) [9], BCI based games [6] and passive BCI [26]. Most data are collected in a clinical or research setting [7, 16]. For other domains, such as ImageNet for image classification, or MNIST for handwritten digit recognition, more data of the same kind can be generated directly from the general end users, and more general patterns could be recognized based on such large scale data. To narrow this gap, we designed a pilot study towards building such a large scale EEG data set, for multi-class classification of user-centered tasks, generated by general end users. This is a simple experiment design with our new algorithm, Time Continuity Voting (TCV), to collect and analyze more data (Fig. 1).

© Springer Nature Switzerland AG 2020
C. Frasson et al. (Eds.): BFAL 2020, LNAI 12462, pp. 24–33, 2020.
https://doi.org/10.1007/978-3-030-60735-7_3

Think (T) For this task, subjects were asked to think of a certain number of random objects, then in following steps they were asked to recall and draw such objects. We asked the participants to think of different objects each time, and different numbers for each session, in session one and two, six objects; three and four, seven objects; five and six, eight objects. Within one minute, they typed these objects down in a text entry box on the screen.

Count (C) Subjects counted numbers aloud, from 200 towards 0, each time subtracting by seven, e.g. 200, 193, 186, 179 ..., the subjects were asked to count as slowly and clearly as possible, with eyes open, and minimize the movements of the body, especially the eyes and jaws.

Recall (R) Each subject recalled the objects they had just typed in the Think (T) task, in the correct order, if possible. The results were again entered in a text entry box through the keyboard.

Breathe (B) Subjects were instructed to breathe deeply with eyes open. They were asked NOT to think about the objects they just thought or recalled in earlier task(s), ideally, they just focused on the breathing task itself.

Draw (D) Each subject was asked to draw the objects they thought about in the earlier task Think (T), with a pen, on a blank A4 paper. The objects were listed on the screen in front of them so they did not need to recall, just focus on drawing.

Fig. 1. Tasks in this experiment

Previous studies [4, 7, 16, 20] demonstrated that EEG signals could successfully be used to distinguish several kinds of cognitive tasks. In this study, we designed these five user-centered tasks, abbreviated them as Think(T), count(C), recall(R), breathe(B) and draw(D). The order of the five tasks was randomly shuffled for each of the six sessions, as shown in Fig. 2.

Our result is that the Time Continuity Voting (TCV) algorithm can recognize the different tasks at a 70% level, compared with 20% by chance.

Beyond the clinical devices with 128 or 64 electrodes, commercial wearable devices for monitoring brain activity (EEG) are now widely available on the consumer market at an affordable price [11, 18], including the Neurosky Mindwave, the Emotiv Epoc, the Open BCI Mark IV headset, and the Muse Headband etc. In this experiment, EEG data were collected using Fig. 3. Muse headsets developed by Interaxon.

Such EEG data collection devices could be used by the general end users in order to support better understanding of cognitive tasks, emotion states, health monitoring, and diagnosis of abnormal states. Also it can be used in the classroom to facilitate teaching and learning [8, 19, 25].

Our long term goal is to 1) develop a personalized EEG-based biofeedback system to help more users better understand their unique individual brain signal patterns; 2) make it easier for general end users to collect, analysis and share more EEG data in daily life, and eventually discover the general patterns for most people based on large scale data.

S/T	1	2	3	4	5
1	T	C	R	B	D
2	B	T	C	R	D
3	T	B	R	D	C
4	T	C	R	B	D
5	C	T	R	D	B
6	T	C	B	R	D

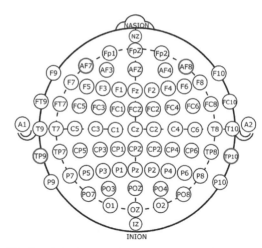

Fig. 2. Session (S) with Task (T) order

Fig. 3. 10–20 System, four electrodes used on shuffled Muse Headset were highlighted

2 Algorithms

We reviewed and implemented several classifiers commonly adopted in the field, as summarized in [16, 17] and [7], such as Linear classifiers, ensemble methods, and deep learning. The code discussed in this paper is available online (the Github link is hidden for the double blind review).

2.1 Existing Algorithms

Linear Classifiers: Both Linear Discriminant Analysis (LDA) and Support Vector Machines (SVM) are discriminative classifiers. Because they use linear functions to classify, the computational requirement is usually low, which make them good for personal computers and smartphones. Previous research has shown the shrinkage LDA (sLDA) and SVM perform from adequately to reasonably well with little data in EEG research. [3, 15].

Nearest Neighbour: Such classifiers look for the nearest neighbours; and we used the k-Nearest Neighbour (kNN) classifier. It is very sensitive to the curseof-dimensionality, especially with a typical 64 or 128 electrodes EEG headset; however, it works well with low-dimensional feature vectors [16, 17]. We suspected that since our headset only has 4 electrodes, it would perform adequately.

Ensemble Classifiers: Boosting [10], bagging and Random Forest [5] are types of Ensemble Machine Learning Algorithms which use a group of weaker learners (e.g. random decision trees) to make a stronger classification. These have been the gold standard for several EEG-based classification experiments, here we implemented Random Forest (RF), Adaboost and RusBoost.

Deep Learning: Deep learning, especially Convolutional Neural Network(CNN) performed well in several previous EEG band power (feature) based research [7, 13]. We implemented it with two layers with maximum pooling layers. We also adopted Long Short Term Memory (LSTM) based on our task type [2, 3, 7, 24]. As motioned in previous research, we expect it to perform well with two recurrent layers followed by two fully-connected layers.

2.2   Our Algorithm

In this paper, we propose a new voting approach based on temporally nearest neighbors. Voting is a popular way of classifier combination, [12]. In EEGbased research, the following approaches have performed well: majority voting, weighted majority voting, and voting based on classification entropy [1, 28].

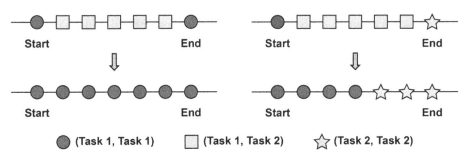

Fig. 4. Time Continuity Voting (TCV)

Time Continuity Voting: As shown in Fig. 4, for each data point, if classifier A and classifier B have the same prediction on a task, e.g. a data point is predicted as task 1, then the prediction result is 1, and it is marked as 'start'. If the two predictions are different. e.g. classifier A predicts this data point as task 1, and classifier B predicts the same data point as task 2, the algorithm then move on to the next data point until find the nearest neighbor, where the two predictions from the two classifiers are the same, and mark it as the 'end', within the task time frame. Because of the time continuity effect [21, 22] of EEG signals, we assume the task and its nearest neighbor have a high probability to have the same label. Thus the algorithm is trying to find the nearest neighbor where both of the classifiers have the same prediction. If there are two such nearest neighbors but they have different classifications at these two different data points, then the algorithm divides the data points in between evenly, first half as the 'start' data point, and second half as the 'end' data point. If the number of data points between 'start' and 'end' is odd, then the middle data point is randomly assigned the same label as either 'start' or 'end' data point.

3 Experiment

In this experiment, scalp-EEG signals were recorded from sixteen subjects. Each one was tested in six sessions, each session is five minutes long, with five tasks, each task is one minute. Tasks were selected by the subjects together with the researchers, based on frequent tasks in study environments for students in their everyday life. Each subject completed six sessions over several weeks.

Each subject first signed the informed consent form. Then, they put on the Muse headbands and test the recording. Subjects then completed an entrance survey. After these preliminaries, Official EEG recording began. Subjects were directed by an online data collection system, which kept track of time and alerted the subjects to change their tasks after every 60 s. After subjects completed all the five tasks, the EEG recording stopped, subjects then completed a short exit survey.

Data Cleaning: When collecting EEG data, one or more electrodes may have momentarily lost contact with the subjects' scalp. The result was that multiple sequential spectral snapshots from one or more electrodes had exactly the same 32 bit value. When we detected this anomaly, we set that entire spectral snapshot of 20 values to 0, while keeping the time-stamped value, even if the anomaly was only detected on one electrode. Such cleaning action resulted in a loss of 43% of the entire data. This result echoed with other researches facing the same challenge of low signal-to-noise ratio.

Subjects: Sixteen healthy subjects finished the experiment. Data from four subjects have less than 35% data points left after removing noises. Thus these four subjects were excluded from subsequent analysis.

Six males and six females are included in the final data set. Ten of the twelve retained subjects were undergraduate students, the other two were graduate students. Seven subjects were computer science majors; the remaining five were math, biology or psychology majors, or had not yet decided on a field of concentration. The average age of the subjects was 20.2.

All twelve subjects completed the six sessions, producing a data set comprising 360 min of EEG recordings (12 subjects × 6 sessions per subject × 5 min per session).

Feature Extraction and Feature Selection: We used the Band Powers (BP) features, the absolute band power for a given frequency range (for instance, alpha, 9–13 Hz) is the logarithm of the power spectral density of EEG signals summed over that frequency range [16]. The Muse headsets, as shown in Fig. 3, are equipped with seven dry electrodes that make contact with the subjects' scalp, three of them are reference, the other four are input. The four input electrode locations corresponded to sites TP9, AF7, AF8, and T10 [23]. The Muse EEG recording application automatically filtered out muscle artifacts, such as eye blinking and jaw movements. The EEG system down-sampled sensor signals from 12 kHz to 220 Hz, with 2 uV (RMS) noise. Spectral analysis was performed on-board the Muse device and then transmitted wirelessly at 10 Hz to the researcher's workstation. Each of these spectral snapshots consists of 20 numeric values – five spectral values for each of the four electrodes. This procedure generated a total of 3,000 spectral snapshots per subject per session (10 snapshots/second * 300 s).

Timewise Cross Validation: Samples, if randomly selected, could be near to each other chronologically in both the training set and the testing set. This may cause over-fitting because EEG signals change slowly. To lessen the possible over-fitting effect, we adopted the timewise cross validation from [21, 22]. For each five minute session there were five tasks, we divided each task into 10 parts, evenly and contiguously, each part had 10% of the task based on time.

Then we did a 10 fold cross validation first, realized the first 20% and last 10% data are demonstrating low accuracy due to the task transition effect. We then cut off these transition time and only use the rest 70% of the data. In each fold, we trained on the six subsets and tested on the left-out subset. Figure 5 showed a graphical representation of this seven-fold timewise cross validation approach. We also did a session-wise cross validation, but the accuracy is average 18% to 25% lower than this within-session cross validation, such results were expected, probably because of the relatively small number of sessions.

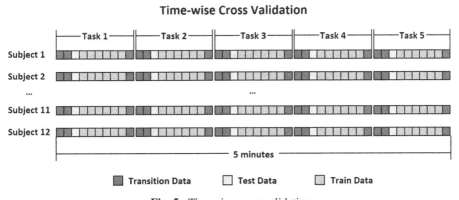

Fig. 5. Timewise cross validation

4   Results

Two main results were observed from the EEG classification. First, the machine learning/deep learning algorithms can distinguish these five tasks fairly well, especially our Time Continuity Voting (TCV) (see Fig. 6). Second, although there are individual differences, (see Fig. 7), the user defined tasks demonstrated general patterns (see Fig. 8) with just six-minute of data from twelve subjects, TCV 0.7, RF 0.64, LSTM 0.64 showed similar trends (see Fig. 6), here we just include the RF figures, the rest figures are available on Github).

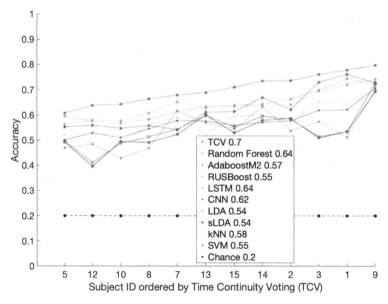

Fig. 6. Compare algorithms

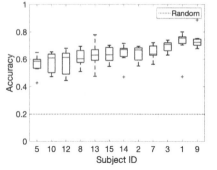

Fig. 7. Subject difference of all twelve subjects.

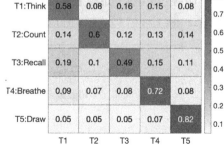

Fig. 8. Task prediction accuracy, average

5   Conclusion and Discussion

The main contributions of this paper are the demonstration that Time Continuity Voting (TCV) algorithm can improve the accuracy of EEG classification of such user-centered tasks. TCV outperformed all other widely adopted classifying approaches in the offline classification task (see Fig. 6). It is voting based on the output of the other individual learners, this version is using the top two: RF and LSTM, it captured the different patterns recognized by these different individual machine learning and deep learning learners, and achieved a six percent increase of classification accuracy.

Figure 6 showed that Linear methods like LDA and SVM still performed adequately. Among all the ensemble methods, Random Forest (Bag) still the best. The two deep learning options, CNN and LSTM, are still very strong predictors even with such a relatively small size of data, but the training time jumped from minutes to hours compared with the traditional machine learning techniques.

The separability of these five different tasks (see Fig. 8, echoed with previous research with clear and distinct EEG patterns from five or more different classes [14, 27], implied that the multi-class task detection could be classified from adequately to good. Although there are still individual difference (see Fig. 7), the similar trends can be observed with these twelve subjects.

Interesting general patterns could be observed from these results (see Fig. 8), such as task Draw and task Breathe are more accurately predicted, possible reasons including muscle related sub-tasks such as inhale, exhale or draw, Also the different objects in each session actually showing the framework is sensitive to the different content subjects are thinking, the low accuracy of task Think and task Recall probably comes from each session the subjects were asked to come up with different objects. The individual difference (see Fig. 7) in task Count is a little surprise to the researchers, we expected it to be as clearly classified as task Breathe, but it was not, probably because the difference of calculating such numbers in mind, between subjects and within subject between sessions, some subjects in some session count it so fast, reaching zero while there were still several second left, while others may just stopped at around a hundred when the time went up, also some subjects count it wrong during the process. These all could lead to the individual difference reflected here.

Such experiment and analysis framework is also sensitive enough to catch the task transition, and early task finishing, as shown in Fig. 5, some subjects finish the task Think, task Recall, task Draw earlier than the designed one minute time, thus the last 10% of time is hard to predict, as subjects could be daydreaming or thinking about something else. Also the transition effect is pretty clear, although we observe the subject switching to the next task pretty fast physically between tasks, it is still an obvious general pattern that the EEG signals changed slowly, it took the first 20% of time, which is twelve second to actually enter the stable states of the next task.

Overall, our Time Continuity Voting (TCV) framework outperformed benchmark individual classifiers in this multi-class task classification experiment. Thus TCV could be a useful option for future research of such EEG classification.

References

1. Ahangi, A., Karamnejad, M., Mohammadi, N., Ebrahimpour, R., Bagheri, N.: Multiple classifier system for EEG signal classification with application to brain–computer interfaces. Neural Comput. Appl. **23**(5), 1319–1327 (2013)
2. Arifoglu, D., Bouchachia, A.: Activity recognition and abnormal behaviourdetection with recurrent neural networks. Proc. Comput. Sci. **110**, 86–93 (2017)
3. Bashivan, P., Rish, I., Yeasin, M., Codella, N.: Learning representationsfrom EEG with deep recurrent-convolutional neural networks. arXiv preprint arXiv:1511.06448 (2015)
4. Bird, J.J., Manso, L.J., Ribeiro, E.P., Ekart, A., Faria, D.R.: A study onmental state classification using EEG-based brain-machine interface. In: 2018 International Conference on Intelligent Systems (IS), pp. 795–800. IEEE (2018)

5. Breiman, L.: Random forests. Mach. Learn. **45**(1), 5–32 (2001)
6. Coyle, D., Principe, J., Lotte, F., Nijholt, A.: Guest editorial: brain/neuronal-computer game interfaces and interaction. IEEE Trans. Comput. Intell. AI Games **5**(2), 77–81 (2013)
7. Craik, A., He, Y., Contreras-Vidal, J.L.: Deep learning for electroencephalogram (EEG) classification tasks: a review. J. Neural Eng. **16**(3), 031001 (2019)
8. Deeb, F.A., DiLillo, A., Hickey, T.: Using spinoza log data to enhance CS1 pedagogy. In: McLaren, B., Reilly, R., Zvacek, S., Uhomoibhi, J. (eds.) International Conference on Computer Supported Education. Communications in Computer and Information Science, vol. 1022, pp. 14–36. Springer, Cham (2018). https://doi.org/10.1007/978-3-030-21151-6_2
9. Devlaminck, D., et al.: From circular ordinal regression to multilabel classification. In: Proceedings of the 2010 Workshop on Preference Learning (European Conference on Machine Learning, ECML), p. 15 (2010)
10. Freund, Y., Schapire, R.E.: A decision-theoretic generalization of on-line learning and an application to boosting. J. Comput. Syst. Sci. **55**(1), 119–139 (1997)
11. Gang, P., et al.: User-driven intelligent interface on the basis of multimodal augmented reality and brain computer interaction for people with functional disabilities. In: Arai, K., Kapoor, S., Bhatia, R. (eds.) Future of Information and Communication Conference. Advances in Intelligent Systems and Computing, vol. 886, pp. 612–631. Springer, Cham (2018). https://doi.org/10.1007/978-3-030-03402-3_43
12. Jain, A.K., Duin, R.P.W., Mao, J.: Statistical pattern recognition: a review. IEEE Trans. Pattern Anal. Mach. Intell. **22**(1), 4–37 (2000)
13. Kwak, N.S., Müller, K.R., Lee, S.W.: A convolutional neural network for steady state visual evoked potential classification under ambulatory environment. PloS One **12**(2), e0172578 (2017)
14. Lindig-León, C., Bougrain, L.: Comparison of sensorimotor rhythms in EEG signals during simple and combined motor imageries over the contra and ipsilateral hemispheres. In: 2015 37th Annual International Conference of the IEEE Engineering in Medicine and Biology Society (EMBC), pp. 3953–3956. IEEE (2015)
15. Lotte, F.: Signal processing approaches to minimize or suppress calibration time in oscillatory activity-based brain–computer interfaces. Proc. IEEE **103**(6), 871–890 (2015)
16. Lotte, F., et al.: A review of classification algorithms for EEG-based brain–computer interfaces: a 10 year update. J. Neural Eng. **15**(3), 031005 (2018)
17. Lotte, F., Congedo, M., Lécuyer, A., Lamarche, F., Arnaldi, B.: A review of classification algorithms for EEG-based brain–computer interfaces. J. Neur. Eng. **4**(2), R1 (2007)
18. Mihajlović, V., Grundlehner, B., Vullers, R., Penders, J.: Wearable, wireless EEG solutions in daily life applications: what are we missing? IEEE J. Biomed. Health Inform. **19**(1), 6–21 (2014)
19. Poulsen, A.T., Kamronn, S., Dmochowski, J., Parra, L.C., Hansen, L.K.: EEG in the classroom: synchronised neural recordings during video presentation. Sci. Rep. **7**, 43916 (2017)
20. Qu, X., Hall, M., Sun, Y., Sekuler, R., Hickey, T.J.: A personalized reading coach using wearable EEG sensors-a pilot study of brainwave learning analytics. In: CSEDU (2), pp. 501–507 (2018)
21. Qu, X., Sun, Y., Sekuler, R., Hickey, T.: EEG markers of stem learning. In: IEEE Frontiers in Education Conference (FIE), pp. 1–9. IEEE (2018)
22. Saeb, S., Lonini, L., Jayaraman, A., Mohr, D.C., Kording, K.P.: Voodoo machine learning for clinical predictions. Biorxiv arXiv:059774 (2016)
23. Seeck, M., et al.: The standardized EEG electrode array of the IFCN. Clin. Neurophysiol. **128**(10), 2070–2077 (2017)

24. Sha, L., Hong, P.: Neural knowledge tracing. In: Frasson, C., Kostopoulos, G. (eds.) International Conference on Brain Function Assessment in Learning. Lecture Notes in Computer Science, vol. 10512, pp. 108–117. Springer, Cham (2017). https://doi.org/10.1007/978-3-319-67615-9_10

25. Tarimo, W.T., Deeb, F.A., Hickey, T.J.: Early detection of at-risk students in CS1 using teachback/spinoza. J. Comput. Sci. Coll. **31**(6), 105–111 (2016)

26. Zander, T.O., Kothe, C.: Towards passive brain–computer interfaces: applying brain–computer interface technology to human–machine systems in general. J. Neural Eng. **8**(2), 025005 (2011)

27. Zeyl, T., Yin, E., Keightley, M., Chau, T.: Partially supervised P300 speller adaptation for eventual stimulus timing optimization: target confidence is superior to error-related potential score as an uncertain label. J. Neural Eng. **13**(2), 026008 (2016)

28. Zhang, J., Wu, Y., Bai, J., Chen, F.: Automatic sleep stage classification based on sparse deep belief net and combination of multiple classifiers. Trans. Inst. Meas. Control **38**(4), 435–451 (2016)

ViewpointS: A Collective Brain

Philippe Lemoisson[1,2] and Stefano A. Cerri[3,4,5](✉)

[1] CIRAD, UMR TETIS, 34398 Montpellier, France
philippe.lemoisson@cirad.fr
[2] TETIS, Univ Montpellier, AgroParisTech, CIRAD, CNRS, IRSTEA, Montpellier, France
[3] DKTS: Digital Knowledge Technologies Services SRL, Via Ampère 61/A, 20131 Milan, Italy
sacerri@didaelkts.it
[4] FBK: Fondazione Bruno Kessler, Trento, Italy
[5] LIRMM, Univ Montpellier and CNRS, 161 Rue Ada, 34095 Montpellier, France

Abstract. Understanding and forecasting brain functions is the major challenge of our times. The focus of this endeavor is understanding and forecasting learning events, such as the dynamic adaptation of beams connecting neuronal cards in Edelman's Theory of Neuronal Group Selection (TNGS). We have conceived, designed and evaluated a new paradigm for constructing and using collective knowledge by Web interactions that we called ViewpointS. By exploiting the similarity with the TNGS we conjecture that it may be metaphorically considered a Collective Brain, especially effective in the case of trans-disciplinary representations. Far from being without doubts, in the paper we present the reasons (and the limits) of our proposal that aims to become a useful integrating tool for future quantitative explorations of individual brain functions as well as of collective wisdom at different degrees of granularity. We are therefore challenging each of the current approaches: the logical one in the semantic Web, the statistical one in mining and deep learning, the social one in recommender systems based on authority and trust; not in each of their own preferred field of operation, rather in their integration weaknesses far from the holistic and dynamic behavior of the human brain.

Keywords: Collective brain · Collective intelligence · Knowledge graph · Knowledge acquisition · Semantic web · Social web

1 Introduction

On one side, today's research on the human brain allows us to visualize and trace the activity along the beams connecting the neural maps. According to the Theory of Neuronal Group Selection (TNGS) that G. M. Edelman made public more than thirty years ago, the dynamic adaptation of these beams is the key of individual learning all lifelong.

Each brain is unique and open on the world, both through the observation/action loop and through social interactions mediated by language. Both loops involve a complex multi layers network of neural maps bi-directionally interconnected by beams of neural terminations, the reinforcement of which is supervised by our homeostatic internal systems, also called system of values. On the other side, we live a digital revolution

© Springer Nature Switzerland AG 2020
C. Frasson et al. (Eds.): BFAL 2020, LNAI 12462, pp. 34–44, 2020.
https://doi.org/10.1007/978-3-030-60735-7_4

where the Web plays an increasing role in the collective construction of knowledge; this happens through the semantic Web and its ontologies, via the indexing and mining techniques of the search engines and via the social Web and its recommender systems based on authority and trust. Our goal is twofold: i) to exploit the metaphor of the brain in order to improve this collective construction of knowledge and ii) to better exploit our digital traces in order to refine the understanding of our learning processes. We have prototyped a Knowledge Graph built on top of Web interactions where resources (agents, documents and descriptors) are dynamically interlinked by beams of digital connections called viewpoints (human viewpoints or artificial viewpoints issued from algorithms). We-as-agents endlessly exploit and update this graph, so that by similarity with the TNGS, we conjecture that it may be metaphorically considered a Collective Brain evolving under the supervision of all our individual systems of values. Moreover, each viewpoint may embed a mental state, either in the shape of an emoticon, or as the result of a measure of brain activity. In the paper we open pathways and show their limits, hoping to have stepped forward in the direction of our goal.

In Sect. 2, we present a schematic view of the biological bases of cognition. We start by the "three worlds" of K. Popper (1978) who sets a simple framework where the interaction between minds can be studied. We re-visit the biological bases of cognition as described by the Theory of Neuronal Group Selection of G.M. Edelman (TNGS). According to the TNGS, the perception-action loop and the social interaction's loop mediated by language are regulated by our homeostatic internal systems, or system of values, that biologically ground our emotions, personality traits, motivation, ethics[1]. We illustrate "learning through interaction" as exposed by D. Laurillard or J. Piaget, in this schematic view.

In Sect. 3, we explore the collective construction of knowledge in the Web paradigm, assuming that a large proportion of the traces we produce and consume today are digital ones, managed by artificial systems governed by algorithms. We distinguish three distinct paradigms, respectively governed by logics, by statistics and by authority and trust. Thus it becomes a challenge to integrate these paradigms and describe how individual systems of values participate to learning events.

Section 4 is dedicated to the ViewpointS approach, as a candidate for answering the challenge. The metaphor of "neural maps interconnected by beams of neurons" led to the design of a graph of "knowledge resources interconnected by beams of viewpoints", where each agent can benefit from the traces of others and react to them by adding new traces. As a result, the combination of all individual "system of values" regulates the evolution of knowledge; we conjecture that it may be metaphorically considered a Collective Brain. In [1] we had presented some reflections about the potential exploitation of our ViewpointS approach as an environment for the elicitation and analysis of brain functions during interaction sessions. In particular, the key question was to understand and forecast – as much as possible supported by empirical evidence – cognitive

---

[1] From: http://www.acamedia.info/sciences/sciliterature/edel.htm#1 « Values - simple drives, instincts, intentionality - serve as the tools we need for adaptation and survival: some have been developed through eons of evolution; and some are acquired through exploration and experience. It needs to be stressed that "values" are experienced, internally, as feelings - without feeling there can be no animal life. »

and emotional events linked to serendipitous learning; we therefore proposed that each viewpoint would embed a mental state, either in the shape of an emoticon, or as the result of a measure of brain activity. It was expected that a "world of knowledge" structured in terms of proximity between and among documents, descriptors (tags) and agents would be likely to trigger serendipitous learning. In this paper we deepen these reflections.

We then conclude by recapitulating our proposal that aims to become a useful integrating tool for future quantitative exploration of individual brain functions as well as of collective wisdom at different degrees of granularity. We are not yet sure if the collective knowledge emerging from our proposed Collective Brain will perform competitively with the existing separate paradigms respectively governed by logics, by statistics and by authority and trust. Our proposal has the limits inherent to any integrator; nevertheless, if it does not ensure scientific discovery, it may facilitate the process.

2   A Schematic View of the Biological Bases of Cognition

In this section, we start by adopting a well-known philosophical position where the questions of cognition and interaction can be addressed. Then we draft a schematic view of the lessons learned from Edelman about the biological mechanisms supporting cognition, and finally we use this representation within D. Laurillard's conversational learning scenario in order to test it against the question of knowledge acquisition through interaction.

2.1   The Three Worlds

To start with our analysis about minds in interaction, we need some philosophical default position; "the three worlds" of K. Popper [2] provides a relevant framework. Such a framework, which had already found an expression in the semantic triangle of Odgen and Richards [3], is in line with what J. Searle writes in [4]. In the following, we shall refer to the three worlds as W_1, W_2 and W_3, with the following definitions:

W_1 is the bio-physical world where objects and events exist independently from us, from our perceptions, our thoughts and our languages. Causal relations, insofar we are not directly implied by some event, are also considered independent from us.

W_2 is the internal world of subjectivity, where the perception of objects and events of W_1 leave traces in memory that are combined in order to participate to the construction of our own knowledge, our consciousness about the world, where intentions appear and the emotions that will be the trigger for our actions.

W_3 is the world of the cultures and languages, made of interpretable traces: signs, symbols, rules of behavior and rules for representing objects and events of W_1. W_3 is the support of communication among individuals; Odgen and Richards call "referencing" the process that binds within each individual W_2 the shared referents of W_1 to the shared symbols of W_3. Within W_3, we find all specialized languages of the scientific disciplines, as well as the language of emotions represented by smileys. Digital images, e.g.: a satellite image or the scan of a document, are traces interpretable by humans or by algorithms (machines).

W_1 is where it happens, W_3 is where we can communicate about what happens, and W_2 is where all the links are … this is why we are going to pay special attention to the internal world W_2.

2.2   The Internal World of the Mind

This section is a synthesis of the work of G.M. Edelman [5, 6], founder of the Theory of Neuronal Group Selection (TNGS).

There is neither correlation between our personality and the shape of our skull (despite the teachings of phrenology), nor localized coding of information; no autopsy will ever reveal any single chunk of knowledge available in the brain. The brain is not a computer, but a highly dynamic, distributed and complex system, maybe the most complex "object" of the known universe.

According to the TNGS, every brain is twice unique: first because its cellular organization results from the laws of morphogenesis. Most important, however, is Edelman's second reason for the brain uniqueness: the brain is a set of "neural maps" continuously selected according to the individual's experiences. These cards, or adaptive functional units, are bi-directionally linked one-another by a fundamental integrating mechanism: the "re-entry". This crucial hypothesis allows a functional integration requiring neither any "super-card" nor any "supervising program": the neural maps are like "musicians of an orchestra linked one-another by wires in the absence of a unique conductor". The bi-directional re-entry links are the result of a selective *synaptic reinforcement among* groups of neurons; similarly: the cards result from a *synaptic reinforcement internal* to each group of neurons composing them. These reinforcements are triggered and managed by the *homeostatic internal systems*, also called "*system of values*" of each individual.

Figure 1 (/left part of the figure) shows an observation-action loop that highlights several brain cards re-entering. The external world's signals enter, in this representation: the perception of an apple, and exit in order to produce a movement: grasping the apple. On turn: the movement modifies the signals perceived. This type of loops originates the *perceptual categorization* event, common to all organisms highly evolved. It is a peripheral process, somehow prisoner of the current time, but correlated in the hippocampus with the system of values and the experience of the past, what allows adaptation of the behavior according to the likelihood of benefits or dangers.

In humans as well as in some higher mammals, there is a second level of categorization, supported by cards situated in the temporal, frontal and parietal areas. Beyond the immediate cartography of the world, humans may shape some durable concepts (*conceptual categorization*) that consider the past and/or the future. The activation of the bi-directional links binding the two zones of categorization - perceptive and conceptual – correspond to the emergence of a primary conscience, as it appears in Fig. 1 (/right part of the figure)

Finally, the human brain parts specialized in language (the Wernicke and Broca areas), also linked bi-directionally to the two categorization areas, play a major role in the emergence of a *consciousness of a higher level*, enabling the human subject to "map" his-her own experience and study him-herself.

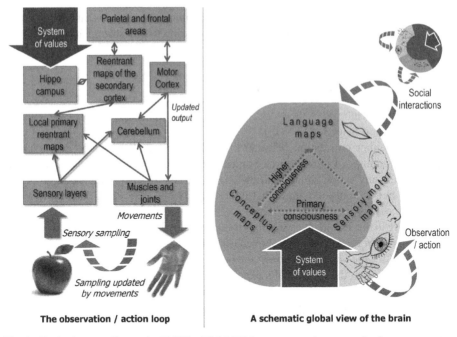

The observation / action loop | **A schematic global view of the brain**

Fig. 1 The brain according to the TNGS of G.M. Edelman: a complex network of re-entrant maps in interaction loops with the world

The basic principles of the TNGS (selective reinforcement and re-entry) can explain all learning processes, from simple memorization to skill acquisition (reacting to a context by updating the perception-action loops) and knowledge acquisition (by evolving the conceptual categorization with the help of language, specifically during social interactions). All these processes are correlated to the memory of internal states, in such a way that learning is selected according to the advantages that they offer to the subject, i.e., is regulated by our system of values.

A kernel element learned from the TNGS, very relevant for us, is the following one. Since the supports for knowledge consist of a "physiological complex and adaptive network of neural maps interconnected", the metaphor of "knowledge graph" seems to us justified. This metaphor, consequently, induces naturally to search for a topology allowing to define distances and proximity, like it was conjectured by the "zone of proximal development" of Vygotsky [7, 8].

2.3 Minds in Social Interaction

According to the two loops at the right of Fig. 1, we always learn through interaction: observation/action versus social interaction. These two loops clearly appear in D. Laurillard's work [9] when she analyzes the acquisition of knowledge in higher education; in her scenario, a student faces his teacher, they share a laboratory experimentation and simultaneously discuss it.

In [10] we have extended this scenario to interactions within a group of peers co-constructing a representation of a shared territory. In this multi-peers scenario, interactions occur through external processes at two levels: i) peers act in the shared territory i.e., act within the world W_1 of objects and events and ii) peers exchange personal views about their perceptions and actions i.e., exchange within the world W_3 of language.

While the actors exchange their inner views of the shared territory in the form of traces interpretable by the others, the assimilation / adaptation processes described by J. Piaget in [11] are activated within their internal worlds W_2. These internal processes can be interpreted in terms of series of re-entry loops according to the TNGS.

As consequence of all the above processes (external and internal), the inner views tend to synchronize and yield a shared representation. This may be called collective knowledge acquisition. We propose that what happens on the Web is a generalization of this prototypical scenario.

3   Humans in Web Interaction

The change in our lives that we have been experiencing since when Internet has gained a significant place, often called the digital revolution, has been theoretically addressed by several authors, among which S. Vial [12] and D. Cardon [13] for respectively the philosophical and sociological approach. This revolution has suggested a significant hope: Internet as a "space of shared knowledge" in the sense given by Gruber in [14] i.e., a space providing tailored advice on top of collected knowledge, structured data and high level automated expertise and able to bring in new levels of understanding. If we refer to the conceptual framework of K. Popper presented previously, Internet as a support for a huge set of digital traces interpretable by humans but also by machines is therefore part of W_3, the world of cultures and languages. This numeric space is far from being homogeneous in its contents however, and the approaches to co-build shared knowledge are multiples. Hereafter, we consider three paradigms.

The first paradigm is governed by the *logical* evidence: we usually call semantic Web this part of Internet logically structured where humans interact with databases encoding the knowledge of experts according to a conceptual scheme or ontology established by consensus. This mode has the advantage to give logical responses to correctly formulated questions (and only to questions with such a property) and allows one to be helped by algorithms during the conversation in order to delegate to them part of the job. But it has problems and limits. The first reason is that each ontology does only represent a fragment of the reality, and the consensus it reflects is necessarily local and temporary. Another reason is that the query languages are formal languages that assume a closed world – what is rarely the case –, at the same time requiring a certain learning effort in order to be used properly. And finally, interconnecting ontologies and supporting their evolution with time in a rapidly changing world are very heavy and costly processes. Various approaches based on automatic alignment [15], machine learning [16] or instance evaluation [17] exist; however the task is huge and never ending, due to the fact that each ontology's evolution is domain-dependent [18].

The second paradigm is governed by the *statistical* evidence. The issue is to exploit techniques of data mining, i.e: scan without too many assumptions a corpus, also called data set, of tweets, sequences, clicks, documents, ... and detect regularities, frequencies, co-occurrences of items or terms. In other words: to feed suitable algorithms with the big data in order to reveal regularities. This approach has the advantage to contribute to make the digital world W_3 visible by reducing it to a synthesis produced by the mining algorithms. However, the simplicity of these descriptions must pay a price to the expressiveness or even to the effectiveness: we often just see the surface, the "syntax" and not the depth, the "meaning". Today, a simple question with three independent keywords on Google may give very disappointing results. Further: what is even worse, is that any inferential statistics – the only one allowing us to take significant decisions - requires to select the data to analyze according to the goal chosen for the analysis, not independently from the objective. Therefore, the statistical space very often has interest for describing some apparent phenomena, rarely for interpreting them in order to abstract and cumulate the knowledge associated to their meaning; i.e., build chunks of science.

The third paradigm is based on authority and *trust*, and builds upon light traces such as 'likes', 'bookmarks' and 'tweets'. The algorithms of the social Web propose services of information search and recommendations by applying methods of graph analysis and exploiting the various personal, subjective and spontaneous contributions available on it. They clearly operate in an open world. However, the quality of their responses is hardly to be evaluated by logical criteria neither their stability assured along time.

The semantic Web project [19] aimed somehow at subsuming the three paradigms described above within the first one i.e., building up upon *logics*. After a first enthusiasm on the integration of ontologies (in order to assure interoperability among subdomains) it seems that the purely logical approach has its limits, even if they are daily pushed forward. In spite of the difficulties, the dream of Gruber and many others to fuse the three spaces: humans, algorithms and contents in order to profit from the emerging collective wisdom is very actual. Due to the digital revolution we have never been so near to the goal, and the following section aims to offer a potential way to explore this intriguing hypothesis and perhaps realize concrete steps towards significant progress in the direction of subsuming the three paradigms within the third one i.e., building up upon *trust* towards 'peers', would they be humans, databases or mining algorithms.

4   The ViewpointS Approach Discussed and Exemplified

This section first briefly recalls the ViewpointS framework and formalism for building collective knowledge in the metaphor of the brain - a detailed description can be found in [20, 21] - and then illustrates them through an imaginary case.

In the ViewpointS approach, the "neural maps interconnected by beams of neurons" are transposed into a graph of "knowledge resources (agents, documents, topics) interconnected by beams of viewpoints". The "systems of values" of the agents influence the viewpoints they emit, but also the way they interpret the graph.

We call *knowledge resources* all the resources contributing to knowledge: agents, documents and topics. We call *viewpoints* the links between *knowledge resources*. Each *viewpoint* is a subjective connection established by an agent (Human or Artificial) between two *knowledge resources*; the *viewpoint* $(a_1, \{r_2, r_3\}, \theta, \tau)$ stands for: the agent a_1 believes at time τ that r_2 and r_3 are related according to the emotion carried by θ. We call Knowledge Graph the bipartite graph consisting of *knowledge resources* and *viewpoints*. Given two *knowledge resources*, the aggregation of the beam of all connections (*viewpoints*) linking them can be quantified and interpreted as a proximity. We call *perspective* the set of rules implementing this quantification by evaluating each viewpoint and then aggregating all these evaluations into a single value. The *perspective* is tuned by the "consumer" of the information, not by third a part "producer" such as Google or Amazon algorithms; each time an agent wishes to exploit the knowledge of the community, he does so through his own subjective *perspective* which acts as an interpreter.

Tuning a perspective may for instance consist in giving priority to trustworthy *agents*, or to the most recent *viewpoints*, or to the *viewpoints* issued from the logical paradigm. This clear separation between the storing of the traces (the *viewpoints*) and their subjective interpretation (through a *perspective*) protects the human agents involved in sharing knowledge against the intrusion of third-part algorithms reifying external system of values, such as those aiming at invading our psyche, influencing our actions [22], or even computing bankable profiles exploitable by brands or opinion-makers [23]. Adopting a *perspective* yields a tailored *knowledge map* where distances can be computed between knowledge resources, i.e. where the semantics emerge from topology as well as from our own system of values expressed by the tuned perspective.

The shared semantics emerge from the dynamics of the observation/action loops. Agents browse the shared knowledge through the *perspectives* they adopt (observation), and reversely update the graph by adding new *viewpoints* expressing their feedback (action). Along these exploitation/feedback cycles, shared knowledge is continuously elicited against the systems of values of the agents in a selection process.

To illustrate this, we develop below an imaginary case where learners have to select resources inside an Intelligent Tutoring System (ITS) to which a Knowledge Graph is associated. They wish to learn about the topic 'apple' and from step1 to step4 the learners adopt a 'neutral' perspective which puts in balance all types of viewpoints (issued from the logical or mining paradigms, or from the emotions of the learners). However at step5 where B chooses a perspective discarding his own viewpoints in order to discover new sources of knowledge. What is figured in the schemas is not the Knowledge Graph itself, but the views (also called Knowledge Maps) resulting from the perspectives; in these maps (Fig. 2), the more links between two resources, the closer they are.

Step1 illustrates the initial state of the knowledge. A, B and C are co-learners in the ITS (linked as such within the logical paradigm); the blue arrows represent their respective systems of values, which play a key role both in the choice of *perspectives* and in the emission of *viewpoints*. D_1, D_2 and D_3 are documents that a mining algorithm has indexed by the topic/tag 'apple'.

Step2: A is a calm person who has time; she browses through D_1, D_2 and D_3 and has a positive emotion about D_1 and D_2 (she likes both and finds them relevant with respect to 'apple'); the capture of this emotion results in linking D_1 and D_2 to her and reinforcing the links between the documents and the topic 'apple'. B is always in a hurry; he asks the Knowledge Graph the question "which is the shortest path between me and the topic 'apple'?". According to the paths in the diagram, he gets a double answer: B-A-D_1-'apple'and B-A-D_2-'apple'.

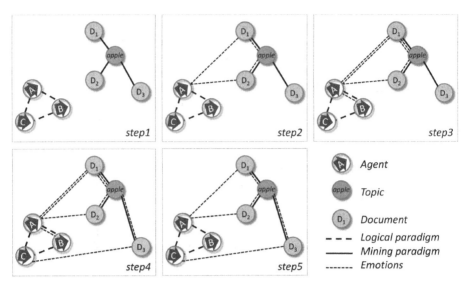

Fig. 2 The network of interlinked resources evolves along the attempts of the learners A, B and C to "catch" the topic 'apple' through performing the modules D_1, D_2 or D_3

Step3: B has a positive emotion about D_1 but not about D_2; this results in reinforcing the path B-A-D_1-'apple'. If he would ask his question now, he would then get only D_1.

Step4: C likes to explore; rather than taking a short path she browses through D_1, D_2 and D_3 and has a positive emotion about D_3 (she likes it and finds it relevant with respect to 'apple'); this results in linking D_3 to her and reinforcing the linking between D_3 and the topic 'apple'. At this stage, if A, B and C would ask for the shortest path to 'apple', they would respectively get D_1, D_1 and D_3.

Step5: B is not fully satisfied by D_1; he asks again for a short path: but in order to discover new sources of knowledge, he changes his perspective: he discards the viewpoints expressing his own emotions. This new perspective yields the view drawn in the figure, B-A-D_1-'apple', B-A-D_2-'apple'and B-C-D_3-'apple' have the same length i.e., D_1, D_2 and D_3 are equidistant from him. He may now discard D_1 (already visited) and D_2 (already rejected) and study D_3.

Along the five steps of this imaginary case, the evolution of "knowledge paths" follows the metaphor of the selective reinforcement of neural beams, except that this reinforcement is not regulated by a single system of values, rather by a collaboration/competition between the three systems of values of A, B and C. The three co-learners learn as a whole, in a trans-disciplinary way: the dynamics are governed by emotions and topology, not by logics.

5   Conclusion

Starting from the three worlds proposed by K. Popper (the external world of objects and events, the internal world of mind and the world of language: interpretable by humans and machines), we have explored the internal world by following the Theory of Neuronal

Group Selection (or Neural Darwinism) of G.M. Edelman. Learning and understanding rely on a complex network of re-entrant neural maps, i.e., maps connected by beams whose force is continuously reinforced – readjusted by the events of our life. These learning phenomena are regulated by our system of values and occur mainly through social interactions.

We have re-visited these elements within the paradigm of the Web and reformulated the question of the emergence of a collective knowledge partially supported by algorithms. The ViewpointS approach offers a formalism as well as a metaphor able to integrate most if not all these elements: we have illustrated through an imaginary case how to produce and consume knowledge in a trans-disciplinary mode.

Within ViewpointS: logical inferences of the semantic Web, statistical recommendations of the mining community, authority and trust of the social Web may all be exploited within the world of digital traces interpretable by human or artificial agents. Since both the construction of the graphs and their use, occur as a result of spontaneous activities of the humans, we conjecture with Edelman that these choices are regulated by the individual system of values that include instincts, culture, personality traits, shortly: affect [24]. As a consequence, we speculate to be facilitated in the goal to measure these values during the interactive activities constructing and using our knowledge graphs and maps in order to understand and forecast human brain behaviors [25].

Since ViewpointS integrates the logical, the statistical and the social Web, it is evident for us that we gain in the integration but we loose with respect to the advantages of each of the three approaches taken individually. For this reason, we are not yet sure if the collective knowledge emerging from ViewpointS graphs and maps (our proposed Collective Brain) will perform competitively with a similar wisdom emerging from each of the three crowds.

Nevertheless: as it has been always the case in the synergies between technological developments and scientific progress, the developments do not ensure scientific discovery, rather may facilitate the process. For instance: Galileo's telescopes did not directly produce the results of modern astronomy, but enabled a significant progress. We hope and believe that our proposed Collective Brain will have a positive impact in understanding and forecasting some aspects of human cognition.

References

1. Cerri, S.A., Lemoisson, P.: Tracing and enhancing serendipitous learning with ViewpointS. In: Frasson, C., Kostopulos, G. (eds.) Brain Function Assessment in Learning. LNAI, vol. 10512, pp. 36–47. Springer, Cham (2017). https://doi.org/10.1007/978-3-319-67615-9_3
2. Popper, K.: The Tanner Lectures on Human Values, pp. 143–167. University of Michigan, Michigan, USA (1978)
3. Hampton, J.A.: Concepts in the semantic triangle. In: The Conceptual Mind : New Directions in the Study of Concepts (2016)
4. Searle, J.: Speech acts: an essay in the philosophy of language. Cambridge University Press, Cambridge, UK (1969)
5. Edelman, G.M.: Neural Darwinism: The Theory of Neuronal Group Selection. Basic Books (1989)
6. Edelman, G.M., Tononi, G.: Comment la matière devient conscience | Éditions Odile Jacob. Sciences, Paris (2000)

7. Vygotski, L.S.: Apprentissage et développement: tensions dans la zone proximale. Paris La Disput. (2ème éd. Augment.), vol. 233 (1933)

8. Vygotsky, L.S.: Mind in Society: The Development of Higher Psychological Processes. Harvard University Press (1978)

9. Laurillard, D.: A conversational framework for individual learning applied to the 'learning organisation' and the 'learning society'. Syst. Res. Behav. Sci. **16**(2), 113–122 (1999)

10. Lemoisson, P., Passouant, M.: Un cadre pour la construction collaborative de connaissances lors de la conception d'un observatoire des pratiques territoriales. Cah. Agric., vol. 21, no. n°1, pp. 11–17 (2012)

11. Piaget, J.: La construction du réel chez l'enfant. Fondation Jean Piaget, Ed. Lonay, Suisse : Delachaux et Niestlé, pp. 307–339 (1937)

12. Vial, S.: L'être et l'écran - Comment le numérique change la perception. Presse Universitaire de France, Paris (2013)

13. Cardon, D. and Smyrnelis, M.-C.: La démocratie Internet. Transversalités, vol. N° 123, no. 3. Institut Catholique de Paris, pp. 65–73. 13 Sep 2012

14. Gruber, T.: Collective knowledge systems: where the social web meets the semantic web. Web Semant. Sci. Serv. Agents World Wide Web **6**(1), 4–13 (2008)

15. Jain, P., et al.: Contextual ontology alignment of LOD with an upper ontology: a case study with proton. In: Antoniu, G., et al. (eds.) The Semantic Web: Research and Applications, pp. 80–92. Springer, Berlin, Heidelberg (2011)

16. Zhao, L., Ichise, R.: Ontology integration for linked data. J. Data Semant. **3**(4), 237–254 (2014)

17. Schopman, B., Wang, S., Isaac, A., Schlobach, S.: Instance-based ontology matching by instance enrichment. J. Data Semant. **1**(4), 219–236 (2012)

18. Karapiperis, S., Apostolou, D.: Consensus building in collaborative ontology engineering processes. J. Univers. Knowl. Manage. **1**(3), 199–216 (2006)

19. Berners-Lee, T., Hendler, J., Lassila, O.: The semantic web. Sci. Am. **284**(5), 34–43 (2001)

20. Lemoisson, P., Surroca, G., Jonquet, C., Cerri, S.A.: ViewpointS: when social ranking meets the semantic web. In: Proceedings of Conference FLAIRS 17, Florida Artificial Intelligence Research Society Conference, North America, May. 2017. <https://www.aaai.org/ocs/index.php/FLAIRS/FLAIRS17/paper/view/15432>. Accessed 17 Aug 2020

21. Lemoisson, P., Surroca, G., Jonquet, C., Cerri, S.A.: ViewpointS: capturing formal data and informal contributions into an evolutionary knowledge graph. Int. J. Knowl. Learn. **12**(2), 119–145 (2018)

22. Duchatelle, V.: Hacker son auto-prophétie. Paris, 2017. https://linc.cnil.fr/fr/peut-hacker-son-auto-prophetie. Accessed 17 Aug 2020

23. Kosinski, M., et al.: Manifestations of user personality in website choice and behaviour on online social networks. Mach. Learn. **95**(3), 357–380 (2014)

24. Bamidis, P.D.: Affective learning: principles, technologies, practice. In: Frasson, C., Kostopoulos, G. (eds.) Brain Function Assessment in Learning. LNAI, vol. 10512, pp. 1–13. Springer, Cham (2017). https://doi.org/10.1007/978-3-319-67615-9_1

25. Shahab, A., Frasson, C.: Using electroencephalograms to interpret and monitor the emotions. In: Frasson, C., Kostopulos, G. (eds.) Brain Function Assessment in Learning. LNAI, vol. 10512, pp. 192–202. Springer, Cham (2017). https://doi.org/10.1007/978-3-319-67615-9_18

Neurocognitive Interventions and Brain Function in Children with Dyslexia

Athanasia Maria Tsiampa[1] and Konstantina Skolariki[2(✉)]

[1] HAU, Hellenic American Union, Athens, Greece
nancytsiampa@gmail.com
[2] Department of Informatics, Ionian University, Corfu, Greece
kskolariki@hotmail.com

Abstract. Dyslexia is a disorder characterized by reading impairment and it is affected by both neurocognitive and developmental factors. The aim of this paper is to present the latest scientific evidence which reveal different neurocognitive interventions that can improve brain function in order for children with reading difficulties and dyslexia to reach long-term reading improvement. As well as to evaluate the level of accomplished results of each neurocognitive intervention. Understanding the difficulties children with dyslexia face on their academic and personal life, it is important to expand research on how to successfully intervene in the process of learning. A variety of interventions such as visual perceptual training, intensive reading training, motor cognition training and several others have been shown to have positive effects on dyslexic children.

Keywords: Dyslexia · Neurocognition · Digital tools · Brain training · Neuroscience · Brain structures · Digital interventions

1 Introduction

Developmental dyslexia is a term used to define a learning disorder which is characterized by a severe disability or impairment in reading [1]. Scientists have given a variety of definitions to the term "dyslexia" over the years. The most widely cited definition asserts that "Dyslexia is a disorder manifested by difficulty in learning to read despite conventional instruction, adequate intelligence and sociocultural opportunity. It is dependent upon fundamental cognitive disabilities which are frequently of constitutional origin" [2]. A more recent definition that incorporates educational and psychological notions states that "dyslexia is a persistent and unexpected difficulty in developing age- and experience-appropriate word reading skills" [3]. Dyslexia has been associated with both neurocognitive and developmental factors.

Speech and language development are multifactorial processes that include cognitive, motor and sensory inputs and involve several brain regions such as the insular cortex, the angular gyrus, the basal ganglia, Wernicke's area and Broca's area [4–6]. The insular cortex has proven to be play a role in language processing [7]. The angular gyrus aids in word/concept comprehension [8]. The basal ganglia are associated with cognitive

© Springer Nature Switzerland AG 2020
C. Frasson et al. (Eds.): BFAL 2020, LNAI 12462, pp. 45–54, 2020.
https://doi.org/10.1007/978-3-030-60735-7_5

functions. Wernicke's area works in collaboration with the insular cortex, the angular gyrus and the basal ganglia for word processing in order to determine their meaning [9]. Broca's area is essential for language formation and expression [10]. A vast body of studies show that the frontoparietal control network (FPN) is responsible for facilitating the neural health in specific brain domains including regions that are linked to the reading ability [11].

One of the major scientific concerns in the field of Developmental Psychology is whether particular neurocognitive interventions can enhance the brain functions of children with neurobiological disorders like dyslexia. The question that arises is whether certain interventions can stimulate the typical neural circuits that are associated with language and reading processes in children with reading difficulties [12]. The aim of this paper is to present the latest scientific evidence which reveal different neurocognitive interventions that can improve brain function in order for children with reading difficulties and dyslexia to reach long-term reading improvement. Another goal of this paper is to ascertain the level of accomplished results of each neurocognitive intervention. A variety of research suggests that there is a broad relationship between educational resilience and FPN involvement while cortical connections allow individuals to regulate the health of neural systems [11]. Thus, through high levels of intervention, the executive function of reading networks can be enhanced in individuals with reading impairment and difficulties.

2 Brain Function

2.1 Brain Function and Language

The process of reading is a complex process that involves several steps and their corresponding brain regions. Initially, the brain needs to detect text. This step involves the optic nerve and other nerve bundles that transport signals from the eyes to the visual cortex. Subsequently, the brain interprets the text via a system of regions including the Broca's area, the angular gyrus, insular cortex, basal ganglia, cerebellum and Wernicke's area. The majority of the areas associated with language and reading are located in the left hemisphere of the brain. The frontal lobe is the largest lobe of the brain and it is responsible for several cognitive functions such speech and emotions regulation, planning and consciousness. The parietal lobe is linked with the conveyance of language inputs to memory for contextual understanding. The occipital lobe is important for letter identification and the temporal lobe is involved in verbal memory.

2.1.1 Broca's Area

Broca's area is located in the frontal lobe and plays a significant role in language formulation and manipulation of language and speech [13]. Broca's area is proposed to be involved in synaptic processing [9, 14]. Studies have also implicated Broca's area with verbal working memory and sentence comprehension [15]. Studies implicate the pars triangularis part of Broca's area with sentence comprehension. Evidence suggests that Broca's area plays a role in the contextual comprehension of sentences [16, 17].

2.1.2 Angular Gyrus (AG)

Dejerine (1891) initially introduced the involvement of the angular gyrus (AG) in reading comprehension [18]. Research shows that reading and writing impairment is associated with AG damage [5, 8, 19]. The angular gyrus (AG) plays a role in a multitude of functions (Fig. 1). Friston, 2010, proposed a framework in which AG stood as an integration step between transforming sensory inputs (bottom-up processing) to cognitive perceptions (top-down processing) [20]. This integration has a significant impact in the comprehension and reasoning of a variety of fundamental processes such as semantic access, fact retrieval, categorization of events and shifting attention to relevant details/events (Fig. 1, orange box). The bottom half of Fig. 1, is a simplified schematic illustration of the multifaceted interactions of the AG with other parts of the brain and their involvement in certain cognitive functions [19, 21].

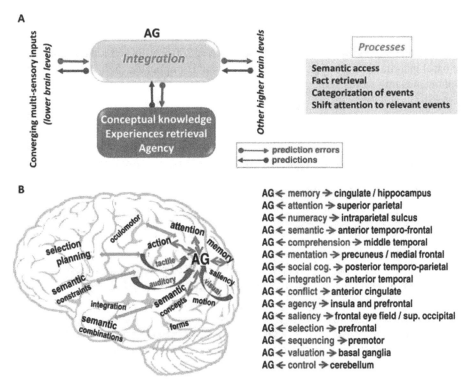

Fig. 1. This figure shows the variety of functions AG is linked to. Top part (A): It illustrates the conversion of multisensory inputs that are integrated in the AG (green box) to top-down predictions (blue box). The integration in the AG occurs from the transformation of bottom-up prediction errors (red arrows) to top-down predictions (blue arrows) until the minimization of the prediction error. The processes in which AG appears to contribute to can be seen in the orange box. Bottom part (B): An illustration of the relationship between the AG and other subsystems. It shows the convergence of different inputs to the AG (red arrows) and the connections with different subsystems (orange arrows). Connections with other potential subsystems are shown with blue arrows. (Taken from [22]) (Color figure online)

2.1.3 Insular Cortex

The insula cortex is part of the cerebral cortex. Evidence shows that the insula is involved in certain aspects of speech and language [23–25]. The role of insula in the production of speech was initially speculated from studies of patients with speech impairment caused by stroke [26]. A meta-analysis of fMRI and PET by Eickhoff et al., 2009, showed that the insular may act as a relay between cognitive-related tasks of language and motor-related aspects for vocalization in basal ganglia and cerebellum [7, 27].

2.1.4 Basal Ganglia

Basal ganglia (BG) are a group of subcortical structures (nuclei) in the cerebral hemispheres. Each nuclei of the basal ganglia acts both individually with particular functions in the brain as well as in an interconnected manner. The nuclei of the basal ganglia form a network that plays significant role in several key functions such as cognitive, emotional, and movement-related functions. Evidence shows that the BG is involved in executive functioning (EF) [28]. Several studies have indicated the role of basal ganglia in several reading and language tasks [29]. Ullman, 2001, proposed a model in which the basal ganglia are part of a cognitive system that is implicated in the transformation of phonemes into words [30].

2.1.5 Cerebellum

A mounting amount of studies implicate the involvement of the cerebellum in several cognitive processes such as language processing [31–36]. Another study by Booth et al., 2007, showed that the cerebellum had reciprocal involvement with brain regions associated with phonological processing [29].

2.1.6 Wernicke's Area

Wernicke's area is located in the temporal lobe on the left side of the and has proven to play a significant role in language development, processing and understanding as well as reading and speech comprehension [13]. It works in collaboration with AG, insular cortex and basal ganglia for word processing in order to comprehend context and meaning [10]. Damage to this particular area can lead to impairment of language development and/or usage [37]. Language aphasia is language impairment that has an impact on the ability to comprehend written and spoken communication [10].

2.2 Comparison with Normal Brain

Lobier et al., 2014, used contrasts in order to identify the main networks of brain regions activated in several tasks in dyslexic and control subjects [38]. Multi-element (ME) visual processing plays a significant role in reading difficulties in dyslexic individuals who present no impairment in their phonological skills [39–41]. Figure 2 shows the brain areas activated in both groups. ME processing lead to the activation of a bilateral cortical network, the occipital extra-striate cortex bilaterally, the pre-supplementary motor area, the right superior and middle frontal gyri and the fusiform and inferior temporal gyri bilaterally in control participants regardless of the stimulus type. In dyslexic subjects the activation included a more limited network including the lingual gyrus, the parietal postcentral gyrus, the left rolandic operculum and supramarginal gyrus.

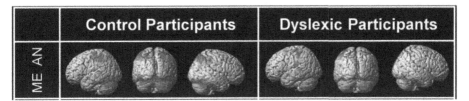

Fig. 2. Activations as a result of multiple element processing for control and dyslexic subjects. Voxel-wise threshold of p < 0.001 uncorrected with an extent threshold correction of p < 0.05 at the cluster level was used. (Taken from [38]).

3 Neurocognitive Interventions in Order to Enhance Learning in Children with Dyslexia

3.1 Cortical Connections

Mental health research suggests that there is a broad relationship between educational resilience and the frontoparietal control network (FPN). FPN plays a significant role in facilitating neural health [11]. Cortical connections allow individuals to regulate the health of neural systems. Therefore, through high levels of intervention in individuals with reading impairments, the executive functions which are considered critical for learning could improve [42, 43]. However, this approach shows inconsistent validity of prediction for the level of improvement through said intervention [44]. This means that isolated cognitive control networks cannot predict the levels of response to the intervention. Cognitive control systems are essential for their role in resilient learning since they strengthen and facilitate connections on critical control networks by creating alternate paths of the reading systems. Therefore, students may benefit from interventions that involve reading and executive functions [45].

3.2 Visual Perceptual Training

According to research, another training that has effectively improved the reading comprehension for dyslexic children is the Visual Perceptual training (VPT) [46]. Although it does not include phonological, orthographic or reading interventions there are significant improvements in fluency compared to established treatments since it develops automatization of visual, perceptual and attentional processing [47], global visual processing [48, 49], rapid endogenous visuospatial orienting and inhibitory-controlled attentional focus [50]. Reading acceleration programs represent letter units, words and sentences which through computerized adaptations stimulate the working memory, attention and executive functions. However, explicit phonological or orthographic training is not included, fact that leads to a gap on the scientific findings in terms of how easy it would be for the children to accurately decode and comprehend morphological, orthographical and then reading processes. Therefore, only tentative conclusions can be drawn regarding the impact of the intervention's efficacy in orthography [46].

3.3 Intensive Reading Training

What has been suggested as an intervention which is also involved in the brain's ability to adapt to environmental changes is Intensive Reading training which stimulates white matter strongly correlated with academic skills. Research suggests that the cross-sectional correlations in tissue properties change from week to week leading to rapid changes across cortical associations [51]. Through the connection of distinct components in certain aspects of reading, phonological awareness is achieved, projecting visual word recognition. By affecting the learning process there are longitudinal changes in many different white matter tracts which arise from common biological mechanisms over a large anatomical scale. Consequently, short-term plasticity which is associated with intensive training on reading skills leads to widespread positive effects in the reading networks [50]. fMRI findings reflect that anatomy-behavior correlation changes over the course of learning. Considering the fact that the posterior corpus callosum is considerably stable during intervention, it is believed to also have a stable correlation with reading skills. Consequently, when the children's educational environment follows a targeted intervention program that involves intensive reading training, white matter tissue properties change, leading to phonological decoding skills. Intensity and repetition, involving 5 h each day for 5 days a week in letters, syllables, words and connected texts through a personalized instruction, become the foundation for spelling and comprehension [51].

3.4 Reading Acceleration Program

The rate in which children can monitor their errors and cognitive abilities is suggested to be another neurocognitive intervention. According to Horowitz-Kraus et al., 2014, greater awareness of the reading errors makes the children more active and efficient during the process of recognizing the desired and actual responses [12]. Several improvements in reading which are related with cognitive abilities occur during the Reading Acceleration Program (RAP) training. On the other side, further research is needed for spatial resolution and change in the brain activation since EEG only provides spatial information which cannot pinpoint possible changes that may occur in the neural circuitries. Detection on the levels of brain activation and specifically on the frontal lobe activation is necessary since it plays a significant role in the reading process. Although these functions were tested, they did not underlie reading therefore there are no specific findings in terms of the level of the improvement they offer and as a result statistical analysis did not reveal any significant interactions. The issue that arises at this point is the way through which a dyslexic child could achieve RAP training when the working memory is impaired.

3.5   Motor Cognition Program

As working memory is considered to play an essential role in information acquisition, intervention programs which enhance its function are believed to be assistive in a dyslexic child's reading skills. Cognitive psychological memory mechanisms are responsible for the observation, rehearsal, encoding and retrieval of information [52]. In order to reach assimilation, a child needs to be able to decompose a task into sensory input in order to register the component into his long-term memory. In the case when children have impaired working memory the Motor Cognition program involves the improvement of the working memory through word decoding for reading. By paying attention to verbally presented digits, encoding them and reciting them verbatim the amount of information that a child can hold in their working memory increases. Consequently, working memory is improved and phonological decoding is built as a skill.

3.6   Computer Programs

Considering the different domains which are responsible for the reading process, a compilation of brain domains that are involved in the enhancement of brain functions would be of great advantage. Composite keys for the reading fluency are considered to be the phonological, orthographical, semantic and basic higher order abilities related to the executive functions such as attention, working memory and the speed of processing [12]. Although research is based on instructional strategies which have proven to be effective for sub-domains of literacy, reading intervention programs should include different combination of sub-components of reading. This would lead to the improvement of several domains of reading. These domains involve reading recovery, multi-components, treatment mastery, discrimination in depth, and fast forward. The drawback at this point though, would be the necessary time required for the intervention in order to train non-impaired domains according to the traditional program curricula. Accepting the fact that the majority of time is devoted to the reading domains with greater impairments, it would be necessary to adjust a traditional school curriculum or the intervention so that it could lead to the future expected outcomes. When human intervention cannot cover the number of students that populate the school environments, computer programs could be created and used in order to further support the intervention. Research suggests that computer programs offer several advantages compared to teachers' interventions alone. Since computers provide manipulations, digitized speech and tailored instructions they can give direct feedback to the students and motivate them to proceed with the relevant tasks more systematically and directly. Mioduser et al., 2000, supported that computer-based instructions bring higher scores in phonological awareness, word recognition and letter naming skills [53]. This brings a successful reading acquisition through the auditory and visual characteristics of the computerized environment.

4   Conclusions

Learning difficulties and specifically dyslexia have been a matter of concern for many years. Many conclusions were drawn about the ways through which teachers and educators could academically approach the learning process. Latest research has guided professionals to consider as major factors that exceed the social and emotional environment, the brain functions and its effects on the learning process. Taking as a fact that each brain is unique and adaptable to the environment, further investigation and research regarding the plasticity of the brain is required. Plasticity and adaptation lead to the formation of neural circuits which are involved in an individual's ability to process, activate and restore information to his memory. Understanding the difficulties children with dyslexia face on their academic and personal life, it is important to expand research on how to successfully intervene in the process of learning. Machine and computerized learning could be implemented for intervention in order to assist educators in their daily responsibilities. Computerized programs that are based on a multisensory approach that affect different brain domains, would achieve the expansion of the neural networks and simultaneously the synergy of the different brain structures that are considered responsible for the reading process. Focusing on certain brain functions, specific computerized tasks could create a new teaching model that would estimate the required time in order to strengthen the auditory, visual and kinesthetic characteristics that are involved in the learning process and give the necessary feedback and scaffolding. The feedback provided is essential not only for the academic achievements but also for the emotional stability of each student so as not to underperform and experience emotional burnout and failure.

A multidisciplinary approach to dyslexia would involve i) the activation of working memory, ii) visuospatial sketchpads, and iii) central executive functions. Early intervention programs in orthographic and morphological spelling, in combination with high intensity reading practices promise new positive future findings in the field of developmental psychology and brain disorders such as dyslexia. What is necessary though to be further investigated are the varying intensities and durations of the interventions in order to measure their long-term effects and automation on larger samples, manipulating other dimensions such as attention and working memory [11].

References

1. Peterson, R., Pennington, B.: Developmental dyslexia. Ann. Rev. Clin. Psychol. **11**(1), 283–307 (2015). Psychology in the Schools, 1970. Critchley, M. The Dyslexic Child. (2nd edn.) Springfield, Ill: Charles C. Thomas, 1970, 137 p., $7.50, vol. 10, issue 2, pp. 264–266
2. Yang, J., Peng, J., Zhang, D., Zheng, L., Mo, L.: Specific effects of working memory training on the reading skills of Chinese children with developmental dyslexia. Plos One **12**(11), e0186114 (2017)
3. Parrila, R., Protopapas, A.: Dyslexia and word reading problems. In: Cain, K., Compton, D., Parrila, R. (eds.) Theories of Reading Development, pp. 333–358. John Benjamins, Amsterdam, The Netherlands (2017)
4. Broca, M.P.: Perte de la parole, ramollissement chronique et destruction partielle du lobe anterieur gauche du cerveau. Bull Soc Anthropol Paris. **2**, 235–238 (1861)
5. Geschwind, N.: The organization of language and the brain. Science **170**(961), 940–944 (1970)
6. Guenther, H.F.: Cortical interactions underlying the production of speech sounds. J. Commun. Disord. **39**(5), 350–365 (2006)
7. Oh, A., Duerden, E., Pang, E.: The role of the insula in speech and language processing. Brain Lang. **135**, 96–103 (2014)

8. Houdé, O., Rossi, S., Lubin, A., Joliot, M.: Mapping numerical processing, reading, and executive functions in the developing brain: an fMRI meta-analysis of 52 studies including 842 children. Dev. Sci. **13**(6), 876–885 (2010)
9. Rogalsky, C.: Broca's area, sentence comprehension, and working memory: an fMRI study (2020)
10. Ardila, A., Bernal, B., Rosselli, M.: The role of Wernicke's area in language comprehension. Psychol. Neurosci. **9**(3), 340–343 (2016)
11. Aboud, K.S., Barquero, L.A., Cutting, L.E.: Prefrontal mediation of the reading network predicts intervention response in dyslexia. Cortex **101**, 96–106 (2018)
12. Horowitz-Kraus, T., et al.: Reading acceleration training changes brain circuitry in children with reading difficulties. Brain Behav. **4**(6), 886–902 (2014)
13. Joseph, J., Noble, K., Eden, G.: The neurobiological basis of reading. J. Learn. Disabil. **34**(6), 566–579 (2001)
14. Grodzinsky, Y.: The neurology of syntax. Behav. Brain Sci. **23**, 1–71 (2000)
15. Martin, A., Kronbichler, M., Richlan, F.: Dyslexic brain activation abnormalities in deep and shallow orthographies: a meta-analysis of 28 functional neuroimaging studies. Hum. Brain Mapp. **37**(7), 2676–2699 (2016)
16. Caplan, D., Alpert, N., Waters, G.S., Oliveri, A.: Activation of Broca's area by syntactic processing under conditions of concurrent articulation. Hum. Brain Mapp. **9**, 65–71 (2000)
17. Rogalsky, C.: Broca's area, sentence comprehension, and working memory: an fMRI study. Front. Hum. Neurosci. **2**, 14 (2008)
18. Dejerine, J.: Sur un cas de cecite verbale avec agraphie, suivi d'autopsie. C.R. Societe de Biologie **43**, 197–201 (1891)
19. Price, C.J.: The anatomy of language: a review of 100 fMRI studies published in 2009. Ann. New York Acad. Sci. **1191**(1), 62–88 (2010)
20. Friston, K.J.: The free-energy principle: a unified brain theory? Nat. Rev. Neurosci. **11**(2), 127–138 (2010)
21. Jung-Beeman, M.: Bilateral brain processes for comprehending natural language. Trends Cogn. Sci. **9**(11), 512–518 (2005)
22. Seghier, M.: The Angular Gyrus. The Neuroscientist **19**(1), 43–61 (2012)
23. Augustine, J.R.: The insular lobe in Primates including humans. Neurol. Res. **7**, 2–10 (1985)
24. Craig, A.D.: How do you feel? interoception: the sense of the physiological condition of the body. Nat. Rev. Neurosci. **3**, 655–666 (2002)
25. Craig, A.D.: Interoception: the sense of the physiological condition of the body. Curr. Opin. Neurobiol. **13**, 500 (2003)
26. Ogar, J., et al.: Clinical and anatomical correlates of apraxia of speech. Brain Lang. **97**(3), 343–350 (2006)
27. Eickhoff, S., et al.: Coordinate-based activation likelihood estimation meta-analysis of neuroimaging data: a random-effects approach based on empirical estimates of spatial uncertainty. Hum. Brain Mapp. **30**(9), 2907–2926 (2009)
28. Tekin, S., Cummings, J.: Frontal–subcortical neuronal circuits and clinical neuropsychiatry. J. Psychosom. Res. **53**(2), 647–654 (2002)
29. Booth, J., Wood, L., Lu, D., Houk, J., Bitan, T.: The role of the basal ganglia and cerebellum in language processing. Brain Res. **1133**, 136–144 (2007)
30. Ullman, M.: A neurocognitive perspective on language: The declarative/procedural model. Nat. Rev. Neurosci. **2**(10), 717–726 (2001)
31. Desmond, J.E., Fiez, J.A.: Neuroimaging studies of the cerebellum: language, leaning and memory. Trends Cogn. Sci. **2**, 355–361 (1998)
32. Fulbright, R.K., et al.: The cerebellum's role in reading: a functional MR imaging study. Am. J. Neuroradiol. **20**(10), 1925–1930 (1999)

33. Moro, A., et al.: Syntax and the brain: disentangling grammar by selective anomalies. NeuroImage **13**(1), 110–118 (2001)
34. Tettamanti, M., et al.: Listening to action-related sentences activates fronto-parietal motor circuits. J. Cogn. Neurosci. **17**(2), 273–281 (2005)
35. Chen, S.H., Desmond, J.E.: Cerebrocerebellar networks during articulatory rehearsal and verbal working memory tasks. NeuroImage **24**(2), 332–338 (2005)
36. Chen, S.H., Desmond, J.E.: Temporal dynamics of cerebro-cerebellar network recruitment during a cognitive task. Neuropsychologia **43**(9), 1227–1237 (2005)
37. Binder, J.R.: The wernicke area: modern evidence and a reinterpretation. Neurology **85**, 2170–2175 (2015). https://doi.org/10.1212/WNL.0000000000002219
38. Lobier, M., Peyrin, C., Pichat, C., Le Bas, J., Valdois, S.: Visual processing of multiple elements in the dyslexic brain: evidence for a superior parietal dysfunction. Front. Hum. Neurosci. **8**, 479 (2014)
39. Valdois, S., et al.: Dyslexia in a French-Spanish bilingual girl: behavioural and neural modulations following a specific visual-attention span intervention program. Cortex **53**, 120–145 (2014). https://doi.org/10.1016/j.cortex.2013.11.006
40. Valdois, S., Bosse, M.-L., Tainturier, M.-J.: The cognitive deficits responsible for developmental dyslexia: review of evidence for a selective visual attentional disorder. Dyslexia **10**, 339–363 (2004). https://doi.org/10.1002/dys.284
41. Bosse, M.-L., Tainturier, M.J., Valdois, S.: Developmental dyslexia: the visual attention span deficit hypothesis. Cognition **104**, 198–230 (2007)
42. Blair, C., Razza, R.P.: Relating effortful control, executive function, and false belief understanding to emerging math and literacy ability in Kindergarten. Child Dev. **78**(2), 647–663 (2007)
43. Diamond, A.: Executive functions. Annu. Rev. Psychol. **64**, 135–168 (2013)
44. Stuebing, K.K., et al.: Are child cognitive characteristics strong predictors of responses to intervention? a meta-analysis. Rev. Educ. Res. **85**(3), 395–429 (2015). https://doi.org/10.3102/0034654314555996
45. Wanzek, J., Wexler, J., Vaughn, S., Ciullo, S.: Reading interventions for struggling readers in the upper elementary grades: a synthesis of 20 years of research. Read. Writ. **23**(8), 889–912 (2010)
46. Peters, J.L., De Losa, L., Bavin, E.L., Crewther, S.G.: Efficacy of dynamic visuo-attentional interventions for reading in dyslexic and neurotypical children: a systematic review. Neurosci. Biobehav. Rev. **100**, 58–76 (2019)
47. DasSmaal, E.A., Klapwijk, M.J., VanderLeij, A.: Training of perceptual unit processing in children with a reading disability. Cogn. Instr. **14**(2), 221–250 (1996)
48. Franceschini, S., Bertoni, S., Gianesini, T., Gori, S., Facoetti, A.: A different vision of dyslexia: local precedence on global perception (2017)
49. Judica, A., De Luca, M., Spinelli, D., Zoccolotti, P.: Training of developmental surface dyslexia improves reading performance and shortens eye fixation duration in reading. Neuropsychol. Rehabil. **12**(3), 177–198 (2002)
50. Huber, E., Donnelly, P.M., Rokem, A., Yeatman, J.D.: Rapid and widespread white matter plasticity during an intensive reading intervention. Nat. Commun. **9**(1), 1–13 (2018)
51. Facoetti, A., Lorusso, M., Paganoni, P., Umiltà, C., Mascetti, G.: The role of visuospatial attention in developmental dyslexia: evidence from a rehabilitation study. Cogn. Brain Res. **15**(2), 154–164, 213 (2003)
52. Ning, L., Liang, J., Crant, J.M.: The role of proactive personality in job satisfaction and organizational citizenship behavior: a relational perspective. J. Appl. Psychol. **95**(2), 395 (2010)
53. Mioduser, D., Tur-Kaspa, H., Leitner, I.: The learning value of computer-based instruction of early reading skills. J. Comput. Assist. Learn. **16**, 54–63 (2000)

Cross-Course and Multi-course Sentiment Classification of Student Posts

Foteini Dolianiti[1,2(✉)] ⓘ, Dimitrios Iakovakis[3] ⓘ, Sofia B. Dias[4] ⓘ,
Sofia Hadjileontiadou[5] ⓘ, José A. Diniz[4] ⓘ, Georgia Natsiou[2],
Melpomeni Tsitouridou[2], and Leontios Hadjileontiadis[3,6] ⓘ

[1] Lab of Medical Physics, School of Medicine, Aristotle University of Thessaloniki,
Thessaloniki, Greece
foteini.dolianiti@gmail.com
[2] Department of Early Childhood Education,
Aristotle University of Thessaloniki, Thessaloniki, Greece
{dolianiti,gnatsiou,tsitouri}@nured.auth.gr
[3] Department of Electrical and Computer Engineering, Aristotle University of Thessaloniki,
Thessaloniki, Greece
dimiiako12@gmail.com, leontios@auth.gr
[4] CIPER, Faculdade de Motricidade Humana, Universidade de Lisboa, Lisbon, Portugal
{sbalula,jadiniz}@fmh.ulisboa.pt
[5] Department of Primary Education, Democritus University of Thrace, Alexandroupolis, Greece
schatzil@eled.duth.gr
[6] Department of Electrical and Computer Engineering, Khalifa University
of Science and Technology, Abu Dhabi, UAE
leontios.hadjileontiadis@ku.ac.ae

Abstract. Affective Computing is one of the most active research topics in education. Increased interest in emotion recognition through text channels makes sentiment analysis (i.e., the Natural Language Processing task of determining the valence in texts) a state-of-the-practice tool. Considering the domain-dependent nature of sentiment analysis as well as the heterogeneity of the educational domain, development of robust sentiment classifiers requires an in-depth understanding of the effect of the teaching-learning context on model performance. This work investigates machine learning-based sentiment classification on datasets comprised of student posts in forums, pertaining to two different academic courses. Different dataset configurations were tested, aiming to compare performance: i) between single-course and multi-course classifiers, ii) between in-course and cross-course classification. A sentiment classifier was built for each course, exhibiting a fair performance. However, classification performance dramatically decreased, when the two models were transferred between courses. Additionally, classifiers trained on a mixture of courses underperformed single-course classifiers. Findings suggested that sentiment analysis is a course-dependent task and, as a rule of thumb, less but course-specific information results in more effective models than more but non-specialized information.

Keywords: Sentiment analysis · Education · Natural language processing

© Springer Nature Switzerland AG 2020
C. Frasson et al. (Eds.): BFAL 2020, LNAI 12462, pp. 55–65, 2020.
https://doi.org/10.1007/978-3-030-60735-7_6

1 Introduction

Affective Computing is a multi-disciplinary field which "*relates to, arises from, or influences emotion*" [1]. Numerous studies have demonstrated the impact of emotions on learning experience and their potential role in promoting or hindering student's academic achievement, self-regulation and higher-order thinking skills [2, 3]. Inspired by experienced human teachers who inform decisions based on both student knowledge and feelings, early works on Affective Computing applications in education had highlighted the potential benefits from creating computer tutors that display empathy and intelligence during their interactions with students [4]. Today, Affective Computing is one of the most active research topics in education, with studies focusing on the design of emotion recognition and expression systems/methods/instruments as well as on examining the relationships between emotion, motivation, learning style, and cognition [5].

Emotions are expressed and communicated through various channels, including text (contextual information), audio (speech), facial expressions and body gestures (visual) and internal neurophysiological changes (brain activity, blood pressure, heart beat rate, etc.) [6, 7]. Systematic reviews of Affective Computing in education have revealed that the textual channel is the most widely-used affective measurement mode within the domain and dimensional models are the most preferred approach for describing students' affective states [5]. This trend towards text data and dimensional models is in line with the growing research interest in sentiment analysis (SA) techniques and applications in education. Although SA is an umbrella term that encompasses many related Natural Language Processing (NLP) tasks [8], it is most commonly used to refer to the task of polarity classification [9]. The latter deals with the automatic determination of the valence of a text, be it positive, negative and/or neutral, and this task is the focus of the present work, as well.

Although NLP researchers have been exploring SA solutions for almost two decades in numerous fields, such as movie reviews, politics, e-commerce and different product reviews, a generally applicable solution does not yet exist. The key barrier lies in the context and its direct impact on word meaning and polarity. Previous studies have demonstrated that SA is domain-dependent, topic-dependent, temporally-dependent and language style-dependent [10]. In the educational domain, dependency may take the form of course discipline and content, since each course has its own technical vocabulary [11]. Nevertheless, SA in education is coarsely approached and studies seem to neglect the high heterogeneity of this domain. As a result, most SA solutions are explored without providing enough information regarding the courses under consideration, while a great amount of the datasets used for training and testing the SA models are multidisciplinary [12]. Examples of studies that focus on the teaching-learning context and dataset origin are scarce (e.g., [13, 14]). However, in order to develop robust tools that will accurately identify positive, negative and neutral sentiment in student-generated texts, an in-depth understanding of the special challenges of the educational domain is needed in the first place.

The purpose of the present work is to investigate machine learning-based sentiment classification in the educational domain, and specifically, to explore the influence of the teaching-learning context on classification performance. Different dataset configurations are tested, aiming:

1. To compare performance between single-course and multi-course classifiers.
2. To compare performance between in-course and cross-course classification.

The rest of the paper is organized as follows: Sect. 2 presents the study methodology, describing the datasets, the model development workflow and the experimental process. Section 3 presents the classification results, which are discussed in Sect. 4. Finally, Sect. 5 concludes this work and poses future research considerations.

2   Materials and Methods

2.1   Datasets

Two educational datasets, previously introduced in [15], were employed. These datasets consisted of student forum posts in Moodle Learning Management System and originated from two academic courses offered by a public Higher Education Institution in Greece. The first dataset came from a postgraduate course on "Affective Computing and Learning" while the second dataset came from an undergraduate course on interdisciplinary approaches to Science and ICT in education, which focused on educational robotics (hereinafter, "Educational Robotics").

Data were collected across a semester, under blended learning. That is, apart from face-to-face lectures, students were also engaged in distant, asynchronous discussions in the courses' forums in Moodle. In both courses, discussion topics fell into two types, i.e., teacher-initiated discussion and student-initiated discussion. Table 1 summarizes the topic categories for each discussion type and includes some representative examples.

Since student posts were written in Greek, Google Translate was used in order to automatically translate them into English and any translation errors were then manually corrected. Previous studies in multilingual SA have demonstrated that machine translation systems can produce datasets that yield similar results as their corresponding native-speaker translations [16].

The datasets were used at sentence level, that is, each dataset instance was a student post's sentence. Each sentence was independently labeled by two annotators, by assigning a sentiment class (i.e., positive, negative or neutral). In order to assess the quality of the dataset labels, percent agreement and Krippendorff's alpha [17] were calculated. Dataset size, class distribution and inter-rater reliability values are provided in Table 2, where "+*tive*" and "–*tive*" signify positive and negative sentiment, respectively.

2.2   Model Architecture

The model architecture for sentiment classification was the same in all experiments conducted. The models were developed using Microsoft Azure Machine Learning Studio (ML Studio)[1], which offers a graphical user interface (GUI)-based environment for constructing and operationalizing Machine Learning workflow. Specifically, Azure ML

---

[1] https://studio.azureml.net/.

Table 1. Discussion types, topic categories and example posts in course forums

Discussion type	Topic category	Examples
Teacher-initiated discussion	Student feedback towards course and activities	*"What were your impressions of our first meeting?"* *"How was the experience of co-creating the online report?"*
	Debate and reflection upon course content and material	*"[…] search for different emotion recognition and recording systems, and discuss […] their potentialities in the educational domain"* *"which concepts/procedures [of the BeeBot] would you need to understand in depth before you carry out educational robotics activities and why?"*
Student-initiated discussion	Technical or administrative issues	*"I would like some clarifications on the conference and mandatory attendance"* *"Girls, I created an email account but I cannot edit the document…Could anyone add me in the group?"*
	Course assignments	*"[…] We would like some information about the software used in the experiment […]"* *"Do you know exactly what the assignment is about?"*

Table 2. Dataset size, class distribution and inter-rater reliability values for each course

Dataset	Size	Class distribution			Percent agreement	Krippendorff's alpha
		+tive	-tive	Neutral		
Affective computing and learning	881	34%	13%	53%	86.8%	0.773
Educational robotics	383	33%	25%	43%	79.6%	0.747

Studio's Text Analytics modules were used for pre-processing the datasets, representing text as feature vector, training the algorithm, testing and validating the models. The workflow is presented in detail in the following subsections.

Data Pre-processing
Pre-processing is a data "cleansing" process in order to reduce the noise caused by the unstructured nature of text. This phase included lemmatization, lowercasing, removing stopwords, numbers, special characters, emails and URLs, and expanding verb contractions (e.g., don't → do not). Additionally, the emoticons that were most commonly used by students in order to express positive or negative sentiment, were extracted using regular expressions and were replaced with the words "posemotion" (for positive emoticons, such as ☺, ♥) and "negemotion" (for negative emoticons, such as ☹).

Feature Extraction
Unigrams, weighted by Term Frequency – Inverse Document Frequency (TF-IDF), were employed for converting input text to feature vector. Unigrams also included the emoticons extracted in the pre-processing phase. During the development process, the model vocabulary was produced by extracting and weighting the unigrams included in the training set and the resulted vocabulary served as an input for representing the test set.

Minority Class Oversampling
Synthetic Minority Over-sampling Technique (SMOTE) [18] was applied on the training sets in order to handle the dataset imbalance problem. SMOTE is an oversampling approach in which the minority class is oversampled by creating new, "synthetic", examples rather than by oversampling with replacement [18]. SMOTE implementation in Azure ML Studio accepts only binary labels and, hence, oversampling was performed in pairs. That is, multi-class oversampling was decomposed into two binary sub-problems and each of the minority classes was oversampled against the prevalent class.

Algorithm
Support Vector Machines (SVM) were selected for building the classifiers, due to their suitability for text categorization tasks [19]. Since the study dealt with multiclass classification, the One-Versus-All (OVA) technique was employed and three different binary classifiers were built, each one trained to distinguish the examples of one class from the examples of other two classes [20]. Thus, an ensemble classifier was built, which combined the hypotheses of the three individual ones. During training, hyper-parameter tuning was performed using the entire grid method. The latter is an exhaustive method which tries all possible combinations over a range or number of parameter values and selects the best performing one. Specifically, grid search was performed for selecting the number of iterations and the value of lambda parameter. The number of iterations controls the trade-off between training speed and classifier performance while the value of parameter lambda defines the weight for L1 regularization, which controls model complexity for avoiding over-fitting and performs a kind of feature selection.

2.3 Experimental Process

The machine learning experiments conducted originated from three factors, namely:

1. The course (Experiment I): classification on the "Affective Computing and Learning" dataset, classification on the "Educational Robotics" dataset.
2. The training data source (Experiment II): single-course data, multi-course data.
3. Model transferring (Experiment III): in-course classification, cross-course classification.

Experiment I was a preparatory analysis to determine the baseline models for each course. Thus, two models were developed in total. Model training and testing was performed with a stratified 3-fold cross-validation.

In Experiment II, one classifier was built for each course, by merging the trainings sets of that course with the dataset of the other course. Thus, multi-source classifiers were developed, meaning that each model vocabulary was produced from data of both courses. Training and testing was again performed with a stratified 3-fold cross-validation. The dataset of the second course was fed into the first course's two-thirds that served as training set, and this process was repeated three times; one for each cross-validation.

In Experiment III, the whole dataset of each course was used for training the algorithm, and each classifier was then transferred from the training course (source course) to the other course (target course). Thus, the model trained on the "Affective Computing and Learning" dataset (source course) was tested on whole "Educational Robotics" dataset (target course), and conversely.

3   Results

Beginning with the baseline models from Experiment I, Table 3 presents the F-measure values for each individual class as well as on average. As Table 3 shows, both classifiers were most successful at predicting the neutral class and least successful at predicting the negative class. F-measure was substantially lower for negative sentiment compared to the other two classes. This is especially true for the "Affective Computing and Learning" classifier, which exhibited a bias towards neutral sentiment. Although average F-measure was higher for the "Affective Computing and Learning" classifier, results for the "Educational Robotics" dataset were more consistent across the three classes.

Table 3. Classification results for the baseline models

Course	F-measure			
	Positive	Negative	Neutral	Average
Affective computing and learning	0.695	0.488	0.806	0.663
Educational robotics	0.637	0.568	0.652	0.619

Regarding Experiment II, Table 4 reports the results from the multi-course classifiers, compared with the performance of the classifiers built from individual course data (baseline models). Both multi-course classifiers scored higher on the neutral sentiment and lower on the negative sentiment, exhibiting a pattern similar to that observed in the baseline models. Bias towards neutral sentiment was reduced for the "Affective Computing and Learning" course while relative consistency across the three classes was maintained for the "Educational Robotics" dataset. Nevertheless, multi-course classifiers' performance was substantially poorer both overall and at each individual class, compared to the performance of the single-course models.

Table 4. Classification results of multi-course and single-course classifiers against each course

Course		F-measure			
	Source data	Positive	Negative	Neutral	Average
Affective computing and learning	Single source	0.695	0.488	0.806	0.663
	Multi source	0.66	0.385	0.738	0.594
Educational robotics	Single source	0.637	0.568	0.652	0.619
	Multi source	0.584	0.508	0.599	0.564

Table 5 presents the results of cross-course classification from Experiment III. As Table 5 shows, both classifiers exhibited an extremely poor performance on negative class. Additionally, neutral sentiment had the highest F-measure score in the "Affective Computing and Learning"-to-"Educational Robotics" transfer scheme while positive sentiment had the highest F-measure in the "Educational Robotics"-to-"Affective Computing and Learning" transfer scheme. Thus, the "Affective Computing and Learning" model maintained the same pattern as the in-course classification while the behavior of the "Educational Robotics" model changed, when transferred to the "Affective Computing and Learning" dataset. In order to get a better insight into that model's behavior, the Confusion Matrix produced when transferred from the source-course to the target-course is presented in Fig. 1. Matrix rows represent the instances in the predicted classes while matrix columns represent the instances in the actual classes. A more intense box color indicates a higher number of instances. As Fig. 1 reveals, when the "Educational Robotics" model was transferred to the "Affective Computing and Learning" dataset, its sensitivity towards neutral instances greatly decreased. Neutral sentiment was confused with positive sentiment and most neutral instances were assigned to positive class rather than neutral class. Regarding the overall cross-course results, Table 6 reports the mean F-measure values for the in-course and cross-course classification, across both courses. As Table 6 shows, classification performance dramatically dropped during model transferring between courses, both overall and at each individual class.

Table 5. Cross-course classification results

Transfer scheme	F-measure			
	Positive	Negative	Neutral	Average
Affective computing and learning → Educational robotics	0.507	0.24	0.536	0.428
Educational robotics → Affective computing and learning	0.536	0.222	0.465	0.408

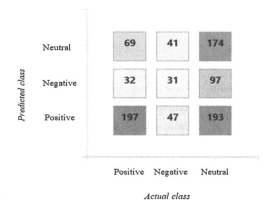

Fig. 1. Confusion matrix of the "Educational robotics" model, when transferred to the "Affective Computing and Learning" dataset

Table 6. Mean in-course and cross-course classification performance across both courses

Test course	F-measure			
	Positive	Negative	Neutral	Average
In-course	0.666	0.528	0.729	0.641
Cross-course	0.522	0.231	0.501	0.418

4   Discussion

The domain-dependent nature of SA and the heterogeneity of the educational domain are the two main points that gave rise to the present work. This study explored machine learning-based SA on datasets comprised of student posts in forums, pertaining to two different academic courses. Cross-course and multi-source classification were tested, in order to promote understanding towards the effect of the teaching-learning context on classification performance.

A sentiment classifier was built for each course, exhibiting a fair performance that ranged from 0.62 to 0.66 in average F-measure. However, classification performance dramatically dropped, when the two models were transferred between courses. Although performance loss was apparent in both transfer schemes (i.e., "Affective Computing and Learning" to "Educational Robotics", and conversely), an interesting model behavior was observed when the "Educational Robotics" model was transferred to the "Affective Computing and Learning"dataset. Specifically, its sensitivity towards neutral instances dramatically decreased, and most neutral instances were assigned to positive rather than neutral class. This finding suggests that neutral discussions around course contents –such as, a student post regarding Positive Psychology stating that "*the positive social environment [...] is a factor in the development of positive emotions*"- were falsely identified as student expressions of positive sentiment. That is, the "Educational Robotics" model missed the contextual information needed to separate actual positive sentiments from neutral instances that simply integrated "positive" words. Previous studies have also demonstrated that each course has its own technical vocabulary, which strongly affects classification performance, both in lexicon-based [11] and machine learning-based methods [13].

A simple approach in overcoming domain dependency and adapt machine learning-based sentiment models to a new context, is training on mixed context data. This approach results in general-purpose classifiers that are less domain-specific than a classifier that has only seen data from one domain [21]. Results from the present study showed that classifiers trained on a mixture of courses underperformed single-course classifiers. Thus, feeding models with more, yet non-specialized, information does not boost classification performance. Findings supporting the peculiarities of SA regarding the choice of training data have also been reported in [14]; model transferring benefits from greater amounts of target-course data, yet it worsens when multi-source, instead of single-source, datasets are employed. However, it is possible that the distribution of features between certain courses is similar enough, allowing out-of-course data to be used to some advantage [21]. In particular, positive features are often shared among different courses [14], indicating that instead of the current practice of fusing whole course datasets [12], a special focus should be placed on which subset of those courses or even which subset of training examples from those courses has a feature distribution most similar to the target domain [21]. Future extensions of this work could adopt a transfer learning approach to deal with data from multiple courses and improve model transferability.

5   Conclusions

This study investigated the transferability of sentiment classifiers between different courses and compared the popular approach of using multi-course and multi-disciplinary educational datasets with course-specific models. Findings suggested that SA is a course-dependent task and, as a rule of thumb, less but course-specific information results in more effective models than more but non-specialized information. The limitation of the small and unbalanced datasets employed in the present study was a result of two factors, i.e., the lack of publicly available educational datasets and the difficulty in collecting data from real-word teaching-learning settings. Similar studies with larger datasets could help determine whether the observed model behaviors are generalized across models with greater vocabulary coverage. Additionally, large datasets enable the deployment of sophisticated deep learning methods, like the case of ConvL model [14], which seems to be a promising solution in the cross-course classification problem. Therefore, there arises the need for properly annotated, open-access affective datasets of student-generated text, to enable standardized SA in education.

References

1. Picard, R.W.: Affective computing. MIT media laboratory perceptual computing section technical report No. 321. Cambridge, MA 2139 (1995)
2. Pekrun, R., Goetz, T., Titz, W., Perry, R.P.: Academic emotions in students' self-regulated learning and achievement: a program of qualitative and quantitative research. Educ. Psychol. **37**(2), 91–105 (2002)
3. Blanchette, I., Richards, A.: The influence of affect on higher level cognition: a review of research on interpretation, judgement, decision making and reasoning. Cogn. Emot. **24**(4), 561–595 (2010). https://doi.org/10.1080/02699930903132496
4. Lepper, M.R., Chabay, R.W.: Socializing the intelligent tutor: bringing empathy to computer tutors. In: Learning Issues for Intelligent Tutoring Systems, pp. 242–257. Springer, New York, NY (1988)
5. Yadegaridehkordi, E., Noor, N.F.B.M., Ayub, M.N.B., Affal, H.B., Hussin, N.B.: Affective computing in education: a systematic review and future research. Comput. Educ. **142**, 103649 (2019)
6. Luneski, A., Konstantinidis, E., Bamidis, P.D.: Affective medicine. A review of affective computing efforts in medical informatics. Methods Inf. Med. **49**(3), 207–218 (2010)
7. Bamidis, P.D., Papadelis, C., Kourtidou-Papadeli, C., Pappas, C., Vivas, B.A.: Affective computing in the era of contemporary neurophysiology and health informatics. Interact. Comput. **16**(4), 715–721 (2004)
8. Liu, B.: Sentiment analysis and opinion mining. Synth. Lect. Hum. Lang. Technol. **5**(1), 1–167 (2012). https://doi.org/10.2200/S00416ED1V01Y201204HLT016
9. Mohammad, S.M.: Sentiment analysis: detecting valence, emotions, and other affectual states from text. In: Meiselman, H.L. (ed.) Emotion Measurement, pp. 201–237. Woodhead Publishing-Elsevier, Sawston, Cambridge (2016)
10. Read, J.: Using emoticons to reduce dependency in machine learning techniques for sentiment classification. In: Proceedings of the ACL Student Research Workshop, pp. 43–48 (2005)
11. Wen, M., Yang, D., Rose, C.: Sentiment analysis in MOOC discussion forums: what does it tell us?. In: Stamper, J., Pardos, Z., Mavrikis, M., McLaren, B.M. (eds.) Proceedings of 7th International Conference on Educational Data Mining, pp. 130–137, London (2014)
12. Dolianiti, F.S., Iakovakis, D., Dias, S.B., Hadjileontiadou, S., Diniz, J.A., Hadjileontiadis, L.: Sentiment analysis techniques and applications in education: a survey. In: Tsitouridou, M., Diniz, J.A., Mikropoulos, T.A. (eds.) TECH-EDU 2018. CCIS, vol. 993, pp. 412–427. Springer, Cham (2019). https://doi.org/10.1007/978-3-030-20954-4_31
13. Bakharia, A.: Towards cross-domain MOOC forum post classification. In: Proceedings of the Third ACM Conference Learning @ Scale - L@S 2016, pp. 253–256 (2016)
14. Wei, X., Lin, H., Yang, L., Yu, Y.: A convolution-LSTM-based deep neural network for cross-domain MOOC forum post classification. Information **8**(3), 92 (2017)
15. Dolianiti, F.S., Iakovakis, D., Dias, S.B., Hadjileontiadou, S.J., Diniz, J.A., Natsiou, G., Tsitouridou, M., Bamidis, P.D., Hadjileontiadis, L.J.: Sentiment analysis on educational datasets: a comparative evaluation of commercial tools. Educ. J. Univ. Patras UNESCO Chair **6**(1), 262–273 (2019)

16. Balahur, A., Turchi, M., Steinberger, R., Ortega, J.M.P., Jacquet, G., Küçük, D., Zavarela, V., El Ghali, A.: Resource creation and evaluation for multilingual sentiment analysis in social media texts. In: Proceedings of Ninth International Conference on Language Resources and Evaluation, pp. 4265–4269. ELRA, Reykjavik, Iceland (2014)
17. Hayes, A.F., Krippendorff, F.: Answering the call for a standard reliability measure for coding data. Commun. Methods Measures 1(1), 77–89 (2007)
18. Chawla, N., Bowyer, K.W., Hall, L.O., Kegelmeyer, W.P.: SMOTE: synthetic minority oversampling technique. J. Artif. Intell. Res. 16, 321–357 (2002)
19. Saleh, M.R., Martín-Valdivia, M.T., Montejo-Ráez, A., Ureña-López, L.A.: Experiments with SVM to classify opinions in different domains. Expert Syst. Appl. 38(12), 14799–14804 (2011)
20. Rifkin, R., Klautau, A.: In defense of one-vs-all classification. J. Mach. Learn. Res. 5(Jan), 101–141 (2004)
21. Aue, A., Gamon, M.: Customizing sentiment classifiers to new domains: a case study. In: Proceedings of Recent Advances in Natural Language Processing, vol. 1, no. 3.1, pp. 2–1 (2005)

Using EEG to Distinguish Between Writing and Typing for the Same Cognitive Task

Xiaodong Qu$^{(\boxtimes)}$, Qingtian Mei, Peiyan Liu, and Timothy Hickey

Brandeis University, Waltham, MA 02453, USA
{xiqu,frankmei,peiyanlilu,tjhickey}@brandeis.edu

Abstract. This study is designed to test the hypothesis of whether writing and typing can be detected as different patterns within the same cognitive task. We designed this pilot study with five frequently-conducted learning-related tasks. We used the four electrode Muse Headset. Sixteen healthy subjects participated in this six-session experiment. In each session, we instructed them to conduct five different one-minute tasks, including reading, copying by writing, copying by typing, answering a question by writing and answering a question by typing. We compared the performance of classifiers of different categories within the same context, including the same users, the same feature extraction approach, and the same training and testing split. Most of the machine learning and deep learning algorithms could correctly classify the five tasks (20% by chance), the best algorithms achieved an accuracy for individual subjects of up to 70% for within session training and 44% for between session training.

Keywords: Machine learning · Deep learning · Classification · ElectroEncephaloGraphy · EEG

1 Introduction

More and more Electroencephalography (EEG) data are available on the web, as we can search from the newly developed Google Dataset Search [16], reflecting the increased interest in EEG in both clinical and nonclinical fields, especially in emotion recognition, motor imagery, event related potential (ERP) detection, mental workload, seizure or stroke detection, Alzheimer's classification, depression, meditation and sleep analysis [8, 13, 20]. In this study we focus more on passive BCI [28], rather than the EEG controlled applications, like BCI based games [7].

Previous studies [5, 18] demonstrated that EEG signals could successfully distinguish several kinds of cognitive tasks. Such as programming in Python vs. solving Math problems; solving Math problems (GRE) vs. solving Reading problems(GRE). These experiments focused on distinguishing different cognitive tasks, but not on whether different communication modes may also have a distinguishable impact on EEG patterns. The experiment in this paper was designed to test the hypothesis of whether AI based EEG markers could distinguish both between two modes of communication: typing vs. writing, and between three cognitive states: reading vs. copying vs. answering.

© Springer Nature Switzerland AG 2020
C. Frasson et al. (Eds.): BFAL 2020, LNAI 12462, pp. 66–74, 2020.
https://doi.org/10.1007/978-3-030-60735-7_7

Read (R) For this task, each subject was asked to read from a PDF file containing a computer science textbook on Data Structures and Algorithms. During each of the six sessions the text varied, and all of the reading material consisted mostly of text with a relatively small amount of computer code or mathematical equations.

Write Copy (WC) Each subject wrote on a blank white paper with a pen, copying the text from the textbook PDF file display on the monitor. We used the same textbook as in the "Read" task, but subjects copied different sections in each session.

Write Answer (WA) Each subject wrote a short essay using pen and paper answer- ing the question: 'Why did you choose your major?' Although one might think that students would produce the same answer in subsequent sessions, we found that their answers in each session were substantially different.

Type Copy (TC) Each subject read a section of the same textbook PDF file, and copied what they read into an Essay Text entry box by typing on the computer keyboard. They copied different sections in each session.

Type Answer (TA) Subjects typed their answers to the question 'What is your aca- demic plan for this semester?' The researcher asked the same question in each session, the answers varied for each session.

Fig. 1. Tasks in this experiment

In this study, each session has five tasks, we use Task Read as the baseline, selected additional four multi-label cognitive tasks that produced a text-based result, and compared the impact of communication mode (typing on a keyboard or writing with pen on paper) and cognitive task (e.g. reading or copying or composing) on the EEG signals, as shown in Fig. 1, the order of the tasks are randomly shuttled in the six sessions. Our main result is that even when the tasks are designed to be similar both in communication mode and in cognitive mode, the AI based EEG markers can clearly recognize the different patterns up to a 70% level for within session training and 44% for between session training, compared with 20% by chance.

Among the frequently used portable and affordable EEG devices [10, 15], including the Neurosky Mindwave, the Emotiv Epoc, the Open BCI Mark IV headset, and the Muse Headband. We selected Muse headsets developed by Interaxon [21] for this study.

2 Algorithms

As many studies focus on designing new algorithms, there is also a need to analyze the existing algorithms and make full use of them. We implemented several highlighted machine learning and deep learning approaches mentioned by [8, 13, 14]. The code mentioned in this paper is available online (the Github link is hidden for the double blind review).

Linear classifiers: Both Linear Discriminant Analysis (LDA) and Support Vector Machines (SVM) still performed fairly well after several decades since they were first implemented in this field [3, 4, 12].

Non-linear Bayesian classifiers: Hidden Markov Models (HMM) is the algorithm we implemented. It observes a given sequence of feature vectors and outputs the probability. HMM is suitable for the classification of time series data, especially in the field of speech recognition. HMMs have performed well in several EEG signal classification studies [27].

Nearest Neighbour: k-Nearest Neighbour(kNN) [13, 14]. Usually performed from adequately to well in our previous research.

Adaboost and Random Forest: Boosting [9], bagging and Random Forest [6] are types of Ensemble Machine Learning Algorithms which use a group of weaker learners (e.g. random decision trees) to make a stronger classification. These have been the gold standard for many EEG classification experiments, including ours.

Transfer Learning: Transfer learning has performed well with EEG data, as mentioned by [2, 13]. We used the training set with labeled data as the source domain and the testing set without labels as the target domain. We selected transductive transfer learning because the source and target tasks are the same, and the source and target domains are different but related.

CNN: Deep learning, especially Convolutional Neural Network(CNN) performed well in many previous EEG research projects [8, 11]. We implemented it with two convolution layers and one fully connected layer.

RNN, LSTM: Long Short Term Memory (LSTM), as motioned in previous research [1, 4, 8, 24], works well with time series data, we implemented it with two recurrent layers followed by two fully-connected layers.

3   Experiment

All subjects first signed an informed consent form. Then, researchers helped them to put on the Muse headbands and test the recording. The Subjects then completed an entrance survey on the computer and became familiar with the online Qualtrics system used in this experiment, especially the sample task switching notice. Next, the Official EEG recording began. A survey in Qualtrics kept track of the time and alerted the subjects to change their tasks after every 60 s. After subjects completed all the five tasks, the Official EEG recording stopped and subjects completed a short exit survey.

Subjects: Sixteen healthy subjects participated the experiment. Of those, data from three subjects were excluded from subsequent analysis; one for failing to participate in one of the required six sessions, and another because of considerable data loss from one of the Muse electrodes, and the third due to a very high level of noise in the electrode recordings.

Seven males and six females are included in the final data set. Ten of the retained subjects were undergraduate students, the other three were graduate students. Eight subjects were computer science majors. The average age of the subjects was 20.9.

Feature Extraction: We used the absolute Band Powers (BP) feature of the Muse head-set, it is the logarithm of the power spectral density of EEG signals summed over that frequency range [13]. The Muse headsets, are using four dry input electrodes, locations corresponded to sites TP9, AF7, AF8, and T10 [23]. The Muse EEG recording application automatically filtered out muscle artifacts, such as eye blinking. Spectral analysis was performed on-board the Muse device and then transmitted at 10 Hz to the EEG recording application on the researcher's computer. Each of these spectral snapshots consists of 20 numeric values – five spectral values for each of the four electrodes.

Data cleaning: During the EEG recording, some electrodes may have temporarily lost contact with the subjects' scalp. The result was that multiple sequential spectral snapshots from one or more electrodes had exactly the same value. When we detected this anomaly, we set that entire spectral snapshot of 20 values to 0, while keeping the time-stamped value, even if the anomaly was only detected on one of the four electrodes. Such data cleaning action resulted in a loss of 27% of the entire data.

Cross Validation: EEG data point samples, if randomly selected, could be near to each other chronologically in both the training set and the testing set. This may cause over-fitting because EEG signals changes slowly. To lessen this possible effect, we first adopted the time-wise cross validation [19, 22].

For each five minute session there are five tasks, we divided each tasks to 10 parts, evenly and contiguously, each part has 10% of the data.

Then we did a 10 fold cross validation first and realized that the first 30% of the data were predicted with low accuracy due to a task transition effect. We then cut off these transition times and only used the rest (70%) of the data. In each fold, We trained on six of the remaining seven subsets and tested on the left-out subset. Figure 2 showed a graphical representation of this seven-fold time-wise cross validation approach. The results reflect some general patterns, as shown in Fig. 9.

Based on that we also did a session-wise cross validation, as shown in Fig. 3, to see how the classifiers work with the data from unseen session. The results are in Fig. 10.

Fig. 2. Time-wise cross validation

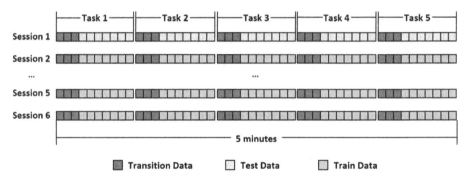

Fig. 3. Session-wise cross validation

4 Results

As shown in Fig. 4, most (nine of the ten) machine learning and deep learning classifiers correctly classified the data into five classes with probability far above chance (20%). Deep learning (LSTM and CNN) and ensemble methods (Random Forest and Adaboost) outperformed other algorithms.

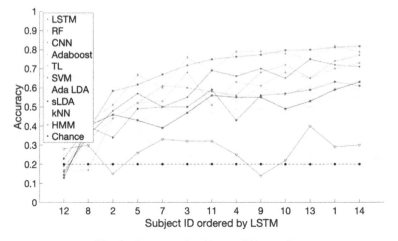

Fig. 4. Compare algorithms, within session

We first implemented the within-session approach, to investigate the general trends. Different individual algorithms generated different accuracies for each subject, such as subject 9 and subject 14, their order is different using LSTM (see Fig. 4) and Random Forest (see Fig. 5), but the general trends for most subjects are still similar to each other, in that some subjects data are more easily classified than others. Also we noticed a significant transition effect, as shown in Fig. 9, even though the subjects physically switched to the next task quickly, the EEG signals changed slowly, in general it took 12 to 18 s to switch to the stable states of the next task, which corresponds to the first 20 to

30 percent of the data for that task. We then cut this first 30 percent off before running the classification algorithms again.

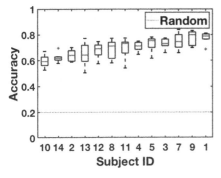

Fig. 5. Within session, by subject, for RF

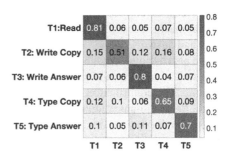

Fig. 6. Within session, by task, for RF

When we averaged the results by task, as shown in Fig. 6, compared with 20 percent by chance, all of the five tasks are classified well with these classifiers, (here we only put RF, the other figures are available on Github).

Previous research [8, 13] has demonstrated there can be significant variations between sessions. We implemented a between session analysis, to see how well the algorithms performed when facing unseen data for the same user but on different sessions The analysis showed that even with just six sessions, the classifiers still classify with accuracies significantly above random, as show in Figs. 7 and 8. Task Read and Task Write Answer are still the highest, Task 2 Write Copy is still the most confusing task, which is similar to pattern in the within session approach shown in Figs. 5 and 6.

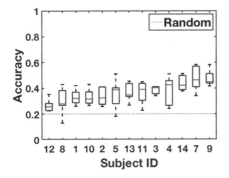

Fig. 7. Between session, by subject, for RF

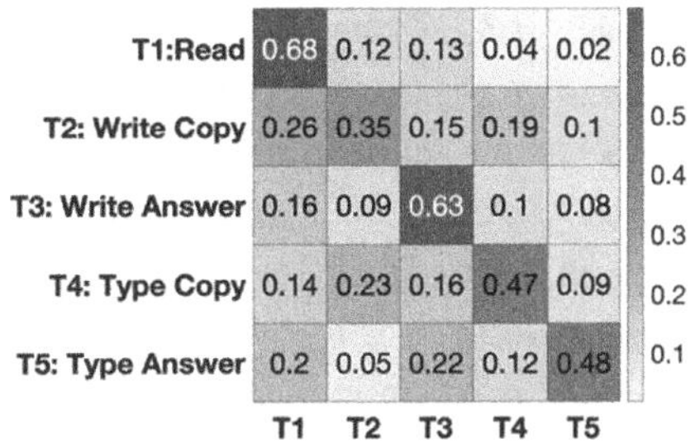

Fig. 8. Between session, by task, for RF

5 Conclusion and Discussion

Our immediate goal was to study the effectiveness of machine learning classification algorithms in distinguishing among different basic communication tasks (write vs. type) and investigate whether the method of communication (write vs. type) and the different cognitive tasks (copy or answer) could be identified. We confirmed previous findings [13, 19] that machine learning with EEG signals could discriminate two cognitive activities (copy and answer).

We also hypothesized that this approach could reliably distinguish the two modes of communication (write and type) from one another even when the cognitive task remained the same. The confirmation of that hypothesis is a suggestion that future studies should control the communication mode variable, also this can be used for multi-label tasks in the experiment design. It is possible that the write and type tasks were distinguished by signals from the motor cortex which is located between the frontal and parietal regions of the brain.

Although these basic tasks may seem similar at the level of cortical activity, we have shown that AI classifiers can successfully capture subtle differences between such tasks. Such result could be used in the online or offline classroom to get better understanding about teaching and learning [17, 25]. Transition effect (Fig. 9) and Session variation (Fig. 10) can also be sensitively detected and integrated to the future experimental design.

The main contributions of this paper are the demonstration that AI classifiers support effective approaches for classifying sets of tasks based on either copying text or answering questions using either handwriting or typing. Random forest is a fast and low-cost solution which works on most mainstream personal computers and smart phones; while LSTM is a slow and expensive solution which currently requires high-end GPUs, or the training time will jump from minutes to hours on the same personal computer compared with other classifiers like RF.

	Fold1	Fold2	Fold3	Fold4	Fold5	Fold6	Fold7	Fold8	Fold9	Fold10
Subject1	0.24	0.52	0.66	0.75	0.82	0.79	0.75	0.77	0.81	0.78
Subject2	0.2	0.44	0.63	0.68	0.62	0.58	0.71	0.67	0.72	0.6
Subject3	0.22	0.49	0.56	0.71	0.73	0.71	0.73	0.79	0.77	0.73
Subject4	0.29	0.36	0.52	0.65	0.75	0.74	0.76	0.71	0.7	0.73
Subject5	0.2	0.5	0.7	0.63	0.74	0.77	0.77	0.74	0.79	0.76
Subject7	0.23	0.45	0.56	0.69	0.67	0.8	0.75	0.82	0.76	0.72
Subject8	0.28	0.47	0.67	0.68	0.74	0.75	0.78	0.71	0.64	0.54
Subject9	0.19	0.51	0.68	0.79	0.79	0.7	0.74	0.8	0.76	0.81
Subject10	0.23	0.42	0.57	0.61	0.6	0.62	0.66	0.61	0.55	0.66
Subject11	0.2	0.36	0.6	0.69	0.76	0.73	0.73	0.7	0.75	0.7
Subject12	0.32	0.52	0.6	0.69	0.7	0.72	0.71	0.74	0.67	0.61
Subject13	0.28	0.49	0.64	0.58	0.61	0.58	0.71	0.7	0.71	0.59
Subject14	0.24	0.33	0.52	0.65	0.67	0.66	0.61	0.62	0.63	0.6

Fig. 9. Transition within session

	Session 1	Session 2	Session 3	Session 4	Session 5	Session 6
Subject 1	0.4	0.5	0.31	0.34	0.44	0.37
Subject 2	0.31	0.49	0.34	0.44	0.33	0.49
Subject 3	0.41	0.43	0.49	0.49	0.48	0.49
Subject 4	0.51	0.51	0.55	0.61	0.32	0.29
Subject 5	0.47	0.48	0.34	0.61	0.46	0.22
Subject 7	0.68	0.7	0.41	0.58	0.53	0.49
Subject 8	0.32	0.46	0.33	0.34	0.51	0.16
Subject 9	0.52	0.54	0.61	0.7	0.54	0.5
Subject 10	0.51	0.42	0.34	0.34	0.45	0.32
Subject 11	0.46	0.54	0.52	0.27	0.47	0.37
Subject 12	0.28	0.42	0.27	0.27	0.33	0.34
Subject 13	0.32	0.52	0.42	0.54	0.41	0.4
Subject 14	0.62	0.53	0.45	0.6	0.46	0.48

Fig. 10. Transition between session

Such passive BCI approaches, as [8, 13, 28] mentioned, could be helpful for a better understanding about real-time brain signals for healthy subjects beyond medical applications[26]. More such non-clinical data sets from healthy users could in the future contribute back to the clinical research with new patterns being recognized or discovered, as well as with more effective AI classification algorithms.

References

1. Arifoglu, D., Bouchachia, A.: Activity recognition and abnormal behaviour detection with recurrent neural networks. Procedia Comput. Sci. **110**, 86–93 (2017)
2. Arvaneh, M., Guan, C., Ang, K.K., Quek, C.: Eeg data space adaptation to reduce intersession nonstationarity in brain-computer interface. Neural Comput. **25**(8), 2146–2171 (2013)
3. Bashivan, P., Rish, I., Heisig, S.: Mental state recognition via wearable eeg (2016). arXiv preprint arXiv:1602.00985
4. Bashivan, P., Rish, I., Yeasin, M., Codella, N.: Learning representations from EEG with deep recurrent-convolutional neural networks (2015). arXiv preprint arXiv:1511.06448
5. Bird, J.J., Manso, L.J., Ribeiro, E.P., Ekart, A., Faria, D.R.: A study on mental state classification using eeg-based brain-machine interface. In: 2018 International Conference on Intelligent Systems (IS), pp. 795–800. IEEE (2018)
6. Breiman, L.: Random forests. Mach. Learn. **45**(1), 5–32 (2001)
7. Coyle, D., Principe, J., Lotte, F., Nijholt, A.: Guest editorial: brain/neuronal-computer game interfaces and interaction. IEEE Trans. Comput. Intell. AI Games **5**(2), 77–81 (2013)
8. Craik, A., He, Y., Contreras-Vidal, J.L.: Deep learning for electroencephalogram (eeg) classification tasks: a review. J. Neural Eng. **16**(3), 031001 (2019)
9. Freund, Y., Schapire, R.E.: A decision-theoretic generalization of on-line learning and an application to boosting. J. Comput. Syst. Sci. **55**(1), 119–139 (1997)
10. Gang, P., et al.: User-driven intelligent interface on the basis of multimodal augmented reality and brain-computer interaction for people with functional disabilities. In: Arai, K., Kapoor, S., Bhatia, R. (eds.) FICC 2018. AISC, vol. 886, pp. 612–631. Springer, Cham (2019). https://doi.org/10.1007/978-3-030-03402-3_43

11. Kwak, N.S., Müller, K.R., Lee, S.W.: A convolutional neural network for steady state visual evoked potential classification under ambulatory environment. PloS one **12**(2), e0172578 (2017)
12. Lotte, F.: Signal processing approaches to minimize or suppress calibration time in oscillatory activity-based brain–computer interfaces. Proc. IEEE **103**(6), 871–890 (2015)
13. Lotte, F., et al.: A review of classification algorithms for EEG-based brain–computer interfaces: a 10 year update. J. Neural Eng. **15**(3), 031005 (2018)
14. Lotte, F., Congedo, M., Lécuyer, A., Lamarche, F., Arnaldi, B.: A review of classification algorithms for EEG-based brain–computer interfaces. J. Neural Eng. **4**(2), R1 (2007)
15. Mihajlović, V., Grundlehner, B., Vullers, R., Penders, J.: Wearable, wireless EEG solutions in daily life applications: what are we missing? IEEE J. Biomed. Health Inf. **19**(1), 6–21 (2014)
16. Noy, N.: When the web is your data lake: creating a search engine for datasets on the web. In: Proceedings of the 2020 ACM SIGMOD International Conference on Management of Data, pp. 801–801 (2020)
17. Poulsen, A.T., Kamronn, S., Dmochowski, J., Parra, L.C., Hansen, L.K.: Eeg in the classroom: synchronised neural recordings during video presentation. Sci. Rep. **7**, 43916 (2017)
18. Qu, X., Hall, M., Sun, Y., Sekuler, R., Hickey, T.J.: A personalized reading coach using wearable EEG sensors-a pilot study of brainwave learning analytics. In: CSEDU (2), pp. 501–507 (2018)
19. Qu, X., Sun, Y., Sekuler, R., Hickey, T.: EEG markers of stem learning. In: 2018 IEEE Frontiers in Education Conference (FIE), pp. 1–9. IEEE (2018)
20. Ranlund, S., et al.: Resting eeg in psychosis and at-risk populations—a possible endophenotype? Schizophr. Res. **153**(1–3), 96–102 (2014)
21. Richer, R., Zhao, N., Amores, J., Eskofier, B.M., Paradiso, J.A.: Real-time mental state recognition using a wearable eeg. In: 2018 40th Annual International Conference of the IEEE Engineering in Medicine and Biology Society (EMBC), pp. 5495–5498. IEEE (2018)
22. Saeb, S., Lonini, L., Jayaraman, A., Mohr, D.C., Kording, K.P.: Voodoo machine learning for clinical predictions. In: Biorxiv, p. 059774 (2016)
23. Seeck, M., Koessler, L., Bast, T., Leijten, F., Michel, C., Baumgartner, C., He, B., Beniczky, S.: The standardized EEG electrode array of the IFCN. Clin. Neurophysiol. **128**(10), 2070–2077 (2017)
24. Sha, L., Hong, P.: Neural knowledge tracing. BFAL 2017. LNCS (LNAI), vol. 10512, pp. 108–117. Springer, Cham (2017). https://doi.org/10.1007/978-3-319-67615-9_10
25. Tarimo, W.T., Deeb, F.A., Hickey, T.J.: Early detection of at-risk students in cs1 using teachback/spinoza. J. Comput. Sci. Coll. **31**(6), 105–111 (2016)
26. Van Erp, J., Lotte, F., Tangermann, M.: Brain-computer interfaces: beyond medical applications. Computer **45**(4), 26–34 (2012)
27. Wang, M., Abdelfattah, S., Moustafa, N., Hu, J.: Deep gaussian mixture-hidden markov model for classification of eeg signals. IEEE Trans. Emerg. Top. Comput. Intell. **2**(4), 278–287 (2018)
28. Zander, T.O., Kothe, C.: Towards passive brain–computer interfaces: applying brain–computer interface technology to human–machine systems in general. J. Neural Eng. **8**(2), 025005 (2011)

Real-Time Gesture Recognition Using Deep Learning Towards Alzheimer's Disease Applications

Marulasidda Swamy Kibbanahalli Shivalingappa$^{(\boxtimes)}$, Hamdi Ben Abdessalem, and Claude Frasson

Département d'Informatique et de Recherche Opérationnelle, Université de Montréal, Montreal, Canada
{marulasidda.swamy.kibbanahalli.shivalingappa,
hamdi.ben.abdessalem}@umontreal.ca, frasson@iro.umontreal.ca

Abstract. There have been significant efforts in the direction of improving accuracy in detecting human action using skeleton joints. Determining actions in a noisy environment is still challenging since the Cartesian coordinate of the skeleton joints provided by depth sense camera depends on camera position and skeleton position. In a few of the human-computer interaction applications, skeleton position and camera position keep changing. The proposed method recommends using relative positional values instead of actual Cartesian coordinate values. Recent advancements in the Convolution Neural Network (CNN) help us achieve higher prediction accuracy using image format input. To represent skeleton joints in image format, we need to represent skeleton information in matrix form with equal height and width. With some depth sense cameras, the number of skeleton joints provided is limited, and we need to depend on relative positional values to have a matrix representation of skeleton joints. We can show near the state-of-the-art performance on MSR 3-Dimensional (3D) data and the new representation of skeleton joints. We have used image shifting instead of interpolation between frames, which helps us have state-of-the-art performance.

Keywords: Human action · Gesture recognition · Real-time · Skelton-joint · Deep learning · Resnet

1 Introduction

Representing skeleton joint information in an image format and utilizing it for human action detection is the most reliable and computationally powerful approach. Processing real images or videos for action detection requires a lot of computation resources [1]. There has been tremendous research effort to improve prediction accuracy in detecting human action with the help of skeleton joint information. CNN (Convolution Neural Network) exploits the spatial relationship between pixels when arranged in matrix representation [2–4]. Shift invariance property possessed by CNN helps in detecting features residing in any part of the image. Encoding spatial and temporal information of skeleton

© Springer Nature Switzerland AG 2020
C. Frasson et al. (Eds.): BFAL 2020, LNAI 12462, pp. 75–86, 2020.
https://doi.org/10.1007/978-3-030-60735-7_8

frames in an image is proven to be the best representation for a deep neural network to understand human action [2–4].

Detecting human action when the camera's position and the position of the skeleton keeps changing is a challenging task [5]. We need to train the CNN model with a lot of training data to understand all variations in the coordinate values of a skeleton. Encoding spatial and temporal information of skeleton frames in an image is not sufficient, and hence we need to consider encoding the difference between joints for the skeleton transformation process. Depth sense cameras provide a limited, varying number of joints [6], and therefore it has become challenging to come with better representation of skeleton information.

We propose a method to encode the difference between 3D coordinates values in an image and train a deep residual neural network [7] for better prediction accuracy. Existing practice insists on adapting interpolation between frames as the approach to fill the picture when we do not have enough frames [3, 4]. CNN can only understand static images, and hence we need to bring in temporal dependency of frames of the current image on previous frames of the skeleton action sequence. We can achieve exploiting a better representation of the picture by shifting earlier frames to the current image.

This method could be used to detect hand gestures and body gestures in many fields, especially for medical applications like to create applications for Alzheimer's disease. The rest of this paper is organized as follows. In Sect. 2, we give an overview of the related works. In Sect. 3, we describe our methodology. In Sect. 4, we detail the Residual Network. In Sect. 5, we detail the experiments, and finally, in Sect. 6, we present the obtained results.

2   Related Works

Skeleton joint information was extensively used for predicting human action and posture detection. Intel Realsense camera [10] provides precise skeleton joints information with third-party SDKs (Software Development Kit). Nuitrack is one of the most reliable SDK's in the market, with which it is easy for a Unity developer to build a skeleton tracking application. Depending on the system's hardware abilities, framerate changes, and it is effortless to develop a hardware-independent software module to capture skeleton frames in real-time with the help of the Unity platform. Kinect [8] of Microsoft provided a skeleton tracking facility for a long time, and it was adopted in most of the research practice. Kinect [8] provides just twenty skeleton joints information; Intel Realsense camera [10] instead can capture twenty-four joints 3D coordinate values. Leap Motion hardware is a dedicated camera for detecting hand joints position along with rotation. There have been efforts to convert 3D coordinate values to RGB (Red, Green, Blue. A color model represents a pixel's color by combining Red, Green, and Blue in different ranges) image representation for training deep neural networks. The transformation step of skeleton information to RGB representation is a significant data pre-processing stage. Encoded RGB image should include extensive temporal and spatial information of skeleton frames in a sequence.

2.1 Realtime Pose Detection

The authors in [8] explain estimating human pose using skeleton data given by the Kinect sensor. Instead of using the temporal sequence of 3D coordinates, relative to the camera position, the authors in [8] uses coordinate values relative to the other joints. Relative coordinate values remove the prediction accuracy dependency on the size and location of the subject. Firstly, three-dimensional skeleton coordinates transformed into a one-dimensional feature vector. The feature vector is the input to a machine learning algorithm with or without pre-processing. The proposed algorithm is assessed on a vocabulary containing eighteen poses and employing machine learning algorithms: Support Vector Machines (SVM), Artificial Neural Network, K-Nearest Neighbors, and Bayes classifier and SVM outperforms on the data set used in experiments. The method explained in [8] works excellently with a predefined set of actions and failed to consider the temporal dependency of frames in predicting human action.

2.2 Skeleton Based Action Recognition Using Translation-Scale Invariant Image Mapping and Multi-scale Deep CNN

Transforming from skeleton information to image representation is a crucial and significant step in human action classification using skeleton data. A sophisticated, promising method of transformation is discussed and demonstrated by the authors in [2] with the help of results. Very few parameters, which plays a vital role in the transformation process, are extracted from each video sequence instead of referring the whole data. The proposed method in [2] helps preserve scale invariance and translation invariance of the training data. The authors in [2] also claim that the complete process of transformation becomes data set independent.

2.3 Recognizing Human Action from Skeleton Moment

Deep learning algorithms need data to be represented in image format so that machine learning models like CNN and its variants can extract image features and classify the image into an available class efficiently. Transforming skeleton joint coordinate values into RGB image space is explained by the authors in [3]. Skelton parts are divided into five significant parts P1, P2, P3, P4, and P5. Each section will have 3D coordinate values of the set of skeleton joints (P1, P2: two arms, P4, P5: two legs, P3: trunk). Transformation module explained by the authors in [3] will convert skeleton joints into an image by arranging pixels in the order of P1->P2->P3->P4->P5. The proposed transformation method helped the authors in [3] achieve the best prediction accuracy with three different variants of Resnet models [7]. The paper [3] fails to effectively incorporate Spatio-temporal information of skeleton motion when the skeleton motion has a higher number of frames.

2.4 Skepxels: Spatio-Temporal Image Representation of Human Skeleton Joints for Action Recognition

We need an effective method to represent skeleton 3D coordinates so that deep learning models can exploit the correlation between local pixels, which helps us have better prediction accuracy. The paper [4] talks about a method that can help us arrange skeleton information like Skepxels [4] in the horizontal and vertical directions. Skepxels [4] in the horizontal direction, carry the frames in skeleton data. Spatial information of the skeleton frame sequence was captured in the vertical direction of the transformed image by rearranging pixels of a skeleton frame at a time 't'. The proposed way of arranging skeleton frames in [4] will increase the prediction accuracy as each image carries rich temporal-spatial information. In [4], the author also explains how using image interpolation between frames can create a full image even though we have a smaller number of frames in a skeleton motion. If the number of frames exceeds the number of frames required to make an image, then the rest of the frames are moved to the next image and labeled with the same class name. NTU 3D action data [9] was used to evaluate the model, and the transformation process generates millions of pictures after the transformation step. For data-augmentation author in [4] has recommended adding Gaussian noise samples to each frame and double the training data size. With all the proposed changes in [4], the Resnet model [7] can achieve state-of-the-art performance. If the position of the camera and skeleton changes, then model prediction accuracy will change to a great extent. With the proposed method in [4], we need to take more data with all possible skeleton positioning to ensure better test accuracy. When the skeleton frame sequence is long, dividing sequence into multiple images will ignore the current picture's temporal dependency information on the previous frames in the series.

3   Our Methodology

Using pixels of training images, CNN tries to build minor and significant features of images. CNN models are translation invariance, and they can recognize trained characteristics anywhere in the pictures. This paper demonstrates how to generate images from skeleton joints information by creating building blocks of a picture called SkepxelsRel. We don't use skeleton joint coordinates; instead, we use a list of 3D coordinate values generated after taking the difference between two joints. We need to group a set of pair of joints which contribute more in deciding the class of action. Combining a couple of skeleton joints is also a hyperparameter during training a Resnet model [7]. Velocity frames generated uses the speed at which the difference of considered skeleton joints changes. As demonstrated in [5], when we take the reference point as other joints, the prediction accuracy does not depend on the camera and skeleton's position. We explain the approach as follows:

3.1   Skeleton Picture Relative Elements (SkepxelsRel)

SkepxelsRel does have a similar structure of Skepxels explained in [4]. SkepxelsRel tensors encode differences of coordinate values along the third dimension (Fig. 1). We follow the same strategy in choosing the best pixels arrangement for filling spatial information of a skeleton frame at time 't'. As shown in Fig. 2, RGB channels encode spatial-temporal information of skeleton joint differences and create an image. Velocity frames (Fig. 3) are constructed using a similar method, as explained in [2], but we use SkepxelsRel values to calculate the rate at which the differences between reference joints change. With the proposed method, we can generate any number of joints required for image representation. As shown in Fig. 1, we created forty relative skeleton joints, which play an essential role in deciding human action. As shown in Fig. 3, velocity frames are generated by taking the difference of successive frames and dividing them by frame rate. In our experiments, we considered the frame rate as 30 frames/second.

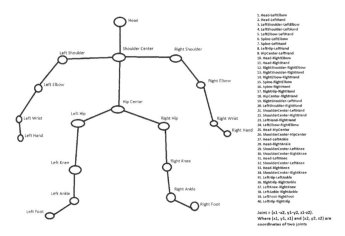

Fig. 1. Skeleton example with relative joints

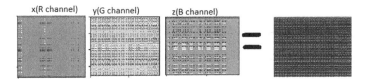

Fig. 2. RGB channels generated with (x, y, z) coordinates of skeleton sequence

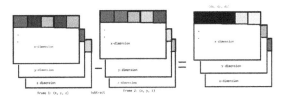

Fig. 3. Velocity frames calculated by subtracting frames

$$Relative\ Joint(x`, y`, z`) = Reference\ Joint1(x, y, z) - Reference\ Joint2(x, y, z) \tag{1}$$

$$Velocity\ of\ a\ relative\ Joint\ at\ time\ t = \frac{Joint(x`, y`, z`)\ at\ t - Joint(x`, y`, z`)\ at\ t-1}{frame\ rate} \tag{2}$$

When the number of frames required to form the image is more than needed, we recommend using frames shifting (Fig. 5) instead of moving the remaining skeleton frames (Fig. 4) to the next image. This way of image construction helps in real-time prediction wherein each image encodes only the original frames of the skeleton motion without adding interpolated frames in between. And this method also helps us to encode temporal dependency information of previous frames in the current image. If the available number of frames for constructing an image is less than the required, we can go with interpolation between frames approach. Figure 5 demonstrates the steps involved in a proper way of adjusting the frames to accommodate all the available skeleton frames.

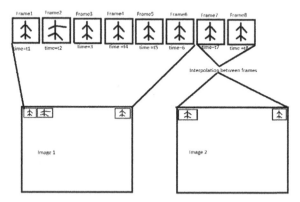

Fig. 4. Existing method: interpolation between frames applied

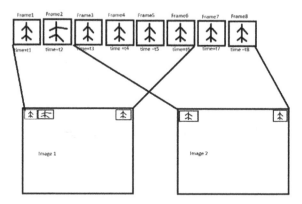

Fig. 5. Frames are shifted to right and temporal dependency of frames is not ignored

3.2 Data Pre-processing

We generated skeleton sequences for primary actions using the Intel Realsense camera [10] with the help of Nuitrack SDK. Hand gesture recognition experiments are conducted on multiple channel images. Each skeleton frame is normalized by making the center of the frame the center of the coordinate system (0, 0, 0) [1].

3.3 Data Augmentation

To increase the training data size, we sampled from a gaussian distribution with mean 0 and a standard deviation of 0.02 and added those noise samples to actual skeleton frames. We have also applied random cropping, horizontal flip, and vertical flip data augmentation strategies (Fig. 6).

Original   Cropped   Vetically Flipped

Fig. 6. Data augmentation

4 Residual Network

Deep neural networks with many more layers stacked, help the model to have a greater number of parameters, and hence degree freedom of a model increases. With the increased complexity of the model, the ability to learn new sophisticated features will also increase. When a neural network has the freedom to choose parameters without regularization, then the chances of finding global minima are less, and the model ends up finding local minima. Hence, we include regularization methods to regulate the most in-depth neural networks and try avoiding model overfitting behavior. Recent experiments and research show that even after having regularization methods in the deep neural network, it is inevitable to have an overfitted model. Researchers have come up with new architecture called Residual Network to avoid such behavior without losing the benefits of deep neural networks [7].

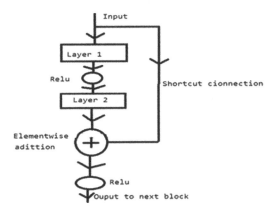

Fig. 7. Residual block

One of the significant problems associated with deep neural networks is vanishing gradients problem, wherein gradients at the last layer will not be able to propagate back to initial layers. Hence, learning will be very slow and improper. Shortcut connections provided in Residual blocks (Fig. 7) make the model learn identity mapping of the input very easily. Also, the shortcut connection helps to carry gradients back to initial layers without vanishing gradients problem. Hence, we have adopted the Residual network [7] in our experiments to learn significant features of skeleton sequence.

5 Experiments

5.1 Real-Time Prediction Using Intel Realsense Camera

We used a setup having Intel Realsense camera [10] for capturing skeleton frames on the Unity platform. 20-layer Resnet model [7] was trained for six basic actions, including Still, Wave Hands, Soothing, Come, Go, Clap. We observed that the trained model could predict all the actions with 100% accuracy in real-time. As stated already, we have used a set of joints that are responsible for deciding pre-decided actions. Other factors also behave as hyperparameters like frame rate (number of frames per second captured by the unity platform, hardware dependent), and image size. As the data available is less with only six human actions, we had to augment data to satisfy Resnet [7] requirements. We tried with different frame rates:30, 20, and 10 and 30 outperformed compared to other framerates. Since we are using differences of coordinates, changing camera position, and skeleton position did not impact prediction accuracy. We also tried with different image sizes 180 * 180, 250 * 250, and 180 * 180 outperformed compared to other image dimensions.

The proposed method does not need the number of joints to be equivalent to the required number of joints to form a SkepxelsRel since we can generate the required number of values by taking differences among responsible joints. Leap motion camera can provide hand joints information along with hand joints rotation information. This set up is used in a different application wherein rotation and moment of joints are very important in deciding hand gestures. Hence, we encoded hand joints position information in the first three channels and rotation information in the next three channels.

5.2 MSR Action 3D Data Set

MSR data set [11] is divided into three data sets, and model performance is evaluated on each data set type. There are twenty actions performed by ten different subjects in generating each dataset type. We use actions from five subjects for generating training data and remaining data used for testing. There is a total of 557 action files having 20 actions performed by different subjects. Generated data is trained and tested with Resnet-20 [7] and Resnet-50 [7] models, and Resnet-20 [7] model outperformed the rest of the models.

6   Results and Discussion

Intel Realsense data: We captured skeleton data for six necessary actions using Intel Realsense depth camera [10]. We have trained 20-layer and 50 Resnet models [7] with a batch size of 64, optimizer as Stochastic Gradient Descent, initial learning rate as 0.01. The accuracy graph (Fig. 8) shows that the model converges very slowly with a lot of variation in validation accuracy. Validation accuracy fluctuation is not an issue. The variation is due to low validation data, the high degree of freedom of the model, large batch size, and high learning rate. This fluctuation gets stabilized with a greater number of epochs. (Data is uploaded here: https://github.com/creative-swamy/IntelReal SenseData). It is evident from the accuracy graph (Fig. 8) that the model can predict the unseen action data efficiently since we see 100% test accuracy with the loss nearing to zero. The data is captured from seven different subjects. Seven different people perform each action, and actions performed by four subjects are considered for training data, and the remaining are regarded as validation data. We made sure that the data used for testing is unseen data and has noise and variation compared to training data. If the model performs better with the test data, then it can be considered for testing in real-time need. We tested the model performance in the Virtual Real environment with two unknown subjects, which are not part of training and testing data, performing actions. The model can predict all the trained actions with 100% prediction accuracy.

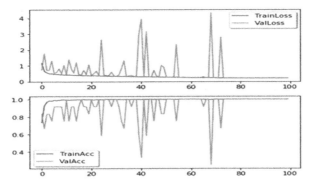

Fig. 8. Intel realsense data, accuracy graph

Leap Motion data: Leap Motion camera provides information about hand joints position and their respective rotation values. We have captured all joints position of two hands and individual rotation values for ten different hand gestures. The data is obtained from ten different subjects. Six subjects are considered for training data, and the remaining subjects are regarded as validation data. We trained the Resnet-20 model [7] incrementally by adding more hand gesture data, and the model behavior is very consistent concerning validation accuracy (Fig. 9). We tested the trained model's performance in a real-time Virtual Reality environment with two unknown subjects, which are not part of training and testing, performing actions. The model can predict all six gestures made by unknown subjects with 100% prediction accuracy, and it is evident from the accuracy graph shown in Fig. 9. (Data is uploaded here: https://github.com/cre ative-swamy/Leap-Motiondata-for-experiments/).

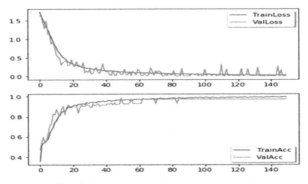

Fig. 9. Leap motion data, accuracy graph

Running Experiments with MSR 3D Action data [11]: We started exploring proposed algorithm behavior with one of the benchmark data set, MSR 3D Action dataset [11]. We tested the model's functioning with a cross data strategy and found that validation accuracy stops at 91%. We have not yet considered converting the skeleton data to scale-invariant and view-invariant [1]. Efficient pre-processing of the skeleton data will make sure proper learning curves to establish. Our research aims to address the moving object and camera position while implementing real-time action or gesture prediction algorithms. We wanted to experiment on the standard dataset to show that our proposed method performs near the state-of-the-art model. We can improve the model performance by enhancing the training data size using more advanced data augmentation methods and extensive hyper-parameters tuning. Our one more research aim is to implement and using a sophisticated, real-time compatible machine learning model in a medical application environment. We concentrated more on experimenting with our prepared dataset and hence did not get more time to tune the model for MSR 3D action dataset. We consider enhancing our model performance in the future to work even better with standard datasets like the MSR 3D action dataset.

7 Conclusion

This paper demonstrated a skeleton-based action detection mechanism using the residual neural network model with a unique way of data representation. The experiments on data captured from Intel Realsense camera [10] and Leap motion prove that the algorithm outperforms real-time prediction. The analysis conducted on a challenging data set, MSR 3D human action dataset, also shows that the proposed algorithm provides near the state-of-the-art performance. Results show that considering relative positional values to construct images provide better accuracy in real-time human action prediction using skeleton joint information. Also, using this method, we can create a medical application for Alzheimer's disease. There are challenges to address when implementing a solution for treating Alzheimer's patients. Existing solutions only provide assisting tools and a virtual environment to help improve cognitive abilities and avoid negative emotions in the participants. Recent research shows that an interactive virtual environment helps a healthcare system treat Alzheimer's effectively, and hence, we have proposed an interactive virtual environment solution for treating Alzheimer's. We can create even a very sophisticated virtual environment for training purposes, but the environment should help Alzheimer's patients overcome negative emotions and improve cognitive abilities. Research work proves that Animal Assisted Therapy allows Alzheimer's patients to improve their mental status. In this project, we have created a virtual dog and a horse character in the VR environment. Research has proved that the Alzheimer's patients will have reduced agitation, increased physical activity, improved eating, and improved pleasure feeling behavior after a real dog visits into the patient's environment. We aim to use our proposed method of human action prediction in a sophisticated Virtual Environment created for Alzheimer's patients and study the impact of a virtual treatment on Alzheimer's mental status.

Acknowledgment. We acknowledge NSERC-CRD (National Science and Engineering Research Council Cooperative Research Development) and BMU for funding this work.

References

1. Simonyan, K., Zisserman, A.: Two-stream convolutional networks for action recognition in videos. In: NIPS (2014)
2. Li, B., He, M., Cheng, X., Chen, Y., Dai, Y.: Skeleton based action recognition using translation-scale invariant image mapping and multi-scale deep CNN. In: CoRR (2017)
3. Pham, H.-H., Khoudour, L., Crouzil, A., Zegers, P., Velasitin, S.A.: Learning and recognizing human action from skeleton momement with deep residual neural networks. In: 8th International Conference of Pattern Recognition Systems (ICPRS 2017) (2017)
4. Liu, J., Akthar, N., Mian, A.: Skepxels: spatio-temporal image representation of human skeleton joints for action recognition. In: CoRR (2017)
5. Choubik, Y., Mahmoudi, A.: Machine learning for real time poses classification using kinect skeleton data. In: 13th International Conference on Computer Graphics, Imaging and Visualization (CGiV) (2016)
6. Du, Y., Wang, W., Wang, L.: Hierarchical recurrent neural network for skeleton based action recognition. In: CVPR (2015)
7. He, K., Zhang, X., Ren, S., Sun, J.: Deep residual learning for image recognition. In: CoRR (2015)
8. Shotton, J., et al.: Real-time human pose recognition in parts from single depth images. In: CVPR (2011)
9. Shahroudy, A., Liu, J., Ng, T.T., Wang, G.: NTU RGB+D: a large scale dataset for 3D huaman activity analysis. In: CoRR (2016)
10. Grunnet-Jepsen, A., Tong, D.: Depth Post-Processing for Inetl RealSense D400 Depth Cameras
11. Li, W., Zhang, Z., Liu, Z.: Action recognition based on a bag of 3D points. In: CVPR Workshops (2010)
12. Wang, F., et al.: Residual attention network for image classification. In: CoRR (2017)

13. Karpathy, A., Johnson, J., Fei-Fei, L.: Visualizing and understanding recurrent networks. In: CoRR (2015)
14. Lun, R., Zhao, W.: A survey of applications and human motion recognition with microsoft Kinect. Int. J. Pattern Recogn. Artif. Intell. **29**(05), 1555008 (2015)
15. Microsoft: Kinect for Windows - Human Interface Guidelines v2.0. Technical report (2014)
16. Chen, C., Liu, K., Kehtarnavaz, N.: Real-time human action recognition based on depth motion maps. J. Real-Time Image Process. **12**(1), 155–163 (2013). https://doi.org/10.1007/s11554-013-0370-1
17. Hochreiter, S., Schmidhuber, J.: Long Short Term Memory, Neural Computation (1997)
18. Vemulapalli, R., Arrate, F., Chellappa, R.: Human action recognition by representing 3D skeletons as points in a LieGroup. In: 2014 IEEE Conference on Computer Vision and Pattern Recognition (2014)

Real-Time Affective Measurements in Medical Education, Using Virtual and Mixed Reality

Panagiotis Antoniou$^{(\boxtimes)}$ ⓘ, George Arfaras ⓘ, Niki Pandria ⓘ, George Ntakakis ⓘ, Emmanuil Bambatsikos ⓘ, and Alkinoos Athanasiou ⓘ

Lab of Medical Physics, School of Medicine, Faculty of Health Sciences, Aristotle University of Thessaloniki, Thessaloniki, Greece

pantonio@otenet.gr, georgearfaras@gmail.com, npandria@gmail.com, gntakakis@outlook.com, manwlisbabatsikos@yahoo.com, alkinoosathanassiou@gmail.com

Abstract. Emotion greatly affects learning. Affective states, such as motivation, interest and attention, have been identified to cause changes in brain and body activity. Heart Rate (HR), Electro-Dermal Activity (EDA), and Electroencephalography (EEG) reflect physiological expressions of the human body that change according to emotional changes. In reverse, changes of bio-signal recordings can be linked to emotional changes. Virtual/Mixed Reality (V/MR) applications can be used in medical education to enhance learning. This work is a proof of application study of wearable, bio-sensor based affect detection in a learning processes, that includes the Microsoft HoloLens V/MR platform. Wearable sensors for HR, EDA and EEG signals recordings were used during two educational scenarios run by a medical doctor. The first was a conventional scenario-based Virtual Patient case for the participant's bio-signal baselines canonization. The second was a V/MR exploratory educational neuroanatomy resource. After pre-processing and averaging, the HR and EDA recordings displayed a considerable increase during the V/MR case against the baseline. The alpha rhythm, of the EEG, had a borderline degrease and the theta over beta ration a borderline increase. These results indicate an increased attention/concentration state. They also demonstrate that the usage of bio-sensors assist in the detection the emotional state and could provide real-time, affective learning analytics using V/MR in medical education.

Keywords: Affective computing · Affective learning · Biomedical signal processing · Educational technology · Electroencephalography · Medical education · Mixed reality · Virtual reality · Wearable sensors

1 Introduction

The affective domain, one of the three main domains of learning according to Bloom's Taxonomy [1], focuses on the learner's feelings, emotions and degree of acceptance of the given learning content [2, 3]. Motivation, attention and interest are linked to the affective domain [4]. It was also stated that learning often occurs during an emotional episode [5]. All these emotions aforementioned, along with the rest of the emotions, are represented

© Springer Nature Switzerland AG 2020
C. Frasson et al. (Eds.): BFAL 2020, LNAI 12462, pp. 87–95, 2020.
https://doi.org/10.1007/978-3-030-60735-7_9

into the Pleasure, Arousal, Dominance (PAD) psychological model of emotional states [6, 7]. Given that "all affective states arise from two fundamental neurophysiological systems, one related to valence (a pleasure–displeasure continuum) and the other to arousal" [8], Pleasure and Arousal are used mainly by researchers [9].

Emotional state changes lead to changes on bio-signals such as Heart Rate (HR), Electrodermal Activity (EDA), and Electroencephalography (EEG) [10]. Analyzing the change of bio-signal recordings can determine the emotional state of the human [11].

Brain activity is, also, affected by emotional states [12, 13]. These changes are associated with the neurophysiological interaction between cortical-based cognitive states and sub-cortical valence and arousal systems [8]. Negative emotion, especially fear, leads to a non-declarative learning condition, which then leads in a functional asymmetry between left and right amygdaloid complex (AC) [14]. Emotional valence is favored by this asymmetry regarding both positive and negative stimuli [15, 16]. Emotional arousal is linked to theta waves generating from amygdala [17–19].

Technology enhanced medical education plays an important role in medical curricula. Current medical technology enhanced education is mostly based on case-based or problem-based learning (CBL/PBL) and other small-group instructional models [20, 21]. Scenario cases, referred as Virtual Patients (VPs), in healthcare are created according to learning objectives, keeping in mind the skillsets of students in order to provide a game–informed, media-saturated learning environment.

The target of this feasibility case study is to gather real-time affective analytics data from a participant while she was experiencing two VP scenarios through the use of commercial wearables and EEG sensors.

2   Materials and Methods

2.1   Demographics and Study Information

One healthy right-handed was the participant of our case study. The participant was a 34yo male medical doctor. He was informed, through the consent form, that he would take part in a VP scenario and an exploratory, holographic neuroanatomy educational scenario. In both scenarios brain activity and bio-signals were recorded, with an EEG device and a wearable wristband.

2.2   Devices

EEG signals were acquired using a Nexus-10 two-channel EEG amplifier [22], connected via Bluetooth to the researcher's PC. EEG electrodes were placed at the Fz and Cz positions, references at the A1 and A2 (earlobes) and ground electrode at Fpz of the international 10–20 electrode placement system. Preprocessing included automatic EEG artifact removal and generation of real-time alpha, beta and theta rhythm. Also, the composite ratio of theta over beta was additionally generated. For continuous, real-time physiological signals for stress detection, the Empatica E4 smart wristband was used [23], where HR (1 Hz) and EDA (4 Hz) were recorded. A Microsoft HoloLens Holographic Computer [24] was used as the Mixed Reality means of the experiment.

Microsoft HoloLens provided holographic experiences in order to empower the user in novel ways. It blends optics and sensors to deliver seamless 3D content interaction with the real world. Advanced sensors capture information about what the user is doing as well as the environment she is in, allowing mapping and understanding of the physical places, spaces and things around the user.

2.3 Software and Hardware

The experimental setup was implemented in two scenarios, a VP and a Mixed Reality scenario. The first scenario is an interlinked web of pages that describe a coherent medical case. The second scenario used for the experiment was an exploratory interactive tutorial on the main central nervous system pathways in the brain and spinal cord (Fig. 1A).

For the needs of this pilot experimental setup, additionally, two standard PC units were used. All real-time signal acquisition and post processing was conducted in a dedicated Signal Acquisition and Post Processing (SAPP) PC Unit while subjective emotion self-reporting, VP educational activity and overall timestamp synchronization was conducted through an Activity and Timestamp Synchronization (ATS) PC Unit. In the ATS unit, the Debut Video Capture software [25] was used to record and timestamp all of the participant's activities on screen for reference and manual synchronization with the internal clocks of the EEG and wearable sensor recorded from the SAPP unit. The overall equipment setup and synchronization is demonstrated in Fig. 1B

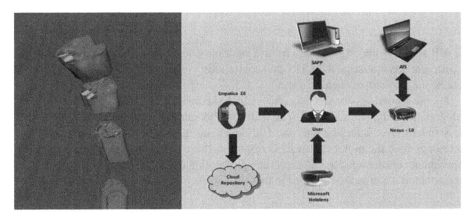

Fig. 1. Mixed Reality (A) visualization and (B) affective analytics setup.

2.4 Experimental Methodology

The experiment took place in two sessions. For the first session, the subject was invited to sit comfortably in front of the ATS unit's screen, at a distance of 60 cm. The participant wore the Empactica E4 sensor, assisted by the experimental team, along with the Nexus-10 EEG electrodes. The ATS unit's screen was set on the starting page of the VP scenario along with a Universal Time (UTC) clock for precise time recording. The user navigated

Table 1. Conventional educational episode biosignal baseline averages

	Seg.1	Seg.2	Seg.3	Seg.4	Average	STDEV
Alpha Cz (µV)	4.886	5.259	4.883	4.921	4.987	0.1822
Theta/Beta Cz	3.198	2.235	3.047	3.584	3.016	0.5675
Alpha Fz (µV)	5.518	5.554	5.334	4.826	5.308	0.3355
Theta/Beta Fz	3.678	3.394	3.654	4.168	3.724	0.3232
HR (bpm)	86	90	88	89	87	1.7
EDA (uSiemens)	0.227	0.209	0.203	0.203	0.215	0.0114

Table 2. V/MR educational episode biosignal averages

	Average	STDEV
Alpha Cz (µv)	4.680	0.711
Theta/beta Cz	3.131	1.137
Alpha Fz (µv)	4.940	0.707
Theta/beta Fz	4.257	1.629
HR	95	1
EDA	3.475	0.865

the VP scenario making choices from a multiple-choice list. The coordinator of the experiment was operating the SAPP unit continuously overseeing the acquisition process outside the participants field of view.

For the second session the only change in the setup was the addition of the HoloLens holographic computer unit that was worn by the subject. Gesture interactions were the standard User Interface with the HoloLens and in order to not contaminate EEG recordings with the motor cortex EEG responses these gestures were conducted by the experiment coordinator after a preset time passed (approx. 4 s). The whole session was time annotated and video recorded to facilitate allow for annotation at a later time.

3   Results

The collected data were annotated according to user activity data, which was taken from the ATS unit, for the first session, and the video recording, for the second session. Those were the Heart Rate (HR), electrodermal activity (EDA), the Alpha amplitude and the Theta/Beta ratio.

Annotation marks in the first session were placed at the time where the user moved to a new node in the VP. HR, EDA, Alpha, Beta and Theta signal values formed the baseline of each bio-signal modality for this user. The data of the second session were annotated with marks placed at time points of the interaction gestures, as they appear in the video recording of the equivalent session. The first session segments were averaged in order to produce a global baseline average for each bio-signal. The data of the HoloLens session were averaged on a per segment basis and the resulting data series (one data point per gesture per signal modality) and explored using descriptive statistics for quantitative differences from the baseline values.

The first scenario (VP scenario) was solved in 4 stages. Thus, after averaging all bio-signal data that were annotated and segmented for these 4 stages we extracted the averages for the bio-signals recorded in this experimental setup presented in Table 1.

The (V/MR neuroanatomy scenario) included 134 annotated segments in total due to its greater educational granularity. Thus the descriptive statistics for this scenario are presented without their original data points in tabular form (Table 2). However, for each segment the EDA, Alpha rhythm and Theta/Beta ratio average values are plotted vs the segment number in Figs. 2, 3.

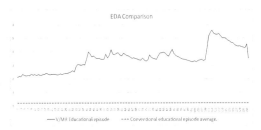

Fig. 2. EDA-Segment plot for the V/MR Educational episode. Dashed line denotes the baseline established in the first experimental session first experimental session. Strong straight line denotes series' average.

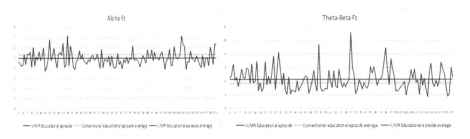

Fig. 3. Alpha amplitude (uV) (A)—Theta/beta ratio (B) segment plot for the V/MR Educational episode for the Fz position. Dashed line denotes the baseline established in the first experimental session. Strong straight line denotes series' average.

4   Discussion

The target of this feasibility case study was to gather real-time affective analytics data from a participant while she was experiencing two VP scenarios. While the EEG data gathering during the first VP scenario was straightforward, that was not the case for the second scenario that required the Microsoft HoloLens device to function upon the Nexus-10 EEG electrodes.

The concept of putting together 3d or even more immersive environments for teaching medicine is not a novel one [26–30]. Even more so, there are a number of studies that involve EEG and pure VR [31, 32]. However, this is among the leading studies that involve a wearable immersive mixed reality holographic computer (the MS HoloLens) along with real-time EEG recordings in an easily transferrable to real world educational settings.

The EEG results of the participant, during the V/MR educational episode, display an increased theta/beta ratio and slightly reduced alpha rhythm in both the central and frontal area when compared to the non-immersive educational activity (the VP) used for establishing a bio-signal baseline in an educational context. Increase of theta power is documented to facilitate both working and episodic memory as well as the encoding of new information [27, 33, 34]. In the frontal-midline brain regions, theta activity is also related to concentration, sustained attention and creativity [35–38]. In line with this suggestion, higher theta activity has been reported in the frontal-midline regions, mainly in Fz, during a task of high cognitive demand, a task with increasing working memory needs [39, 40] or even a high attention process [41–43]. Furthermore, engagement in attention-demanding tasks or judgment calls is reported to lead to alpha power suppression [44, 45]. In light of this literature, our pilot findings point towards an increased concentration and attention potential in the V/MR educational session than in the conventional one that was used as the base of comparison.

The EDA, as well as the HR results were increased in the V/MR session compared to the baseline educational episode. These increased bio-signals results indicate high arousal, independent of valence (c.f. [46, 47]). This can be due to the immersion and excitement of the interaction with the V/MR educational resource, along with the sensation of wearing a sense altering digital device.

Amongst the limitations of this study is that it was run by one participant. A bigger participant pool will provide statistically verified results. While this pilot scenario provided specific results for the user's affective state, during the interaction with a V/MR educational scenario against a conventional educational scenario, there is the need for extended research regarding the scenarios' impact in the affective state of the participants.

Regarding future work, the use of different immersion systems, such as 3D virtual environments, can be explored. Also, enhanced emotional content could be implemented in these scenarios in order to trigger increased bio-signal variations.

Mixed reality affective analytics is a field open to further exploration. It provides a way of enhancement of the educational process, over the conventional way, improvement of decision-making skill due to the impact in users' affective state and manual practice through immersive simulations.

References

1. Bloom, B.: Bloom's taxonomy of learning domains: the three types of learning (1956). http://www.nwlink.com/~donclark/hrd/bloom.html. Accessed 13 May 2018

2. Krathwohl, D.R., Bloom, B.S., Masla, B.B.: Taxonomy of Educational Objectives, the Classification of Educational Goals. Handbook II: Affective Domain. David McKay Co., Inc, New York (1964)
3. Bamidis, P.D.: Affective learning: principles, technologies, practice. BFAL 2017. LNCS (LNAI), vol. 10512, pp. 1–13. Springer, Cham (2017). https://doi.org/10.1007/978-3-319-67615-9_1
4. Picard, R.W., et al.: Affective learning—a manifesto. BT Technol. J. **22**(4), 253–269 (2004)
5. Stein, N.L., Levine, L.J.: Making sense out of emotion. In: Kessen, W., Ortony, A., Kraik, F. (eds.) Memories, Thoughts, and Emotions: Essays in Honor of George Mandler, pp. 295–322. Erlbaum, Hillsdale (1991)
6. Mehrabian, A., Russell, J.A.: An Approach to Environmental Psychology. MIT Press, Cambridge (1974)
7. Russel, J.A.: A circumplex model of affect. J. Pers. Soc. Psychol. **39**(6), 1161–1178 (1980). http://psycnet.apa.org/record/1981-25062-001
8. Posner, J., Russell, J.A., Peterson, B.S.: The circumplex model of affect: an integrative approach to affective neuroscience, cognitive development, and psychopathology. Dev. Psychopathol. **17**(3), 715–734 (2005)
9. Bakker, I., van der Voordt, T., Vink, P., de Boon, J.: Pleasure, arousal, dominance: Mehrabian and Russell revisited. Curr. Psychol. **33**, 405–421 (2014)
10. Chang, C.-Y. Zheng, J.-Y., Wang, C.-J.: Based on support vector regression for emotion recognition using physiological signals. In: The 2010 International Joint Conference on Neural Networks (IJCNN), pp. 1–7. IEEE. https://doi.org/10.1109/IJCNN.2010.5596878
11. Niu, X., Chen, L., Chen, Q.: Research on genetic algorithm based on emotion recognition using physiological signals. In: 2011 International Conference on Computational Problem-Solving (ICCP), pp. 614–618. IEEE (2011). https://doi.org/10.1109/ICCPS.2011.6092256
12. Lane, R., Reiman, E.M., Ahern, G.L., Schwartz, G.E., Davidson, R.J.: Neuroanatomical correlates of happiness, sadness and disgust. Am. J. Psychiatry **154**, 926–933 (1997)
13. Damasio, R., et al.: Subcortical and cortical brain activity during the feeling of self-generated emotions. Nat. Neurosci. **3**, 1049–1056 (2000)
14. Phelps, E.A., O'Connor, K.J., Gatenby, J.C., Gore, J.C., Grillon, C., Davis, M.: Activation of the left amygdala to a cognitive representation of fear. Nat. Neurosci. **4**, 437–441 (2001)
15. Lanteaume, L., Khalfa, S., Régis, J., Marquis, P., Chauvel, P., Bartolomei, F.: Emotion induction after direct intracerebral stimulations of human amygdala. Cereb. Cortex **17**, 1307–1313 (2007)
16. Markowitsch, J.H.: Differential contribution of right and left amygdala to affective information processing. Behav. Neurol. **11**, 233–244 (1998)
17. Paré, D., Collins, D.R., Pelletier, J.G.: Amygdala oscillations and the consolidation of emotional memories. Trends Cogn. Sci. **6**, 306–314 (2002)
18. Bamidis, P.D., Dimitrova, V., Treasure-Jones, T., Poulton, T., Roberts, T.: Augmented minds: technology's role in supporting 21st century doctors. In: Workshop on European TEL for Workplace Learning and Professional Development (TEL@ Work). Leeds (2017)
19. Dafli, E., Fountoukidis, I., Hatzisevastou-Loukidou, C., Bamidis, P.D.: Curricular integration of virtual patients: a unifying perspective of medical teachers and students. BMC Med. Educ. **19**(1), 416 (2019)
20. Williams, B.: Case based learning—a review of the literature: is there scope for this educational paradigm in prehospital education? Emerg. Med. J. **22**(8), 577–581 (2005). https://doi.org/10.1136/emj.2004.022707 [Medline: 16046764]
21. Larson, J.R.: In Search of Synergy in Small Group Performance. Psychology Press, New York (2010)
22. Nexus-10 product page. https://www.mindmedia.com/en/products/nexus-10-mkii/

23. Empatica E4 product page. https://www.empatica.com/en-eu/research/e4/
24. Microsoft Hololens product page. https://www.microsoft.com/en-us/hololens
25. Debut Video Capture Software product page. http://www.nchsoftware.com/capture/index.html
26. Dafli, E.L., Vegoudakis, K.I., Pappas, C., Bamidis, P.D.: Re-purposing cardiology to psychiatry sessions in a 3D based virtual learning environment. Bio-Algorithms Med-Systems **6**(11), 9–13 (2010)
27. Karrasch, M., Laine, M., Rapinoja, P., Krause, C.M.: Effects of normal aging on event-related desynchronization/synchronization during a memory task in humans. Neurosci. Lett. **366**(1), 18–23 (2004)
28. Antoniou, P.E., Sidiropoulos, E.A., Bamidis, P.D.: DISCOVER-ing beyond OpenSim; immersive learning for carers of the elderly in the VR/AR era. In: Beck, D., et al. (eds.) iLRN 2017. CCIS, vol. 725, pp. 189–200. Springer, Cham (2017). https://doi.org/10.1007/978-3-319-60633-0_16
29. Antoniou, P.E., Athanasopoulou, C.A., Dafli, E., Bamidis, P.D.: Exploring design requirements for repurposing dental virtual patients from the web to second life: a focus group study. J. Med. Internet Res. **16**(6), 1–19 (2014)
30. Antoniou, P.E., Dafli, E., Arfaras, G., Bamidis, P.D.: Versatile mixed reality medical educational spaces; requirement analysis from expert users. Pers. Ubiquit. Comput. **21**(6), 1015–1024 (2017). https://doi.org/10.1007/s00779-017-1074-5
31. Charalambous, E.F., Hanna, S.E., Penn, A.L.: Visibility analysis, spatial experience and EEG recordings in virtual reality environments: the experience of 'knowing where one is' and isovist properties as a means to assess the related brain activity. In: Proceedings of the 11th Space Syntax Symposium 3 July 2017, vol. 11, p. 128-1. Instituto Superior Técnico, Departamento de Engenharia Civil, Arquitetura e Georrecursos, Portugal
32. Lin, C.-T., Chung, I.-F., Ko, L.-W., Chen, Y.-C., Liang, S.-F., Duann, J.-R.: EEG-based assessment of driver cognitive responses in a dynamic virtual-reality driving environment. IEEE Trans. Biomed. Eng. **54**(7), 1349–1352 (2007)
33. Klimesch, W.: EEG alpha and theta oscillations reflect cognitive and memory performance: a review and analysis. Brain Res. Rev. **29**(2–3), 169–195 (1999)
34. Klopfer, E., Squire, K.: Environmental detectives—the development of an augmented reality platform for environmental simulations. Educ. Technol. Res. Dev. **56**(2), 203–228 (2008)
35. Kubota, Y., et al.: Frontal midline theta rhythm is correlated with cardiac autonomic activities during the performance of an attention demanding meditation procedure. Cogn. Brain Res. **11**(2), 281–287 (2001)
36. Başar-Eroglu, C., Başar, E., Demiralp, T., Schürmann, M.: P300-response: possible psychophysiological correlates in delta and theta frequency channels. A review. Int. J. Psychophysiol. **13**(2), 161–179 (1992)
37. Lagopoulos, J., et al.: Increased theta and alpha EEG activity during nondirective meditation. J. Altern. Complement. Med. **15**(11), 1187–1192 (2009)
38. Gruzelier, J.: A theory of alpha/theta neurofeedback, creative performance enhancement, long distance functional connectivity and psychological integration. Cogn. Process. **10**(1 SUPPL.), 101–109 (2009)
39. Jensen, O., Tesche, C.D.: Frontal theta activity in humans increases with memory load in a working memory task. Eur. J. Neurosci. **15**(8), 1395–1399 (2002)
40. Grunwald, M., et al.: Theta power in the EEG of humans during ongoing processing in a haptic object recognition task. Cogn. Brain Res. **11**(1), 33–37 (2001)
41. Gevins, A.S., et al.: EEG patterns during 'cognitive' tasks. I. Methodology and analysis of complex behaviors. Electroencephalogr. Clin. Neurophysiol. **47**, 693–703 (1979)

42. Gevins, A.S., Zeitlin, G.M., Doyle, J.C., Schaffer, R.E., Callaway, E.: EEG patterns during 'cognitive' tasks. II. Analysis of controlled tasks. Electroencephalogr. Clin. Neurophysiol. **47**, 704–710 (1979)
43. Gevins, A.S., et al.: Electroencephalogram correlates of higher cortical functions. Science **203**(4381), 665–668 (1979)
44. Adrian, E.D., Matthews, B.H.: The interpretation of potential waves in the cortex. J. Physiol. **81**(4), 440–471 (1934)
45. Niedermeyer, E., Lopes da Silva, F.: Electroencephalography: Basic Principles, Clinical Applications, and Related Fields, 5th edn. Williams & Wilkins, Baltimore (2004)
46. Fowles, D.C.: The three arousal model: implications of Gray's two-factor learning theory for heart rate, electrodermal activity, and psychopathy. Psychophysiology **17**(2), 87–104 (1980)
47. Drachen, A., Nacke, L.E., Yannakakis, G., Pedersen, A.L.: Correlation between heart rate, electrodermal activity and player experience in first-person shooter games. In: Proceedings of the 5th ACM SIGGRAPH Symposium on Video Games 28 July 2010, pp. 49–54. ACM (2010)

Hypocrates+: A Virtual Reality Medical Education Platform with Intelligent Real-Time Help System

Qiang Ye$^{(\boxtimes)}$, Hamdi Ben Abdessalem$^{(\boxtimes)}$, and Marwa Boukadida$^{(\boxtimes)}$

Université de Montréal, Montréal, Canada
{qiang.ye,hamdi.ben.abdessalem,marwa.boukadida}@umontreal.ca

Abstract. Virtual reality, an immersing and interactive information communication technology, is changing the fundamental of medical education by creating more astonishing vivid realistic clinical environment and cases. Here, we proposed a virtual reality medical education platform with intelligent real-time emotion evaluation and help system, named Hypocrates+. By this platform, medical students can gain their medical knowledge and experience through well designed virtual clinical cases and environments with less frustration. Experiments shows that the overall mean frustration before getting the help was 0.53 and the mean frustration after was 0.50; better performance is related to lower frustration. We concluded that Hypocrates+ is a good start for developing a popular virtual medical education platform.

Keywords: Virtual reality · Medical education · EEG · Real-time help system · Intelligent agent

1 Introduction

Virtual reality (VR) technology is changing the style of medical education [1] with its powerful capability of simulating the clinical environments and clinical cases. By using a virtual medical education platform, medical students have an opportunity to do clinical reasoning on virtual cases instead of on real patient. It is much safer to make mistakes on virtual patients during the long-time medical learning process.

In our previous work [2], we proposed a virtual reality platform with several well-designed virtual clinical environments and clinical cases, Hypocrates, where a medical student can experience virtual clinical cases and learn medical knowledge while a real-time emotion analysis of the student can also be performed by the electroencephalographic (EEG) signal [3] collected from the users' interaction as well. Our further research shows that, during interaction between a medical student and the platform, positive emotion has a strong correlation to better learning result, and vice versa. Can we improve our platform to reduce students' negative emotion so that they can interact with the platform and learn medical knowledge in a more peaceful and positive mood? Is it possible to help students in order to reduce their negative emotions?

C. Frasson et al. (Eds.): BFAL 2020, LNAI 12462, pp. 96–101, 2020.
https://doi.org/10.1007/978-3-030-60735-7_10

In this article, we imported a real-time emotion analysis and a real-time help system to our existed Hypocrates, and we call it Hypocrates+. When interacting with Hypocrates+, medical students' EEG signals are collected simultaneously and sent to the real-time emotion analysis system, where a decision of whether a help is needed for the student is making. If such a help is needed, the help system will provide the student related useful medical information intelligently acquired from internet in real time.

2 Related Works

2.1 Real-Time Help Systems

Learning new things usually is a long-term process. Repetition is required, help is often useful, and correction is essential when mistakes are made. In which situation and how frequently a repetition, help, or a correction is required is a subject of research. A real-time help system provides timely information to learners when they get stuck during a learning process, which often saves time for learners. Moreover, a real-time help system may also provide targeted and personalized help information if an intelligent analysis component is equipped.

Due to the development of information technology, medical education is changing its style: from traditional paper books and real clinical practice to electronical resources and virtual standardized patient model [4]. By interacting with well-designed electronical and virtual clinical cases, students are more easily to master medical knowledge and apply them to real clinical cases correctly [5]. Students are also aware of medical errors; however, remaining tensions may limit learning [6]. In such situation, a real-time help system may help maintain students' positive emotion.

2.2 Virtual Reality

Virtual reality is more and more used in different domains and it proved its efficiency due to its advantages. Its main advantage is the possibility to isolate the user from any external visual distraction and thus making them believe they are in a real world [7]. Some researchers generated sensorimotor illusions giving the user a sense of presence in the environment by manipulating multimodal stimulus inputs thanks to virtual reality [8]. This technology has been used to treat various psychological disorders including brain damage [9], anxiety disorders [10] and alleviation of fear [11]. Moreover, some researchers designed real-time editable virtual reality environment in order to change its parameters according to the user's brain activity.

3 "Hypocrates+": Methodology

3.1 Environment: "Hypocrates+"

We created an interactive virtual reality environment. The choice of virtual reality is based on the fact that it ensures a total isolation from external distraction, as seen in a previous section, and thus increase concentration on the task. This environment is a dynamic system able to present various medical cases in real-time. The student initially goes through an introductory scene in which we explain the tasks to be done. Subsequently, they are immersed in a virtual operating room or a doctor's office, depending on the type of the medical case. The participant interacts with the virtual environment through a virtual reality headset and a gamepad.

For each medical case, we start by exposing a panel in which we display to the student information about the patient and their symptoms, a reliability score gauge, an "Analysis" and a "Diagnosis" buttons. The score of reliability gauge decreases every time the student selects a wrong choice.

The student must read the displayed symptoms, then they can click on one of the buttons ("Analysis" or "Diagnosis" buttons) depending on whether they want to ask for analysis or directly choose a diagnosis. If the student asks for analysis, a panel containing a checklist of analysis will appear where they can check one or more analysis and then can see a panel displaying the results by clicking on the "Results" button. If the student clicks on the "Diagnosis" button, a panel displaying four medical diagnosis appears and they must choose the correct one by clicking on it. Once the diagnosis is selected a series of panels appear one at a time. Each one of these panels contains 3 possible actions (one correct, and two wrong). The number of actions' panels depends on the number of actions to perform in the medical case being resolved. For example, if the number of actions needed to be performed is three, three panels will appear, one by one, containing each one three actions. Every time the student chooses an action the next actions' panel will appear.

3.2 Real-Time Help System

Within Hypocrates+, the real-time help service functions as a server, providing help content to its client: the other parts of the whole platform. Figure 1 briefly shows the architecture of the real-time help system and how it communicates with its client. It includes three main components: a communication component, an intelligent content generating component, and a log component. When a client asks for a help, it sends a message to the real-time help server. When receiving this message, the communication component enqueues this message to a queue; meanwhile, the content generating component continuously checks the message queue, dequeues a request, and intelligently produces response content. Once a response content is prepared, communication component will send the content back to the client who requested it. All communication history is recorded by the log component for future analysis. The whole system is capable to provide the service stably and robustly to multiple clients.

Intelligent content generating component is another major module of the real-time help server. It parses the request, invokes Wiki search API to acquire most related Wiki pages, analyzes the pages and selects most meaningful, high-related text within a certain length as a response and sends it back to the endpoint who requests it. Figure 2 briefly shows how this component works. Having considered the characteristics of the description of a clinical disease in a Wiki Page, we designed and implemented section recommendation and best response decision intelligent algorithms to produce best response accurately and quickly.

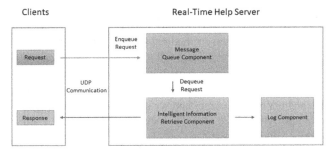

Fig. 1. Architecture of the real-time help system for Hypocrates+

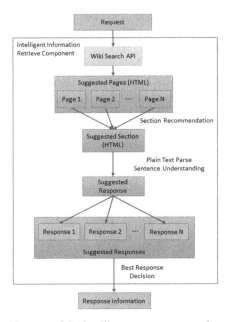

Fig. 2. Architecture of the intelligent content generating component

3.3 Neural Agent

The neural agent in Hypocrates+ is responsible for communicating with the real-time help system and the virtual environment. By receiving the EEG signal of a Hypocrates+ user who is interacting with the virtual environment, the neural agent calculates the emotional state of the user and makes decisions on whether a real-time help request is needed according to an inner intelligent algorithm. If this request is needed, the agent will send a request to the real-time help server, then receive a help information and display it on the virtual environment to the user.

4 Experiments

We conducted experiments involving 5 medical students (4 females) in order to test our approach. The experimental protocol is the following. In the first step of the experiment, the participant signs an ethic form which explains the study and fills a pre-session form. In the second step, we install an Emotiv EPOC headset. In the third step, the participant is equipped with the FOVE VR headset and we give him a wireless gamepad to interact with the environment. After these steps, we start the "Hypocrates" environment, the Real-time help service and the Neural Agent.

5 Results and Discussion

The objective of this study was to discover whether it is possible to help student in order to reduce their negative emotions. To this end, we analyzed the mean frustration level of the participants before and after they received a help information. The results show that the overall mean frustration before getting the help was 0.53 and the mean frustration after was 0.50. More detailed results are shown in Fig. 3 where we note that the frustration decreased for all the participants expect P2.

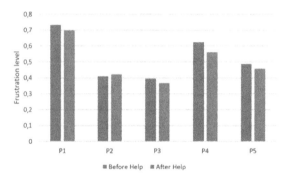

Fig. 3. Histogram of mean frustration level before and after the help

This effect obtained in our first analysis lead us to analyze the performance of each participants. The highest performance was made by the participant 1 with a mean score of 72.77% and the worst performance was made by participant 2 with a mean score of 55%. This result may be explained by the frustration that was not decreased by the help.

6 Conclusion

In this paper, we presented a novel approach to help medical students resolving medical cases by importing a real-time help service in our platform: Hypocrates+. We conducted experiments, and results show that the emotional state of a medical student is easy to keep stable and positive, which provides more peaceful and positive mood for learning. Besides, it is also possible to help reduce mistakes when the student makes clinical reasoning on virtual clinical cases presented by 3D virtual environment. Hypocrates+ is a good start for developing a popular virtual medical education platform.

Acknowledgment. We acknowledge NSERC-CRD (National Science and Engineering Research Council Cooperative Research Development) and BMU for funding this work.

References

1. Khan, R., Plahouras, J., Johnston, B.C., Scaffidi, M.A., Grover, S.C., Walsh, C.M.: Virtual reality simulation training for health professions trainees in gastrointestinal endoscopy. Cochrane Database Syst. Rev. **8**, CD008237 (2018)
2. Ben Abdessalem, H., Frasson, C.: Real-time brain assessment for adaptive virtual reality game: a neurofeedback approach. In: Frasson, C., Kostopoulos, G. (eds.) Brain Function Assessment in Learning. LNCS, vol. 10512, pp. 133–134. Springer, Cham (2017). https://doi.org/10.1007/978-3-319-67615-9_12
3. McFarland, D.J., Sarnacki, W.A., Wolpaw, J.R.: Electroencephalographic (EEG) control of three-dimensional movement. J. Neural Eng. **7**, 036007 (2010)
4. Moran, J., Briscoe, G., Peglow, S.: Current technology in advancing medical education: perspectives for learning and providing care. Acad. Psychiatry **42**, 796–799 (2018)
5. Dyer, E., Swartzlander, B.J., Gugliucci, M.R.: Using virtual reality in medical education to teach empathy. Virtual Proj. **518**, 498–500 (2018)
6. Fischer, M.A., Mazor, K.M., Baril, J., Alper, E., DeMarco, D., Pugnaire, M.: Learning from mistakes - factors that influence how students and residents learn from medical errors. J. Gen. Int. Med. **21**(5), 419–423 (2006)
7. Biocca, F.: The cyborg's dilemma: progressive embodiment in virtual environments [1]. J. Comput.-Mediat. Commun. **3** (2006)
8. Bohil, C.J., Alicea, B., Biocca, F.A.: Virtual reality in neuroscience research and therapy. Nat. Rev. Neurosci. **12**, 752–762 (2011)
9. Rose, F.D., Brooks, B.M., Rizzo, A.A.: Virtual reality in brain damage rehabilitation: review. Cyberpsychol. Behav. **8**, 241–262 (2005)
10. Gorini, A., Riva, G.: Virtual reality in anxiety disorders: the past and the future. Expert Rev. Neurother. **8**, 215–233 (2008)
11. Alvarez, R.P., Johnson, L., Grillon, C.: Contextual-specificity of short-delay extinction in humans: renewal of fear-potentiated startle in a virtual environment. Learn. Mem. **14**, 247–253 (2007)

A Personalized Brain-Based Quiz Game for Improving Students' Cognitive Functions

Akrivi Krouska, Christos Troussas[(✉)], and Cleo Sgouropoulou

Department of Informatics and Computer Engineering, University of West Attica,
Egaleo, Greece
{akrouska,ctrouss,csgouro}@uniwa.gr

Abstract. Brain-based learning is the understanding of the human brain functions and its application in educational environments for meaningful learning. Brain-Based Learning adapts the learning process based on the function of human brain, providing a learner-centered tutoring environment. To this direction, a personalized brain-based quiz game was developed applying the principles of brain-based learning and Marzano Taxonomy for promoting meaningful learning and improving students' higher order cognitive functions. Thus, the system adapts quiz content based on student knowledge level, emotional state and the learning goal set. Regarding the control grouped pre-test and post-test experiment; the results reveal that this approach has a positive effect on students' performance, outperforming the traditional e-assessment systems.

Keywords: Brain-based learning · Cognitive functions · E-learning · Marzano Taxonomy · Personalized learning

1 Introduction

Information and Communication Technologies (ICT) have evolved rapidly affecting all fields, such as learning technology [1]. The educational challenges in digital learning require new pedagogical approaches combined with technological advances for providing innovative learning environments and improving learning outcomes [2]. Therefore, helping students to reach their highest potential has been of great importance in the development of effective e-learning systems [3].

Nowadays, some methods and strategies in learning process are revised based on the research in neuroscience field. The findings in this field have provided a better understanding of the human brain and how individuals learn. Thus, a new learning approach has arisen, namely Brain-based Learning [4]. This strategy admits the brain's rules for meaningful learning instead of memorization, adapting teaching methods based on these rules, namely the principles of brain-based learning [5, 6]. Brain-based learning is oriented to maximize learning and tutoring through a motivating and positive process. Several studies indicate the positive impact of this approach on academic achievement compared to traditional instruction [4, 7–9].

© Springer Nature Switzerland AG 2020
C. Frasson et al. (Eds.): BFAL 2020, LNAI 12462, pp. 102–106, 2020.
https://doi.org/10.1007/978-3-030-60735-7_11

In brain-based learning model, the learning environment should be developed in such way that it should: (1) challenge students' cognitive skills; (2) be pleasant and learner-centered; (3) promote active and meaningful learning [10]. These facts provide opportunities for students to advance their cognitive functions.

In view of the above, this work presents a personalized quiz game based on the brain-based learning theory in order to provide a brain-based assessment which promotes meaningful learning. The aim of this system is to improve students' cognitive functions instead of memorization on which traditional approaches mainly focus. Thus, the Marzano Taxonomy was applied to the design of assessment items for corresponding to the four level of cognition, namely knowledge retrieval, comprehension, analysis and knowledge utilization. Moreover, appropriate hints messages were designed for each assessment item in order to motivate students and help them to improve their learning outcomes. Thus, the system adapts quiz content based on student knowledge level, emotional state and the learning goal set. For system evaluation, control grouped pre-test and post- test experiment has been applied on undergraduate students of computer science in a public university. The research reveals that the personalized brain-based quiz has a positive effect on improving students' learning outcomes and obtaining higher order cognition.

2 Personalized Brain-Based Quiz Game

Brain-based learning involves tutoring practices, curriculum designs, and programs that focus on the current scientific research about how the brain learns, including several aspect, such as cognitive development, i.e. how students learn in a different way as they become older, grow, and mature socially, emotionally, and cognitively.

The logic architecture of the personalized brain-based quiz game developed for improving students' cognitive functions is shown in Fig. 1.

The system takes into consideration three characteristics regarding students, as follows:

- Knowledge level: This is a key characteristic for the assessment of students [2]. For example, difficult assessment units are more suitable for students who have a high knowledge level and easy assessment units can be better targeted to students who have a lower knowledge level. The system defines three knowledge levels for students, namely beginner, intermediate and expert.
- Emotional state: Emotional state is an important determinant for students' assessment [11]. Indeed, emotion is significant in education—it drives attention, which in turn drives learning and memory. For instance, if a learner is happy, s/he will probably have a better performance in assessment. The system specifies several basic emotions, such as happiness, sadness, boredom, and anger.
- Learning goal: Learning goals help learners to target to what they are supposed to learn [1]. Furthermore, they are closely related to the efforts of students. Based on specific learning goals, assessment can be more accurate by considering students' abilities. The system offers the possibility to students to select the level of learning goals that they want to achieve using the choices "Easy", "Normal" and "Challenging".

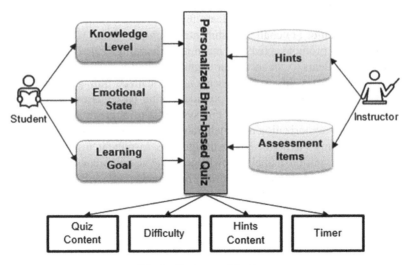

Fig. 1. System architecture.

Furthermore, the system holds two repositories that can assist the process of personalized brain-based assessment, as follows:

- Hints repository: This repository holds information about the hints and feedback that can be delivered to students based on their personal model. Hints can be seen as a valuable tool in the process of assessment since it can help students to have a better performance, when needed. Especially in brain-based assessment, hints can play an important role since they are adapted to the different way each brain learns. Examples of the personalized hints to students delivered by the system are: "Very good effort! But you have to clear you mind while studying!", "Good! You can try more while you were not very well-prepared", etc.
- Assessment items repository: This repository holds units, tailored to the brain-based assessment of units. To achieve this, the Marzano's New Taxonomy is used [12]. In particular, the assessment items are designed based on the levels of cognition defined by Cognitive System of this taxonomy, namely Knowledge Retrieval, Comprehension, Analysis, and Knowledge Utilization (Table 1). Therefore, the quiz provides content that leads the students to achieve higher order cognitive skills instead of memorization.

Table 1. Level of cognition based on Marzano Taxonomy.

Level of cognition	Description
Knowledge Retrieval	Recall of knowledge previously learned
Comprehension	Identify the key elements of information
Analysis	Examine knowledge in detail and come to new conclusions
Knowledge Utilization	Apply or use knowledge in a new or specific situation

The outputs of the system are the question items of the quiz, its difficulty level, the content of the hints provided during the quiz, and the available time for answering it. These outputs are adjusted to students' characteristics in order to provide more personalized brain-based assessment units that aim to the improvement of students' cognitive functions.

3   Evaluation and Discussion

The population of the experiment consists of 100 undergraduate students of computer science in a public university, dividing into two groups of 50 students each one, namely the experimental and control group. This division was made by the instructors based on students' characteristics in order the two groups to be equal. Both groups used an e-assessment system for testing their knowledge in each course's chapter. In particular, the experimental group used the personalized brain-based quiz, whereas the control group used a conventional version providing to students simple tests.

For evaluating the effect of personalized brain-based quiz on learning outcomes, a control grouped pre-test and post-test experimental design has been used. In particular, the same pre-test and post-test, examining the 4 level of cognition based on Marzano Taxonomy, were given to students of the two groups at the beginning of the course and after its completion, respectively. Comparing the pre-test and post-test scores of each level of cognition for both groups, a paired t-test is applied (Table 2).

Table 2. Comparing pre-test and post-test scores of each level of cognition.

Level of cognition	Group	Pre-test Mean	Post-test Mean	Diff.	t Stat	P value
Knowledge Retrieval	Exp.	6,24	8,46	2,22	-22,1638	3,44E-27
	Con.	5,98	7,2	1,22	-11,2957	3,03E-15
Comprehension	Exp.	6,08	8,26	2,18	-23,3365	3,4E-28
	Con.	5,82	6,92	1,1	-10,5768	3,03E-14
Analysis	Exp.	5,96	8,12	2,16	-17,6435	7,19E-23
	Con.	5,74	6,86	1,12	-9,60969	7,42E-13
Knowledge Utilization	Exp.	5,92	8,04	2,12	-22,7475	1,07E-27
	Con.	5,56	6,64	1,08	-10,1607	1,18E-13

The results showed that the average scores of post-test had a significant improvement in all levels of cognition for both groups. However, these of the experimental group were greater than those of the control group, indicating that the personalized bran-based quiz played an important role in the development of higher order cognitive functions. The possible reason of this superior is that in the proposed system, the quiz content is designed based on Marzano Taxonomy and adapted according to student characteristics.

4 Conclusions

Brain-Based Learning adjusts the learning process according to the function of human brain, providing techniques and strategies for a more learner-centered educational environment. Thus, a personalized brain-based quiz game was developed following the principles of brain-based learning. This system aims to improve students' cognitive functions instead of memorization on which traditional approaches mainly focus. For this purpose, the quiz content was designed based on Marzano Taxonomy and adapted to student characteristics, namely knowledge level, emotional state and learning goal. The control grouped pre-test and post- test experiment reveals that this approach has a positive effect on students' performance, outperforming the traditional e-assessment systems in improving students' higher order cognitive functions.

References

1. Krouska, A., Troussas, C., Virvou, M.: SN-Learning: An exploratory study beyond e-learning and evaluation of its applications using EV-SNL framework. J. Comput. Assist. Learn. **35**(2), 168–177 (2019)
2. Troussas, C., Krouska, A., Sgouropoulou, C.: Collaboration and fuzzy-modeled personalization for mobile game-based learning in higher education. Comput. Educ. **144**, 103698 (2020)
3. Troussas, C., Krouska, A., Virvou, M., Sougela, E.: Using Hierarchical Modeling of Thinking Skills to Lead Students to Higher Order Cognition and Enhance Social E-Learning. IISA 2018, pp. 1–5 (2018)
4. Thomas, M., Swamy, S.: Brain based teaching approach—a new paradigm of teaching. Int. J. Educ. Psychol. Res. **3**(2), 62–65 (2014)
5. Caine, R.N., Caine, G.: Making Connections: Teaching and the Human Brain. Association for Supervision and Curriculum Development, Alexandria, VA (1991)
6. Jensen, E.(ed.): Brain-Based Learning: The new Paradigm of Teaching, 2nd edn. (2008)
7. Gözüyeşil, E., Dikici, A.: The effect of brain based learning on academicachievement: a meta-analytical study. Educ. Sci. Theor. Pract. **14**(2), 642–648 (2014)
8. Tafti, M., Kadkhodaie, M.: The effects of brain-based training on the learning and retention of life skills in adolescents. Int. J. Behav. Sci. **10**(4), 140–144 (2016)
9. Tüfekçi, S., Demirel, M.: The effect of brain based learning on achievement, retention, attitude and learning process. Proc. Soc. Behav. Sci. **1**(1), 1782–1791 (2009)
10. Yulian, V.N., Hayati, N.: Enhancing students' mathematical connection by brain based learning model. J. Phys. Conf. Ser. **1315**(1), 012029 (2019)
11. Krouska, A., Troussas, C., Virvou, M.: Comparative evaluation of algorithms for sentiment analysis over social networking services. J. Univ. Comput. Sci. **23**(8), 755–768 (2017)
12. Marzano, R., Kendall, J.: The New Taxonomy of Educational Objectives. Corwin Press, Thousand Oaks, CA (2001)

Virtual Savannah: An Effective Therapeutic and Relaxing Treatment for People with Subjective Cognitive Decline

Caroline Dakoure[1]([⊠]), Hamdi Ben Abdessalem[1], Marwa Boukadida[1], Marc Cuesta[2], Marie-Andrée Bruneau[2], Sylvie Belleville[2], and Claude Frasson[1]

[1] Département d'Informatique et de Recherche Opérationnelle, Université de Montréal, Montreal, QC, Canada
{caroline.dakoure,hamdi.ben.abdessalem,
marwa.boukadida}@umontreal.ca, frasson@iro.umontreal.ca
[2] Centre de Recherche de l'Institut de Gériatrie de Montréal, Montreal, QC, Canada
marc.cuesta@criugm.qc.ca,
{marie.andree.bruneau,sylvie.belleville}@umontreal.ca

Abstract. In an attempt to make the therapeutic aspect less aversive, more attractive and engaging, virtual reality, an increasingly popular application in healthcare, offers an interesting alternative to pharmacological treatments. Positive emotions may improve the cognitive abilities of people suffering from cognitive impairment. Virtual reality can provide immersive and efficient relaxation tool. This paper presents an experiment where 19 people with Subjective Cognitive Decline (SCD) were immersed in a virtual environment representing a savannah. The hypothesis is that the environment may help them reducing their frustration by relaxing. Participants' brain activity was recorded using the Emotiv Epoc headset and the virtual savannah experience lasted 10 min. Results suggest that frustration decreased when participants were surrounded by the virtual savannah and that the positive effects continued afterwards.

Keywords: Cognitive impairment · Virtual reality therapy · Emotions · EEG · Savannah · Cognitive decline · Healthcare application · Brain activity · Relaxation · Frustration

1 Introduction

As the global proportion of older people is increasing rapidly, attention should be paid to cognitive impairment, as it particularly affects older people. According to the World Health Organization, the world population aged 65 or older was 703 million in 2019 [1]. This number is expected to double to 1.5 billion by 2050. Worldwide, approximately 50 million people (91% over 65 years of age) suffer from dementia causing cognitive decline. By 2050, this number is estimated to triple [2].

New forms of non-drug treatments are in great demand to relieve patients, this study will focus on one of them: Virtual reality therapy is the use of virtual environments for health applications. Virtual reality (VR) environments have the advantage that they can be designed, controlled and configured more easily than real environments. With their immersive experience, they are proven to be effective in treating psychiatric disorders by inducing relaxation [3]. Reducing stress by reducing negative emotions not only can reduce cognitive decline and increases memory performance, but also improves mood and quality of life, thus reducing treatments related to anxiety and agitation [4, 5].

The aim of this study is to assess the impact on frustration of the developed VR environment (Savannah VR) for people with Subjective Cognitive Decline (SCD). The paper is organized as follows. First section introduces research that led to the design of Savannah VR. Savannah VR is presented in the second section. A third section describes the experiments conducted and the results are reported and discussed in the last section.

2   Design of the Virtual Environment: Conducted Research

2.1   From Savannah Preference to a Soothing Virtual Reality Environment

Wilson introduced the word biophilia in 1984, that is an innate affinity people have with nature [6]. Savannah preference is a tendency to prefer savannah landscapes because early humans lived for thousands of years in the African savannahs [7]. The term savannah refers here to open environments where the grass is short, with deciduous green trees, water and animal life. Ancient survival challenges led to a correlation between natural landscapes and positive feelings. Savannah as a natural environment brings back the feeling of tranquility and peace [8]. Spreading trees in savannah give a feeling of security because they provide to early humans a place to observe or hide from predators. Savannah is an ideal place to travel and explore, it attracts attention and relaxes thanks to its varied and pleasant landscapes. Therefore, it is assumed that it can be a beneficial virtual environment for people with cognitive impairment.

2.2   Audiovisual Research: Concept Art Based on Drone Videos

The components of the environment were chosen to minimize stress. The main consideration in the choice of animals was to find animals perceived as harmless. Following animals have been chosen to be part of Savannah VR: hornbills, starlings, giraffes, antelopes, gazelles, small elephants and zebras. The key factors in the choice of the graphical user interface were clarity and readability. The Wii Sports game was very popular with the elderly [9]. It has a clear and simple interface, so a similar interface for text and explanations was adopted.

3   Savannah VR: A Soothing Environment

3.1   Overview

Savannah VR was developed at the Heron Laboratory of the Department of Computer Science and Operations Research of the University of Montreal using C# with Unity3D

2017.1.4 engine. It is a therapeutic virtual experience designed to relax and unwind. Participants follow an avatar walking through a savannah speaking in a soft and reassuring voice. As a way of attracting participants' attention and reassuring them, the avatar asks users how they feel and gives clear and concise indications, both in writing and speaking, to ease information processing. The Windows-based environment that requires only a virtual reality headset and a mouse has been designed with cognitively impaired people in mind. The dominant colors are warm, the animals are calm, their movement is slow. A soothing piano tune is played in the background at a volume low enough to appreciate the sound of each animal. Figure 1 below illustrates the visual aspect of a part of the environment.

Fig. 1. Screenshots of Savannah VR

3.2 Navigating in the Environment

Participants automatically follow a gazelle that moves along a precise path with breaking points. They can only look around them without controlling movements. To avoid nausea caused by movement in virtual reality, users follow the gazelle at low speed. The animal is in front of them to imitate a third person view that is less likely to cause motion sickness [10]. The participant's vision has been adjusted to be more pleasant.

3.3 Real-Time Environment Modifications

Real-time changes of the environment are possible with a view to future research. Functions have been implemented that enable environment parameters to be modified by pressing a key. One of the adjustable parameters is the color and intensity of the light because light influences perception and decision-making [11]. Its color can also improve learning [12] and relieve stress more quickly [13]. Also, it is important to choose the volume carefully; too high volume can cause noise pollution [14] so sound volumes can be changed. An environment with more trees can also relieve stress more quickly and effectively [15], it is therefore possible to increase the number of trees in the environment. The number of animals can also be decreased, and the sky and colors can be changed to have a soothing sunset (Fig. 2).

Fig. 2. Screenshots of real-time changes in Savannah VR

4 Experiments

To test whether the virtual environment may reduce frustration, we conducted experiments on 19 participants (12 females) with SCD and a mean age = 71 (SD = 8,39). The participants went through two sessions. The first session was the pre-experimental session in which we made sure that they were eligible for the study. Participants with SCD were eligible to the study and were invited to take part of the experiment.

In the second session which is the experimental session, the participants were first invited to fill out pre-session forms. They were then equipped with an EEG headset and asked to solve attention and memory exercises. Following these tests, a FOVE VR headset was installed and the Savannah VR began. The savannah exploration lasted about 10 min. Afterwards, the participants completed again different examples of the same attention and memory tests. Lastly, they were asked to fill out post-session forms.

5 Results

The objective of this study was to analyze the effect of Savannah VR on the emotions of the participants and check whether the environment decreases the negative emotions. To this end, we started by analyzing the emotions of the participants before, during and after the Savannah VR. We analyzed the frustration extracted from Emotiv EEG. The preliminary results show that the mean frustration before Savannah was 0.68 (0.24 min and 0.98 max). The mean frustration during the Savannah was 0.57 (0.31 min and 0.88 max). After the Savannah, the mean frustration level was 0.55 (0.28 min and 0.91 max). Figure 3 shows a boxplot of the mean frustration before, during and after the Savannah.

Overall, the frustration decreased when the participants were immersed in Savannah VR and the positive effect was still observed after Savannah VR.

In addition to using data extracted from Emotiv EEG, we asked questions at the beginning and end of the virtual experience to find out how the participants felt. At the beginning of the virtual experience, 63.2% of participants reported feeling very good, 36.8% reported feeling good and 0% reported feeling bad. After being immersed in Savannah VR, 68.4% of participants reported feeling very well, 31.6% reported feeling good and 0% reported feeling bad.

As mentioned in the introduction [4], by decreasing stress and negative emotions, memory performance could increase. It is therefore likely that Savannah VR, which decreased frustration, could also improve cognitive performance.

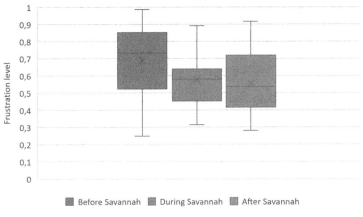

Fig. 3. Boxplot of general mean frustration

6 Conclusion

In this paper, we introduced Savannah VR, a virtual reality therapeutic environment whose purpose is to relax the user. Experiments were conducted during which the participants were first asked to perform attention and memory exercises, then immersed in Savannah VR to reduce their negative emotions. Results showed that the virtual environment helped reducing negative emotions most notably frustration. As it is mentioned by reducing negative emotions memory performance may be improved, so it is likely that Savannah VR may help in reducing cognitive decline. Future work should benefit from an analysis of the results of the attention and memory tests carried out by the participants. Subsequently, reminiscence therapy, which uses memories of the past to relieve people with dementia, may also be beneficial. For example, personalized virtual worlds could be developed to remind patients of their childhood and allow them to stimulate their memory and engage in conversation.

Acknowledgment. We acknowledge NSERC-CRD (National Science and Engineering Research Council Cooperative Research Development) and BMU for funding this work.

References

1. United Nations, Department of Economic and Social Affairs, Population Division: World population ageing, 2019 highlights (2020)
2. Dementia: number of people affected to triple in next 30 years. https://www.who.int/news-room/detail/07-12-2017-dementia-number-of-people-affected-to-triple-in-next-30-years
3. Maples-Keller, J.L., Bunnell, B.E., Kim, S.-J., Rothbaum, B.O.: The use of virtual reality technology in the treatment of anxiety and other psychiatric disorders. Harvard Rev. Psychiatry **25**, 103 (2017)
4. Ben Abdessalem, H., Byrns, A., Cuesta, M., Manera, V., Robert, P., Bruneau, M.-A., Belleville, S., Frasson, C.: Application of virtual travel for Alzheimer's disease: In: Proceedings of the 9th International Conference on Sensor Networks, pp. 52–60. SCITEPRESS - Science and Technology Publications (2020)

5. Russell-Williams, J., Jaroudi, W., Perich, T., Hoscheidt, S., El Haj, M., Moustafa, A.A.: Mindfulness and meditation: treating cognitive impairment and reducing stress in dementia. Rev. Neurosci. **29**, 791–804 (2018)

6. Wilson, E.O.: Biophilia. Harvard University Press, Massachusetts (1984)

7. Balling, J.D., Falk, J.H.: Development of visual preference for natural environments. Environ. Behav. **14**, 5–28 (1982)

8. Frumkin, H.: Beyond toxicity: human health and the natural environment. Am. J. Prev. Med. **20**, 234–240 (2001)

9. Glännfjord, F., Hemmingsson, H., Larsson Ranada, Å.: Elderly people's perceptions of using Wii sports bowling–A qualitative study. Scand. J. Occup. Ther. **24**, 329–338 (2017)

10. Monteiro, D., Liang, H.-N., Xu, W., Brucker, M., Nanjappan, V., Yue, Y.: Evaluating enjoyment, presence, and emulator sickness in VR games based on first-and third-person viewing perspectives. Comput. Animation Virtual Worlds **29**, e1830 (2018)

11. Song, S., Yamada, S.: Ambient lights influence perception and decision-making. Front. Psychol. **9**, 2685 (2019)

12. Choi, K., Suk, H.-J.: Dynamic lighting system for the learning environment: performance of elementary students. Opt. Express **24**, A907–A916 (2016)

13. Minguillon, J., Lopez-Gordo, M.A., Renedo-Criado, D.A., Sanchez-Carrion, M.J., Pelayo, F.: Blue lighting accelerates post-stress relaxation: results of a preliminary study. PloS One **12** (2017)

14. Burden of disease from environmental noise - Quantification of healthy life years lost in Europe. https://www.who.int/quantifying_ehimpacts/publications/e94888/en/

15. Jiang, B., Li, D., Larsen, L., Sullivan, W.C.: A dose-response curve describing the relationship between urban tree cover density and self-reported stress recovery. Environ. Behav. **48**, 607–629 (2016)

Introducing Drugonfly; A Novel Computer-Aided Drug Repurposing Pipeline Based on Genomic, Structural and Physicochemical Profiles

Dimitrios Vlachakis[1,2,3](✉) (iD)

[1] Genetics and Computational Biology Group, Laboratory of Genetics,
Department of Biotechnology, School of Applied Biology and Biotechnology,
Agricultural University of Athens, Iera Odos 75 Street, 11855 Athens, Greece
dimvl@aua.gr
[2] Laboratory of Molecular Endocrinology, Division of Endocrinology and Metabolism, Center
of Clinical, Experimental Surgery and Translational Research, Biomedical Research Foundation,
Academy of Athens, Soranou Ephessiou Street, 11527 Athens, Greece
[3] University Research, Institute of Maternal and Child Health and Precision Medicine,
Medical School, National and Kapodistrian University of Athens,
Thivon 1 & Papadiamantopoulou Street, 11527 Athens, Greece

Abstract. Herein, we are proposing a novel and radical pipeline that will facilitate the repurposing of approved drugs in an unprecedented way that will eventually yield invaluable insights and results that will aid the pharma-medical domain to tackle many more pathologies using weaponry that has already been approved, is safe for the public, is very rapid relatively to conventional drug design and requires no further significant investment to be made. The ultimate goal is to develop a novel clinical concept and establish a computer-aided pipeline that will facilitate and rationalize the repurposing of approved drugs, orphan drugs and generics. The end result of the described pipeline is a competitive and reliable software that will be made available for the scientific community.

Keywords: Drug design · Drug repurposing · Bioinformatics · Metagenomics · Data mining · Data analytics

1 Introduction

Finding new pharmacological targets and new active ingredients as pharmaceutical and biological agents is an ever-evolving field of science with great interest and a global marketplace. Billions of euros have been invested in the pharmaceutical industry in recent years. The journey is long, the destination uncertain and requires high resources, infrastructure and human resources. Too often, research teams coordinate their efforts to find new drugs or improve and develop commercial drugs [1]. The cutting-edge science and economic displacement of the field has led the pharmaceutical industry to

© Springer Nature Switzerland AG 2020
C. Frasson et al. (Eds.): BFAL 2020, LNAI 12462, pp. 113–121, 2020.
https://doi.org/10.1007/978-3-030-60735-7_13

great specialization and competition. This fierce competition has brought astronomical investment in the pharmaceutical industry, and the legislature, in its quest for protection and sustainability, has patented all commercial preparations for several years. So, there is depreciation and profit from these multi-million dollar investments. But the huge market has created a whole science of pharmaceuticals-manoeuvres, which has now brought many small and large industries into the field of medicine into a stalemate. Multiple different preparations can be given for the same use and the notice difference left the field of drug science, marketing and trade. Thus, many pharmaceuticals with millions of investments are in danger of being out of competition due to competition.

The answer to this problem can only be given by a holistic and coordinated effort by the sciences of medicine, biology, mathematics and computer science. The redefinition of drug use promises a way out of this great problem by giving new clues and new opportunities for access to markets in unsustainable formulations [2]. The aim of the development of this system is, on one hand, the detection of new pharmacological targets in disease-related proteins, and on the other hand, the reassessment and utilization of currently approved pharmacological substances based on their unknown properties, in order to apply them to "target" proteins. The system will have as a given input the three-dimensional structure of a "target" protein, i.e. a new protein that will be associated with a disease or a group of diseases (metabolic syndrome), and will return to the user its candidate functional areas, but also a group of approved pharmacological substances that will be able to suppress the action of its respective functional area. In this way, approved compounds will be proposed as new candidate drugs against specific diseases that were not known to be used [3–5]. Thus, for the first time, it will be possible to test known pharmacological compounds against incurable diseases and diseases, saving resources and human resources. In addition, all pharmacological compounds that will be included in a unified database in the system will already have been approved and no new approval will be required from the national drug organization. By avoiding the approval process of the pharmacological association, the long time required to approve a drug is gained, and also, studies and results of previous research in which many resources have been invested, are used [6–8]. In this way we will be able to bridge the knowledge that has been extracted so far from previous studies on different types of experiments and diseases. The final gain will be very large, as many of the unsustainable drugs will be able to be re-marketed for a different purpose.

2 Overview of the Drugonfly Pipeline

The structure of the implementation of the integrated system for the detection of known pharmacological substances suitable for the inhibition of the action of protein targets related to diseases will be divided into a series of distinct steps and processes (Fig. 1).

First step is to gather all the known approved pharmacological substances that are recorded in the databases of the International Medicines Agency, and to create a new database that will be used by the system. For each entry in the system database, information on each pharmacological substance from the literature will be collected, such as, mode of action, disease used, similar pharmacological substances, chemical composition, production costs, year of approval and side effects after use, and the physico-chemical properties of the preparation will be calculated [9]. To determine the additional

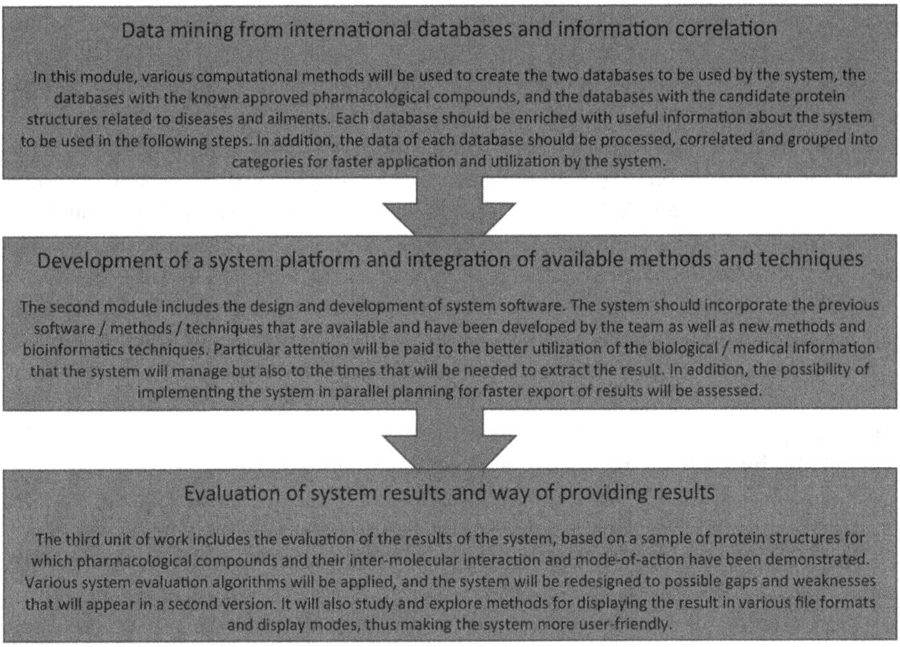

Fig. 1. A schematic overview of the distinct actions in the Drugonfly drug repurposing pipeline.

physicochemical properties, tools developed and used by the team will be applied. In addition, based on the above characteristics, an attempt will be made to group all the approved known pharmacological substances collected into clusters and categories.

Next step involves the creation of a second database in which known protein "targets" related to diseases will be collected, as well as proteins in which we have suppressed their action in order to stop various pathological conditions. To this end, neural networks will be developed to detect all candidate proteins associated with diseases and ailments. Enzymes have a great and primary role in the design of well-known drugs to date, in many cases due to their nature in catalysing chemical reactions. For this reason, the results of previous research conducted by the laboratory and related to the collection and grouping of structurally soluble protein enzyme biomolecules will be used [10]. In addition, machine learning methods will be applied to extract knowledge through bibliography related to the protein targets that will be gathered to enrich the database by category. Finally, all known protein targets will be grouped into categories using classifiers and bio-tools developed by the team.

At this point the analysis and processing of the three-dimensional protein structure "target" that will be given by the user to the system will be employed. It will include many sub-processes/flows that will be performed depending on the "target" protein. Initially, a rapid classification of the target protein will be made based on the protein targets collected by the system as described in process two, in order to find homologous proteins. For the correlation of the "target" protein with the existing proteins, smart similarity algorithms will be applied at the sequence and structure level. In addition, in case of non-similarity of the "target" protein with the proteins of the system, various evolutionary algorithms and available bio-tools will be applied to gather additional information. The functional areas of the "target" protein will then be calculated and evaluated based on the software developed by the team and adapted to the system [11].

In this direction the next step will handle the assessment and calculation of the "target" protein based on its functional areas and the selection of the most appropriate pharmacological substances that could interact with them. The pharmaceutical surfaces will be calculated based on the physicochemical properties and the three-dimensional space of each functional area of the protein using a specific bio-tool that has been developed in the team and that will be integrated into the system [12]. In addition, all known well-known approved pharmaceutical associations will be tested based on process one in the system, in order to find the most suitable candidates to suppress the action of the functional areas of the target protein. The evaluation of the most suitable candidate pharmacological substances will be done with bio-tools that have been developed by the team but also by applying methods of molecular dynamics and quantum physics.

The last procedure involves extracting the results of the techniques/algorithms proposed in process three. Comparing the results, the best and fastest techniques/methods will be chosen to suggest the implementation of the system. In order to evaluate the results given by the system, various assessment parameters will be applied, such as the percentage of incorrect results, based on a sample that will have been collected in known protein structures related to known approved pharmacological compounds. Repeated sampling methods will be used to estimate the estimation parameters.

3   Scientific Application of the Drugonfly Pipeline

The expected results after the completion and operation of the integrated system for detecting known pharmacological substances suitable for inhibiting the action of "target" proteins related to diseases and illnesses will be numerous and will be provided indirectly and directly to several groups of researchers in the pharmaceutical industry. This comprehensive system will be a reliable and effective tool to easily and quickly relate and use existing approved pharmaceutical compounds in many cases of incurable diseases and ailments that cannot be treated to date. It is a very promising computational method through which the commercial value and exploitation of many approved pharmaceutical compounds will be reconsidered, minimizing the cost and time required to create novel pharmaceutical compounds.

This platform will be a key to detecting new pharmacological targets, but also a good guide to the real cases that need more research to fill potential gaps in science that are currently unknown in the pharmaceutical industry. Also, by comparing the functional areas of proteins to date, it is possible to associate proteins that are unknown to each other in terms of functionality, thus better interpreting the mechanisms of action behind them. New drugs may emerge through the whole process in cases of partial efficacy of well-known approved drug types that are potentially modified in structure or pharmaceutical form. In addition, it will be possible to associate similar approved drugs that demonstrate a similar profile of side effects in the human body, thus giving the opportunity to understand possible combinations of chemical compounds that work negatively.

With the development of the two integrated databases that will be used in the system, we will have for the first time a complete database that will cover all approved pharmaceutical associations and on the other hand all the proteins related to pathological conditions and diseases. The above database can be used commercially for other purposes in the development of biomedical tools. Finally, with this tool it will be possible to relate bio-computationally to the concepts of "pharmacological compound", "pharmacological target" and "protein target".

The processing and analysis capabilities that will be provided to each user will be many that in the future it can stand as a reference tool in the field of bioinformatics and the science of redefining the use of drugs. The efficiency of this application is very high compared to other computational approaches, as the final result will refer to already approved, reliable and safe pharmacological compounds. So, this system will be easy to use immediately.

Many of the tools and methodologies described in the implementation of this system are now well known in the field of bioinformatics and computational biology. With this project, for the first time, we will have the combination of most of them, to achieve a common goal. Noteworthy, the cost of implementing this idea is very low, considering the future contribution to the performance of new indications of well-known approved pharmaceuticals.

4   The Drugonfly Drug Repurposing Pipeline

The methodology of drug repurposing as implemented in the Drugonfly pipeline is a seven-step process:

1. Drug detection/clustering

   - The drug or set of drugs under investigation are imported into the pipeline and the pre-processing phase is initiated. Pre-processing involves checking to missing or erroneous data and retrieving the full Summary of Product Characteristics (SPC) and pharmacology for each entry by accessing genomic, proteomic, drug-compound repositories and pharmacological databases (i.e. the Protein Data Bank, the National Cancer Database). Moreover, all pharmacodynamic information is retrieved and the drugs are accordingly classified based on their mode of action (i.e. direct or indirect). The lead compounds accompanied by their full formulation are stored in a dedicated local database for further analysis.

2. Stereochemistry/Physicochemical analysis

   - The physicochemical properties of each one of the drugs in the database of step 1 are calculated and the compounds are profiled. Consequently, a multidimensional matrix is generated for each entry that will be later used as input for the repurposing analysis engine. Note that physicochemical parameters are calculated for all kind of drugs, regardless to their biochemical properties and molecular weight. Our pipeline will cover all cases from single ions and cations to multi-domain protein complexes.

3. Semantics/Text mining

- Having acquired all information from the drug SPC it is then feasible to track and retrieve all relevant information for each drug from various sources. Namely, a repertoire of chemical databases is accessed depending on the drug instance:

  i.   If the drug is a low molecular weight compound, the NCI (or equivalent) database is accessed.
  ii. If the drug is a protein, the PDB (or equivalent) database is accessed.
  iii. If the drug is an antibody, the IMGT (or equivalent) database is accessed.

  Regardless the type of drug information text will be mined and analyzed from genomic databases (i.e. Genecards) and literature databases (i.e. PubMed). Genomic databases will be used for gene and tissue specificity determination and literature databases will be used to extract scientific information for each entry (for example: type of clinical trial, formulation, ADME).

4. Molecular docking – High Throughput Virtual Screening (HTVS)

- In the case of low molecular weight drugs (that account for 90% of commercial compounds) a High Throughput Virtual Screening pipeline is established. The compound is screened against all known pharmacological targets available in structural databases that contain the three-dimensional information of proteins from X-ray crystallography, NMR and electron microscopy.
- If the drug is a protein or an antibody the screening approach will be based on protein similarity searches. More specifically this task is broken down in two steps:

  i.   First, the overall conformation of the protein or antibody is used as query against the abovementioned structural databases, in an effort to identify entries of similar structure, 3D arrangement and folding.
  ii. Then depending on whether it is a protein or an antibody there are two options:

       1. For proteins: any active site is identified, and all relevant information is harvested (i.e. presence of ligand, shape, size, type of amino acid composition, coordinate info).
       2. For antibodies: the CDR (Complementarity Determining Region) sequence and structure is captured and analyzed alongside the detection of putative sites for anchoring compounds and the design of ADCs.

5. Pharmacological target detection – Evolutionary analysis

- The putative pharmacological targets that have been identified in steps 1–4 are automatically entered into a phylogenetic study. Based on sequence and structural evolutionary linkage, all available homologous proteins and enzymes will be identified, thus providing insights for possible cross-associations to relative proteins and enzymes. The latter can be used either for repurposing or side effect prevention reasons. The phylogenetic study is performed as follows:

i.   The resulting multiple sequence alignment is used to determine the optimal model for protein evolution.
ii. A pharmacological target specific phylogenetic tree is constructed.
iii. Statistical evaluation of the tree from step (ii) defines the reliability of the evolutionary model.

6. Structure optimization – Molecular Dynamics

- The top hit pharmacological targets in their bound form (complexed to the drug) is structurally optimized in an *in silico* system, to evaluate the association and confirm and validate the discovered interaction. This is applied in all interaction cases (i.e. immediate bonding to long distant associations) and to all modes of drug action (i.e. direct or indirect pharmacological activity).

  Energetic calculations and minimizations will be applied in each molecular complex to remove any residual geometrical constrains.
  Molecular Dynamics are used to assess in a simulated environment the affinity and specificity of interaction using a variety of force-fields and thermodynamic parameters.

7. Drug repurposing scoring

- All the information and analyses performed in steps 1–6 is fused together and scored to produce the final repurposing output.

5 Conclusions

Drug design is a very exciting field, with uncountable applications and a huge worldwide market. However, designing a new drug is a very high risk and laborious task that rarely has a happy ending. It is estimated that the average time it takes from the designing board to the market is somewhere between 12–14 years. The average investment for each drug is 1.4 billion USD and the most optimistic stats conclude that less than 1 in 10.000 candidate drugs actually makes it to the market. So, it is a long and winding road that very rarely pays back. The pharma industry that is already weakened by a declining economy and rising inflation now faces a new threat from the academic world. Due to lack of funds and future uncertainty even fewer scientists take on such a difficult task. The number of NME (New Medical Entities) in the market has plummeted from 55 in 1995 to less than 5 in 2015. So, there is great need for new strategies to be deployed in the field of drug design.

One of the most promising and cost-efficient alternatives is the so-called drug repurposing domain. Instead of starting from scratch, our proposed drug repurposing pipeline will make use of only those drugs that have already made it to the market. The benefits are huge. Firstly, those are FDA or EMA approved drugs (i.e. they are safe). Then there is no need for costly and timely investments in basic research, since those drugs have successfully been though all stages of *in silico, in vitro, in vivo* and clinical trials and formulation and pharmacokinetics stages. The main concept is that approved drugs are tested in an efficient computer-based drug scoring pipeline that will provide insights for other putative pharmacological targets and pathologies. There will be three levels of repurposing: a) All approved drugs currently in the market will be assessed against new protein targets using molecular dynamics and bioinformatics, b) A special effort will be made to test and repurpose the drugs that EMA announced this year in the Orphan Drugs list, thus providing a sustainable solution to a huge problem in pharma industry, and c) A database of generics will be established and then those compounds will be assessed against all known pharmacological targets in comparison to the original patented compounds, thus providing cost-efficient alternatives as early as in the *in silico* platform. The proposed pipeline herein, will be based on the Drugster computer-aided drug design platform with some implementations.

References

1. Dalkas, G.A., Vlachakis, D., Tsagkrasoulis, D., Kastania, A., Kossida, S.: State-of-the-art technology in modern computer-aided drug design. Briefings Bioinf. **14**, 745–752 (2013). https://doi.org/10.1093/bib/bbs063
2. Tsagrasoulis, D., Vlachakis, D., Megalooikonomou, V., Kossida, S: Introducing Drugster: a comprehensive and fully integrated drug design, lead and structure optimization toolkit. Bioinformatics **29**, 126–128 (2013e). https://doi.org/10.1093/bioinformatics/bts637
3. Antoniou, N., et al.: A motif within the armadillo repeat of Parkinson's-linked LRRK2 interacts with FADD to hijack the extrinsic death pathway. Sci. Rep. **8** (2018). https://doi.org/10.1038/s41598-018-21931-8
4. Amidi, A., Amidi, S., Vlachakis, D., Megalooikonomou, V., Paragios, N., Zacharaki, E.I.: EnzyNet: enzyme classification using 3D convolutional neural networks on spatial representation. PeerJ (2018). https://doi.org/10.7717/peerj.4750
5. Kontopoulos, D.G., Vlachakis, D., Tsiliki, G., Kossida, S.: Structuprint: a scalable and extensible tool for two-dimensional representation of protein surfaces. BMC Struct. Biol. **16** (2016b). https://doi.org/10.1186/s12900-016-0055-7
6. Papageorgiou, L., Cuong, N.T., Vlachakis, D.: Antibodies as stratagems against cancer. Mol. BioSyst. **12**(7), 2047–2055 (2016). https://doi.org/10.1039/c5mb00699f
7. Papageorgiou, L., Vlachakis, D.: Antisoma application: a fully integrated V-like antibodies platform AIMS. Med. Sci. **4**, 382–394 (2017). https://doi.org/10.3934/medsci.2017.4.382
8. Tsiliki, G., Vlachakis, D., Kossida, S.: On integrating multi-experiment microarray data. Philos. Trans. R. Soc. A Math. Phys. Eng. Sci., 372 (2014). https://doi.org/10.1098/rsta.2013.0136
9. Vlachakis, D.: Theoretical study of the Usutu virus helicase 3D structure, by means of computer- aided homology modelling. Theor. Biol. Med. Model. **6,** 9 (2009). https://doi.org/10.1186/1742-4682-6-9
10. Vlachakis, D., Bencurova, E., Papangelopoulos, N., Kossida, S.: Current state-of-the-art molecular dynamics methods and applications. In: Advances in Protein Chemistry and Structural Biology, vol. 94, pp. 269–313. Academic Press (2014b). https://doi.org/10.1016/b978-0-12-800168-4.00007-x

11. Vlachakis, D., Fakourelis, P., Megalooikonomou, V., Makris, C., Kossida, S.: DrugOn: a fully integrated pharmacophore modeling and structure optimization toolkit. PeerJ (2015). https://doi.org/10.7717/peerj.725

12. Vlachakis, D., Koumandou, V.L., Kossida, S.: A holistic evolutionary and structural study of flaviviridae provides insights into the function and inhibition of HCV helicase. PeerJ (2013c). https://doi.org/10.7717/peerj.74

Learning

Serendipitous Learning Fostered by Brain State Assessment and Collective Wisdom

Stefano A. Cerri[1,2,3]([✉]) and Philippe Lemoisson[4,5]

[1] DKTS: Digital Knowledge Technologies Services SRL, Via Ampère 61/a, 20131 Milan, Italy
sacerri@didaelkts.it
[2] FBK: Fondazione Bruno Kessler, Trento, Italy
[3] LIRMM, Univ Montpellier and CNRS, 161 Rue Ada, 34095 Montpellier, France
[4] CIRAD, UMR TETIS, 34398 Montpellier, France
philippe.lemoisson@cirad.fr
[5] TETIS, Univ Montpellier, AgroParisTech, CIRAD, CNRS, IRSTEA, Montpellier, France

Abstract. *Serendipitous* discovery, invention or artistic creation are among the most exciting and utmost relevant phenomena strongly related to human *learning*. At the moment, there are very few measurable criteria helping to understand and foster serendipity. In other papers [1–3] we have presented, discussed and exemplified a new paradigm/model/method/system/environment – called ViewpointS – that represents our efforts to overcome many current existing limitations in generic Information Systems or search engines (e.g.: Google) as well as in other social media (e.g.: recommender systems) offering information retrieval solutions based on the *proximity* of available resources. We also have also exposed how ViewpointS may facilitate serendipitous discovery in an unprecedented way. In this paper, we wish to further motivate this last conjecture by proposing to explore two main research directions that did not convey sufficient attention by previous researchers (in particular those active in recommender systems): 1. *assessing brain states* in order to understand and forecast serendipitous human learning events triggered by emotions; 2. *enhancing collective wisdom*, since Human-Computer Interactions do not occur today between a human and a single machine (or algorithm), but within a community of humans and machines that continuously update "knowledge" beyond the scene. Both directions (assessment of brain states, collective wisdom) are currently on separate ways; we propose to combine them within one unified approach called ViewpointS.

Keywords: Collective intelligence · Human learning · Serendipity triggered by brain states · Socially driven serendipity

© Springer Nature Switzerland AG 2020
C. Frasson et al. (Eds.): BFAL 2020, LNAI 12462, pp. 125–136, 2020.
https://doi.org/10.1007/978-3-030-60735-7_14

1   Introduction

This paper aims to identify, motivate and document some necessary requirements for the success of a research challenge[1] that is ongoing since many years: understanding and forecasting serendipitous learning.

Understanding human learning is one of the priorities of the next century if we consider the complexity of the subject and the impact that any progress may have.

In its essence, human learning may occur as a result of interactions with the external world[2], either because an external agent "communicates" some information, concept, relation, attribute, way-to-do (learning by being told) or because the subject constructs some chunk of knowledge (concept, how-to-do, relation, property, …) in his/her mind. This latter event may be associated to the known theories of human learning by Piaget or Vygotsky. Both events occur by interaction. It has been demonstrated that animals (and humans) that are not exposed to a rich interactive environment do not learn as well as those that are immersed in knowledge-rich interactive scenarios.

Independently from "how" learning occurs, we may ask a question about "what is" human learning. Under the hypothesis that at higher cognitive levels the natural location representing and producing human cognitive behavior – including learning - is the brain, we are aware that the brain is not a computer, and concepts, relations, procedures, facts, … are all represented and stored in a highly distributed and temporally mutable way [4]. Therefore, we may for the moment only reason by looking at individual's cognitive behavior *before* and *after* a learning event. We come to the conclusion that learning is a "state change" measurable only – for the moment – by looking at its effects: changes in human knowledge, know-how, reaction times to questions, … As it was stated by various authors in the Web Science movement, the Web is the most interesting laboratory ever invented for studying Human-Computer and Human-Human interactive phenomena.

Considering self-awareness, learning may occur when humans are aware: they wish to learn, they positively engage their resources in order to reach the goal to learn: it is the case of the school, learning to play an instrument, to improve the performance in a physical activity, such as a sport, etc. However, *most* of human learning occurs when the learner is not aware i.e.: informally or incidentally. Serendipity, explored in the following section, represents not only a phenomenon of informal learning useful for the subject, but one of extreme importance as it impacts the whole community.

In Sect. 2 we give a short, historically supported introduction to the concept of serendipity. In Sect. 3 we discuss some early research in linking Information retrieval and serendipity, including general remarks and recent analogies about the interest of serendipitous behavior even in service-oriented computing. Section 4 is dedicated to some recent serendipity research in recommender systems. The three "introductory"

---

[1] This paper has the objective to stimulate reflections about an ambitious, but equally modest and feasible, collaborative, large, long term research project for understanding, forecasting and stimulating *serendipitous learning*, i.e.: discovering, inventing, creating. At the same time we claim this project to be a concrete step *towards digital sovereignty* since it enables to personalize -thus control and trust- effectively the individual and collective information spaces, differently from current search engines, social networks and recommender systems.

[2] From: https://en.wikipedia.org/wiki/Learning: *Humans learn before birth and continue until death as a consequence of ongoing interactions between people and their environment.*

Sects. 2, 3 and 4 are rich of excerpts from the literature in order to justify the primary interest of serendipity studies today and the minimal requirements for stimulating human serendipitous learning. These are identified to consist of measurements of emotions - *brain state assessment* in the title- and interactions within a knowledge space fed by trusted peers and regulated by a subjective topology (proximity of resources: concepts, agents and documents) – *collective wisdom* in the title-. Within this frame, the ViewpointS paradigm is briefly introduced in Sect. 5 ending with an annotated, toy example of a process facilitating serendipitous discoveries, inventions or creations. Section 6 concludes the paper.

2   The Concept of Serendipity

One of the early authoritative sources [5] reports that: *Serendipity can be defined as the supposed capacity to discover, invent, create or imagine **something important** without deliberately being in quest for it. If somebody discovers, invents, creates or imagines something of general value, without being deliberately in quest of it then his finding can be called serendipitous. So, we speak about a serendipitous discovery, invention, creation or thought.* Later, in another paper [6] where the author identifies 17 serendipity patterns, he specifies: *If I define true serendipity as the art of making an 'unsought finding', what do I mean by a 'finding'? I speak of a 'finding' when two or more elements (observations, hypotheses, ideas, facts, relations or insights) are combined originally, for the finder or anybody, to something new and true (science), new and useful (technology), or new and fascinating (arts).* The number, quality and interest of serendipity examples described 30 years ago is astonishing.

A "recent" paper [7] (archived from 2014 and updated till 2019) reporting about several projects (British but also EU FET) has a rather complete bibliography about serendipity research and systems (more than 100 papers quoted). While in their projects the goal was to define a formal model of serendipity and an associated creative computational system, we focus here on understanding, forecasting and facilitating *human* serendipitous learning behavior: we believe to have different goals and preconditions - "what" and "why" - and different means - "how" -, even if their work is highly valuable for us as well.

Another convincing statement – about progress as reported in scientific papers - from Pek Van Andel [6], is the following one: *In general the role of serendipity in science, technology and art is underestimated. This is mainly and unintentionally caused by the way we rationalize "a posteriori" about theoretical and experimental research and its results, when we publish. The not strictly rational, chronological or searched components (like chance, fortuitous, accidental, surprising, unsought (n)ever dreamt of, unknown, etc.), which have led to these results are therefore underestimated and sometimes even banned from the theater and totally hidden behind the décor. The next step is that pure rationality becomes the norm, not only regarding the results, but also regarding everything that has led to these results. Scientists then report their results as following directly and logically*[3] *from their initial hypothesis, omitting possibly crucial (pseudo)serendipitous events. Reading and interpreting such articles as 'the inside story' about the discovery, can unwillingly brainwash the researcher in such a way and to such an extent that he neglects during his own research the flowers along the road that can form a nicer bouquet than those he is looking for. This can cause a loss of serendipity: the aim and/or plan spoils the journey. A successful researcher or manager has one open eye for sought findings and another open eye for unsought findings.*

So, in the following we feel encouraged to talk about serendipity in information systems, in particular recommender systems, even if we did not explore the whole gigantic literature about those systems, but just a minimal part of it, necessary and sufficient for our goals. Our rationality is limited, we admit, but accompanied by very well founded feelings and curiosity about our conjectures.

These feelings started years ago when the Web was in its early stage [8]. The research on ViewpointS [1–3] was motivated by an attempt to bypass the "intractable" problem of "domain, time and author's dependent ontologies" and respect the conviction that humans in the loop are a much better source of intelligence. Its main result was a unified (logical, statistical, social) and personalized context of knowledge construction. The serendipity potential was a fortuitous side effect of very different initial goals.

3   Serendipity in Information Retrieval

Another early author [9] gives clues to understand the interest (and the resistances) to study, accept and facilitate serendipity in information systems: *The acquisition of information is generally thought to be deliberately sought using a search or query mechanism or by browsing or scanning an information space. People, however, find information without seeking it through accidental, incidental or serendipitous discoveries, often in combination with other information acquisition episodes. The value of this phenomenon to an individual or an organization can be equated with the impact of serendipitous breakthroughs in science and medicine. Although largely ignored in information systems development and research,* **serendipitous retrieval complements querying and browsing**, *and together they provide a holistic, ecological approach to information acquisition and define the key approaches to a digital library.* Further: *In essence, there are three ways in which people acquire information, each of which should be supported by a digital library: 1. from the search for information about a well-defined and known object(s); 2. from the search for information about an object that cannot be fully described, but will be recognized on sight; and, 3. from the accidental, incidental, or serendipitous discovery of an object. Systems that support the first prompt users for search terms and keywords and provide options for manipulating the query and the result. Hypermedia, visualization and menu-driven systems that provide views and overviews of the data facilitate the second. In both cases, the next step taken, e.g., next index term selected, next page*

---

[3] Rationalism and empiricism exist and balance each other since centuries in the philosophy of Science, as much as idealism and materialism. In the brain, logical thinking is associated to emotions; in Society it occurs probably the same. It is not rational to negate the interest of serendipitous events and the associated processes.

examined or information node accessed has a conceptual and/or a semantic relationship with the previous one. In the first, that relationship is predetermined by the system's response to the query; while in the second, the relationship is enabled for the most part by directed pathways through the system. While the process of information seeking is more complex than this, the outcome is generally the same: to locate the information object; this is a highly purposive task. The third type, the serendipitous approach, is a type of information seeking that is not traditionally examined in information retrieval research and has received little attention by both developers and researchers. The same author, under the heading "facilitating serendipity" explains: *In the case of my study, the **serendipitous activity** was stimulated and triggered by a list of articles that bore some **degree of similarity** to the one currently displayed.* Further, she quotes another aspect of serendipity: creativity: *Just as the creative process must result in new ideas that are intelligible to the creator and understood in terms of prior knowledge (Boden, 1996[4]), so too must the results of a chance encounter.* Apparently, there is a need to link the new "idea" or "concept" to previous knowledge, a conjecture very similar to Vygotsky's "law of proximal development". E.G. Toms concludes: *Serendipitous retrieval demands approaching information retrieval in an unorthodox manner, one that does not tightly couple the explicit match of query with result, but instead takes a fuzzy approach to the problem.* Yet, there is no link with "the brain's state" neither with any "social context".

Other authors [10] have attempted to propose an empirically founded model for serendipity that emerged from several interviews: *Our empirically-grounded process model of serendipity (Fig. 1 below, by courtesy of the authors) focuses on the mental connection that is sparked by circumstances that are to some extent unexpected. A **new connection** is made between an informational or non-informational need and a 'thing' (e.g. person, event, place, information, object) with the potential to address the need. The circumstances that led to the connection are subsequently (and subjectively) considered to have involved an amount of unexpectedness. The making of the connection itself is subjectively considered to have involved an amount of insight.*

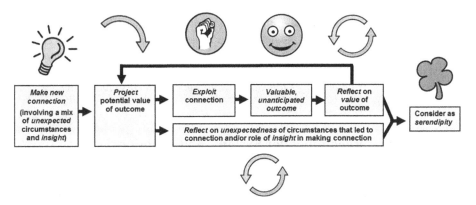

Fig. 1. <An> empirically-grounded process model of serendipity <from: [10]>

---

[4] Margaret Boden is a major actor in the historical development of Artificial Intelligence.

The model is the result of a long empirical research based on interviews that not only produced the model but also a classification of different serendipity events.

However, differently from Toms, the authors do not offer suggestions in this paper about how to organize information spaces in order to support serendipity.

In a subsequent paper [11] there is finally some clear roadmap about how to proceed: *While initial discussions on accidental information discovery in digital environments focused on concerns about the loss of serendipity as a result of digitalization, most current discussions accept that digital information environments can and, where useful, should create opportunities for serendipity. As Lori McCay-Peet notes in her essay "Digital Information Environments That Facilitate Serendipity", "It is no longer about whether technologies are helping or hurting serendipity. That question is too broad and not helpful." A more helpful question, and one that is answered in this chapter, is "how can we design digital information environments to (best) cultivate serendipity?"* This is also our concern.

The message has been adopted by other researchers [12] that conclude their work with a strong support to "prioritization": *In this paper we have extended our earlier model for information seeking in large-scale digital libraries with new strategies and modes of contextual browsing, showing their consistency with behaviors supporting serendipitous discovery set out by Makri et al. We have described how contextual browsing requires prioritization to remain feasible in large-scale scenarios and have proposed the application of **contextual similarity metrics** to this purpose.* However, the system "proof of concept" they used (Compage) did neither capitalize from the dynamic behavior of communities, nor from the assessment of brain mental states.

The interest of serendipity is also addressed recently by other authors [13] that relate serendipity to service-oriented computing: *In service-oriented computing, software applications evolve dynamically to meet their goals through discrete reconfigurations triggered by the need for an external resource and realized through a three-fold process of discovery, selection and binding of service modules. To model creative systems, we regard concepts as modules and concept discovery as service discovery.*

The analogy with human serendipity is striking: *One salient feature of this approach is the **unpredictability of the interactions** between service entities. The continuous change in the availability of modules places us in a dynamic context where chance plays an important role in the evolution of systems. The selection of a most promising concept (provider of a resource) is based on the semantic compatibility of specifications. Because applications change over time, the evaluation of concepts can change as well, generating a focus shift.*

4   Serendipity, Recommender Systems and Emotions

A rather recent study [14] addresses the issue not just of information retrieval, rather of recommender systems, a kind of proactive systems. The essence is contained in their abstract: *Most recommender systems suggest items similar to a user profile, which results in boring recommendations limited by user preferences indicated in the system. To overcome this problem, recommender systems should suggest serendipitous items, which is a challenging task, as it is unclear what makes items serendipitous to a user and how to measure serendipity. The concept is difficult to investigate, as serendipity includes an emotional dimension and serendipitous encounters are very rare. In this paper, we discuss mentioned challenges, review definitions of serendipity and serendipity-oriented evaluation metrics. The goal of the paper is to guide and inspire future efforts on serendipity in recommender systems.*

The authors finally admit that: *Relevance of an item for a user might depend on user mood <...omissis...> This contextual information is difficult to capture without explicitly asking the user. As serendipity is a complex concept, which includes relevance <...>, this concept depends on the current user mood in a higher degree.* **An emotional dimension makes serendipity unstable** *and therefore difficult to investigate <...>.*

The first conclusion of this study is that the system should recommend serendipitous items, a challenging task; because items similar to a user profile result in boring recommendations. The second is that serendipity depends on the emotional state of the subject that is not only hard to evaluate by interviewing the subjects, but also unstable.

In [15] the authors propose "a theoretical model of surprise" (in recommender systems) that includes the following properties: surprise must be subjective, surprise must be dynamic, surprise is related to the notion of distance. The paper includes several measures of surprise and a list of specific and recent references. In the scenarios there is a clear exploitation of collective behavior (the Movie Lens dataset used contains 3883 items, 6040 users and over 1 million ratings) but no suggestion about the influence of emotions in "surprise", thus in serendipity.

Taking the challenge indicated by these authors, we aim to suggest "serendipitous items" that should have three properties:

1. be linked to the previous user knowledge and experience;
2. be dependent from the user's emotional state;
3. be exciting and new for the user, not boring.

5   ViewpointS: Emotions and Collective Wisdom for Serendipity

This section first briefly recalls the ViewpointS[5] framework and formalism for building collective knowledge in the metaphor of the brain (a detailed description can be found in [1–3] but also [17, 18] and then illustrates through an imaginary toy example the specific interest of ViewpointS for facilitating serendipitous learning.

In the ViewpointS approach, the "neural maps interconnected by beams of neurons" [4] are transposed into a graph of "knowledge resources (Agents, Documents, Topics) interconnected by beams of viewpoints". Agents (Human or Artificial) are the only active resources. The "systems of values" of the Agents influence the viewpoints they emit, but also the way they interpret the graph.

We call *knowledge resources* all the resources contributing to knowledge: Agents, Documents and Topics. We call *viewpoints* the links between *knowledge resources*.

---

[5] This section is a revised, annotated version of the similar section of another paper. On purpose, we use the same very simple example in order to support quite different conjectures about the properties of ViewpointS; in this case serendipity.

Each *viewpoint* is a subjective connection established by an Agent (Human or Artificial) between two *knowledge resources*; the *viewpoint* (a_1, {r_2, r_3}, θ, τ) stands for: the Agent a_1 believes at time τ that r_2 and r_3 are related according to the emotion carried by θ. Agents entitled to feed *viewpoints* are selected by the user according to his/her *preferences* (they are *trusted* Agents).

We call Knowledge Graph (KG) the bipartite graph consisting of *knowledge resources* and *viewpoints*. Given two *knowledge resources*, the aggregation of the beam of all connections (*viewpoints*) linking them can be quantified and interpreted as a proximity (or, inversely, as a distance). We call *perspective* the set of rules (defined by the user) implementing this quantification by evaluating each viewpoint and then aggregating all these evaluations into a single value: the single value is associated to the two resources. The graph resulting from the transformation activated on the KG by the rules of the *perspective* is called Knowledge Map; since the KG is continuously updated by trusted Agents, the KM is also continuously updated.

Notice that there are two sources of subjectivity: the choice of the trusted Agents that feed the KG (*preference*) and the rules transforming the KG into the KM (*perspective*). This double subjectivity represents the user's *system of values*. Both are chosen by the "Agent-consumer" of the information, not by a third-part "Agent-producer" such as a Google or Amazon algorithm. Each time an Agent wishes to exploit the knowledge acquired from the community of *trusted* Agents, he does so through his own subjective *perspective* which acts as an interpreter.

Tuning a perspective may for instance consist in giving priority to selected trustworthy *agents*, or to the most recent *viewpoints*, or to the *viewpoints* issued from the logical paradigm. This clear separation between the storing of the traces (the *viewpoints*) and their subjective interpretation (through a *perspective*) protects the human agents involved in sharing knowledge against the intrusion of third-part algorithms reifying *external systems of values*, as it is the case for most recommender systems. Adopting a *perspective* yields a tailored KM: *knowledge map* where distances can be computed between knowledge resources, i.e. where the semantics emerge from the topology as well as from our own subjective system of values expressed by the perspective and by the choice of the trusted Agents (preference).

To illustrate this, we develop below an imaginary case where learners have to select resources inside an Intelligent Tutoring System (ITS) to which a Knowledge Map is associated. They wish to learn about the topic 'apple' and from step1 to step4 the learners adopt a 'neutral' perspective which puts in balance all types of viewpoints (issued from the logical or mining paradigms, or from the emotions of the learners). However, at step5, B chooses a perspective discarding his own viewpoints in order to discover new sources of knowledge. What is figured in the schemas (see Fig. 2) is not the KG itself, but the KM resulting from the perspectives; in these maps, the more links between two resources, the closer they are.

Step1 illustrates the initial state of the knowledge. A, B and C are co-learners of an ITS[6] (linked as such within the logical paradigm: they belong to the same group); the blue arrows represent their respective systems of values, which play a key role both in the choice of *perspectives* and in the emission of *viewpoints* (Agents trusted to feed the

---

[6] This is obviously an extremely simplified tutoring system!

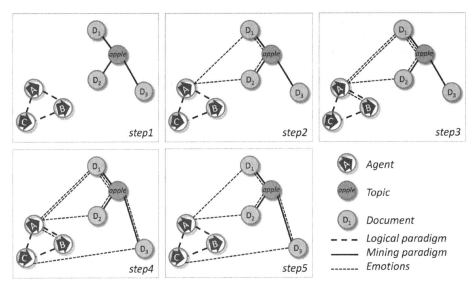

Fig. 2. The network of interlinked resources evolves along the attempts of the learners A, B and C to "catch" the topic 'apple' through accessing the modules D_1, D_2 or D_3. (Color figure online)

KG). D_1, D_2 and D_3 are documents that a mining algorithm has indexed by the topic/tag 'apple'. So, in Fig. 2 you notice the three types of resources: topics (one, in green: apple), documents (three, in orange: D1, D2, D3) and agents (three, in blue: A, B, C). In the example each of the three agents consider each other agent as trusted and adopts the same preferences so that we may say that there is a unique KM seen by each agent. This not necessarily true but simplifies once more the example without sacrificing the evidence of situations of potential serendipitous behavior.

Step2: A is a calm person who has time; she browses through D_1, D_2 and D_3 and has a positive emotion about D_1 and D_2 (she likes both and finds them relevant with respect to 'apple'); the capture of this emotion results in linking D_1 and D_2 to her and reinforcing the links between the documents and the topic 'apple'. B is always in a hurry; he asks the KM the question "which is the shortest path between me and the topic 'apple'?"[7]. According to the paths in the diagram, he gets a double answer: B-A-D_1-'apple'and B-A-D_2-'apple'. *B is exploiting the behavior of A in order to answer a question. This is already a source of potential "surprise". In general, the introduction of Agents in the KG and KM as first-class citizens is the major potential source of surprise and serendipity. There is a second major difference with traditional search engines: B (like A) can as well directly access D1, D2 and D3 by launching a query; but "trusts" the search done by A reducing in this way the overload of the group of trusted Agents (A, B and C).*

---

[7] This is obviously an oversimplification: in the real prototype available, the KM is visualized and the notion of proximity (short path) is reified by real distances in the visualized graph. Another way to convey the same message without visualization is to give a list of answers in order of increasing distance. In this case the difference with Google's answers is evident.

Step3: B has a positive emotion about D_1 but not about D_2; this results in reinforcing the path B-A-D_1-'apple'. If he would ask his question now, he would then get only D_1. *The system's behavior depends on the history of interactions, adapts to the user's historical behavior.*

Step4: C likes to explore; rather than taking a short path she browses through D_1, D_2 and D_3 and has a positive emotion about D_3 (she likes it and finds it relevant with respect to 'apple'); this results in linking D_3 to her and reinforcing the linking between D_3 and the topic 'apple'. At this stage, if A, B and C would ask for the shortest path to 'apple', they would respectively get D_1, D_1 and D_3. *Notice that these modifications occur as a result of asynchronous, unforeseeable Agent's interactions with the KM generated by the KG fed by three autonomous Human Agents that activate an Artificial Agent: the search engine. The example concerns a minimal number of resources; when the size of the resources increases significantly, we may envision the emergence of a "collective wisdom of the crowd" where the "crowd" is controlled by each one's preferences and perspectives, not by external algorithms.*

Step5: B has read again D1 and is not fully satisfied by D_1; he asks again for a short path: but in order to discover new sources of knowledge, he changes his perspective: he discards the viewpoints expressing his own emotions. ***The KM is dynamic,*** *changes not only as a function of the peer's behavior but also our own history.* This new perspective yields the view drawn in the figure, B-A-D_1-'apple', B-A-D_2-'apple'and B-C-D_3-'apple' have the same length i.e., D_1, D_2 and D_3 are equidistant from him. He may now discard D_1 (already visited) and D_2 (already rejected) and study D_3. ***B has a chance of discovering what C has found interesting****: serendipity may be triggered NOT as a consequence of an available "serendipitous object" proposed by an algorithm that finds something "similar in its essence" and "compatible (relevance) with the user" -as most recommender systems propose- but capitalizing on the autonomous behavior of trusted peers that may depend on much more sophisticated (and unforeseen) choices, previous knowledge, emotional states etc. For instance, if Agent C is an artist, she may find D3 interesting and relevant for "apple" because D3 is a famous painting of Cezanne or Renoir, not a biologist's classification of diverse apple types (D1 for instance) or an cook's story of how to exploit apples for making cakes (D2 for instance).*

Along the five steps of this imaginary case, the evolution of "knowledge paths" follows the metaphor of the selective reinforcement of neural beams [4], except that this reinforcement is not regulated by a single system of values, rather by a collaboration/competition between the *three systems of values* of A, B and C. The three co-learners learn as a whole, in a trans-disciplinary way: the dynamics are governed by emotions and topology, not by logics.

Emotions influence the KM that each "learner" sees, i.e.: the distance (s)he perceives from the available resources (Agents, Topics and Documents). This, however, occurs in the community of trusted agents, not in the single one. Each learner is influenced by the choices made by other agents, with an indirect effect on his/her exposure to unexpected resources (Agents, Documents, Topics) that may trigger his/her "new connection" (see the lamp in Fig. 1, often associated to Archimede's EUREKA!).

6 Conclusion

We have presented our new paradigm/model/method/system/environment called ViewpointS and the opportunities offered with respect to possibly understand, forecast and foster serendipitous learning, a conjecture that we consider very likely to be true. This potential was not among the initial goals of the work, so we may state that it has been a serendipitous encounter. In this paper, we have made an effort to motivate *retrospectively*, on the basis of part of the available literature, the adequacy of our conjecture.

The foundations of our conviction reside on two properties that ViewpointS may include: the assessment of brain states relating to emotions, to be associated to single viewpoints, and the collective wisdom embodied in the model. These components have been described in fine detail in a toy example that has been annotated in order to unveil its potential application.

We conclude that such a proposal would not be acceptable just a few years ago when measurements of brain functions were much harder to assess and the Web did not have the size it has today ("big" data but also "big" people!).

Concerning the last phenomenon, we believe that the construction of a "protected knowledge space" such as the one envisaged by ViewpointS is today non just an issue of optimization and personalization of the access to information, but a real challenge for the defense of digital sovereignty from the control of external undesired or irrelevant agents.

Regarding the first – brain state measurements - we have been encouraged and fully convinced by the results of Conferences such as: [16] that show the current availability of equipment and of human expertise for assessing and exploiting brain state measurements in real time interactive applications including biofeedback.

References

1. Cerri, Stefano A., Lemoisson, P.: Tracing and enhancing serendipitous learning with view-pointS. BFAL 2017. LNCS (LNAI), vol. 10512, pp. 36–47. Springer, Cham (2017). https://doi.org/10.1007/978-3-319-67615-9_3
2. Lemoisson, P., Surroca, G., Jonquet, C., Cerri, S.A.: ViewpointS: when social ranking meets the semantic web. In: FLAIRS 17 Conference Proceedings, Florida Artificial Intelligence Research Society Conference, North America, May 2017. https://www.aaai.org/ocs/index.php/FLAIRS/FLAIRS17/paper/view/15432. Accessed: 17 Aug 2020
3. Lemoisson, P., Surroca, G., Jonquet, C., Cerri, S.A.: ViewPointS: capturing formal data and informal contributions into an evolutionary knowledge graph. Int. J. Knowl. Learn. **12**(2), 119–145 (2018)
4. Edelman, G. M.: Neural Darwinism: The Theory of Neuronal Group Selection. Basic Books (1989)
5. Van Andel, P.: Serendipiteit: de paradox van de ongezochte vondst: 'toevallige' ontdekkingen, uitvindingen en creaties uit wetenschap, techniek en kunst, PhD thesis, Un. Groningen (1989), also published (in Dutch) as a book with Bert Andreae
6. Van Andel, P.: Anatomy of the unsought finding. serendipity: origin, history, domains, traditions, appearances, patterns and programmability. Br. J. Philos. Sci. **45**(2), 631–648 (1994). Oxford University Press. http://www.jstor.org/stable/687687. (verified 8 March 2020)

7. Corneli, J., et al.: Modelling serendipity in a computational context (2014). https://arxiv.org/abs/1411.0440. (Submitted on 3 Nov 2014 (v1), last revised 30 Aug 2019 (v7))
8. Cerri, S.A., Loia, V., Maffioletti, S., Fontanesi, P., Bettinelli, A.: Serendipitous acquisition of web knowledge by agents in the context of Human Learning. In: THAI−ETIS, Varese, Italy; June 21−22, 1999, pp. 1–25 (1999)
9. Toms, E.G.: Serendipitous information retrieval. In: Proceedings of the First {DELOS} Network of Excellence Workshop on Information Seeking, Searching and Querying in Digital Libraries, {DELOS} 2000, Zurich, Switzerland, December 11–12, 2000, ERCIM Workshop Proceedings, 01/W001, ERCIM (2000)
10. Makri, S., Blandford, A.: Coming across information serendipitously - Part 1: a process model. J. Doc. **68**(5), 684–705 (2012). http://dx.doi.org/10.1108/00220411211256030
11. Makri, S., Tammera, T.M.: Serendipity in future digital information environments. In: Accidental Information Discovery, pp. 81–114. Chandos Publishing (2016). http://www.sciencedirect.com/science/article/pii/B9781843347507000054. (verified 11 March 2020)
12. Weigl, D.M., Emsley, I., Page, K.R.: Serendipity in context: prioritised contextual browsing in large-scale digital libraries. In: Proceedings of the Association for Information Science and Technology, vol. 55, 1, pp. 544–553 (2018). https://doi.org/10.1002/pra2.2018.14505501059. (verified 16 March 2020)
13. Chirita, C.: Modelling serendipity in a service-oriented context. In: AISB Symposium (2017). http://ccg.doc.gold.ac.uk/serendipitysymposium/. (verified 11 March 2020)
14. Kotkov, D., Veijalainen, J., Wang, S.: Challenges of serendipity in recommender systems. In: Majchrzak, T.A., Traverso, P., Monfort, V., Krempels, K.-H. (eds.) WEBIST 2016: Proceedings of the 12th International Conference on Web Information Systems and Technologies, vol. 2, pp. 251–256. SCITEPRESS, Setúbal (2016)
15. de Lima, A.P., Marques Peres, S.: Limits to Surprise in Recommender Systems. eprint = {1807.03905}, archivePrefix = {arXiv}, primaryClass = {cs.IR} (2018)
16. Frasson, C., Kostopoulos, G.: Brain function assessment in learning. In: First International Conference, BFAL 2017, Patras, Greece, September 24–25, 2017, Proceedings. Lecture Notes in Artificial Intelligence, vol. 10512, pp. XV, 215. Springer International Publishing (2017)
17. Lemoisson, P. and Cerri, S.A.: ViewpointS: a Collective Brain. This volume
18. Lemoisson, P., Rakotondrahaja, C.M.H., Andriamialison, A.S.P., Sankar, H.A., Cerri, S.A.: VWA: viewpoints web application to assess collective knowledge building. In: Nguyen, N.T., Chbeir, R., Exposito, E., Aniorté, P., Trawiński, B. (eds.) ICCCI 2019. LNCS (LNAI), vol. 11683, pp. 3–15. Springer, Cham (2019). https://doi.org/10.1007/978-3-030-28377-3_1

Chatbots in Healthcare Curricula: The Case of a Conversational Virtual Patient

Foteini Dolianiti[1] , Iraklis Tsoupouroglou[1], Panagiotis Antoniou[1(✉)] ,
Stathis Konstantinidis[2], Savvas Anastasiades[1], and Panagiotis Bamidis[1]

[1] Lab of Medical Physics, School of Medicine, Faculty of Health Sciences,
Aristotle University of Thessaloniki, Thessaloniki, Greece
foteini.dolianiti@gmail.com, irtsoup@gmail.com,
pantonio@otenet.gr, sanastas@auth.gr, bamidis@med.auth.gr
[2] School of Health Sciences, Faculty of Medicine and Health Sciences,
The University of Nottingham, Nottingham, UK
Stathis.Konstantinidis@nottingham.ac.uk

Abstract. Artificial Intelligence (AI) is among the top technological trends that are expected to shape the future of teaching and learning. Chatbots, or conversational agents, are software that can interact with a human user turn by turn using natural language, and they are considered as exemplar utilization of AI and Machine Learning (ML) in education. Despite the increased interest around educational applications of chatbots, there is a lack of chatbot integration into formal learning settings. This work introduces the case of a Conversational Virtual Patient (CVP) prototype for training decision-making skills regarding thromboembolism in medical students. In contrast to typical virtual patients which rely on predefined, multiple-choice input, the proposed CVP employs Natural Language Processing and ML techniques to allow students to formulate their own utterances and interact with the virtual patient in natural language. In view of employing participatory design and co-creating open access chatbots for healthcare curricula, this CVP prototype will form the basis for the co-creation sessions, by familiarizing stakeholders with the chatbot technology and enabling the requirement elicitation process. Future steps in further co-developing the CVP prototype are discussed.

Keywords: Chatbot · Virtual patient · Medical education

1 Introduction

Educational technology research reflects upon the advances in the field of Artificial Intelligence (AI) to feed the educational sector with cutting-edge tools for helping teachers and learners meet the new demands and challenges of the digital era. Recently, the 2020 EDUCAUSE Horizon report has placed AI among the top technological trends that are expected to shape the future of teaching and learning, and has featured chatbots as exemplar utilization of AI and machine learning in education [1].

Chatbots or conversational agents are software that can interact with a human user turn by turn using natural language [2]. Although bibliometric studies have revealed that

© Springer Nature Switzerland AG 2020
C. Frasson et al. (Eds.): BFAL 2020, LNAI 12462, pp. 137–147, 2020.
https://doi.org/10.1007/978-3-030-60735-7_15

the current applications of chatbots are mainly in the educational sector [3], chatbots are in the very beginning of entering education [4] and they are most often designed for non-formal and informal learning settings [5]. To fill this gap between increased interest in educational applications of chatbots and lack of chatbot integration into formal education, CEPEH (Chatbots Enhance Personalised European Healthcare Curricula)[1], a research project funded by the European Commission (EC) through the Erasmus+ programme, was recently launched.

A mix of partners with technical, educational, medical and nursing expertise participate in the CEPEH project, aiming to co-design and implement new pedagogical approaches in order to promote innovative practices in utilizing AI and open access chatbots for healthcare curricula. To engage stakeholders in co-designing chatbot scenarios and interfaces, the Lab of Medical Physics, of the Aristotle University of Thessaloniki, has developed a chatbot prototype, for familiarizing stakeholders with the chatbot technology and enabling the requirement elicitation process. Specifically, this piece of work introduces the case of a Conversational Virtual Patient (CVP) prototype, which enables natural language-based interaction between the medical student and the Virtual Patient (VP).

The rest of the paper is organized as follows: Sects. 2, 3 and 4 contextualize this work, by summarizing the educational potentialities of chatbots (including CVPs in medical education), providing the technological background, and reviewing existing frameworks and chatbot development systems, respectively. Section 5 is dedicated to the proposed system and details the implementation of the CVP prototype. Finally, Sect. 6 discusses this work and outlines future research directions.

2 Educational Potentialities

2.1 Chatbots for Question-Answering and Lower-Order Thinking Tasks

Among the six levels of Bloom's taxonomy within the cognitive domain, remembering and understanding represent the lowest-level learning, which relates to recalling previously learned material and grasping their meaning [6]. To achieve these goals, students often utilize popular search engines to look for information and find answers to their questions in informal learning sources. In fact, information-retrieval systems have become part of their daily study routine. The massive corpus of question-answer pairs produced by students in online learning environments can promote the emergence of data-driven Question-Answering (Q&A) chatbots, for effectively supporting students' self-directed learning. In this vein, chatbots can serve as student-tailored information systems for providing domain-specific information. In [7], for example, a discussion-bot system was presented, which tries to match student questions with archived data (course documents and past discussions) in order to generate an answer and present it to the student as a human-like reply. Studies have shown that students exhibit an increased memory retention and significantly higher learning outcomes when they solve problems using a course-specific Q&A chatbot compared to a conventional search machine [8]. At the same time, this type of Q&A chatbots may alleviate teachers' workload, especially

---

[1] http://cepeh.eu/.

in large-scale educational paradigms such as MOOCs, where manual monitoring and response to student questions is infeasible. An experimental work on a "teacherbot" implementation for automatically sending predetermined answers to MOOC students seeking help can be found in [9].

2.2 Chatbots as Intelligent and Affective Tutors

A substantial body of research in AI applications in education focuses on adaptive learning environments capable of deriving models of learners and providing personalized learning experiences [10]. Instead of the merely information system presented in the previous subsection, Conversational Intelligent Tutoring Systems (CITS) are able to personalize the learning experience by adapting contents and tutoring based on student characteristics. Oscar is an example of a CITS, which uses cues from students' dialogue and behavior to predict their learning style and adapt its tutoring accordingly, with promising results in learning outcomes [11]. To model student profile, CITS may utilize input not only from student actions within the e-learning environment (e.g., quiz scores, engagement time, and other aspects of quality of interaction [12]), but also from typed input, which can provide further insights into both "*what*" students say (i.e., textual cues in student-chatbot dialogues) and "*how*" they say it (e.g., keyboard input to detect typing patterns and deviations from typical typing behavior, like in [13]). The latter elicits potentialities towards incorporating the affective learning dimension into CITS, by augmenting students' profile with information regarding their affective state. Apart from keystroke dynamics, which have been shown to be a successful affect recognition modality, sentiment analysis is an affect measurement tool tailored to text-based communication environments. The utilization of sentiment analysis in CITS exhibits two principle advantages, i.e., i) the capability to automatically analyze text data in real-time, a task that would otherwise be difficult, labor and time-intense to handle, and ii) the opportunity to unobtrusively record and study student emotions without interrupting the learning process [14]. On the one hand, furnishing CITS with affective capabilities may help timely detect and restore cognitive disequilibrium before confused students become bored and disengaged [15]; on the other hand, it could enhance students' social presence [16], by enabling chatbots to respond emotionally to students' feelings and actions and, thereby, to project their "*personality traits*" into the discussion (e.g., enthusiasm, when the student is doing particularly well, boredom if the student is not responding to the system, like in [13]).

2.3 Chatbots for Fostering Reflection and Meta-Cognition

Opportunities for learner reflection and metacognition can be found in conversational agents that incorporate open learner modeling as well as in conversational teachable agents. Beginning with open learner modeling, students actively participate in learner model construction, by inspecting, discussing and altering the learner model [17]; and this is what it differentiates these systems from the CITS presented in the previous subsection. A representative example of a chatbot that opens the learner model to the student can be found in [18], demonstrating positive results in increasing the accuracy of both student's self-assessment and system's inferences. CALMsystem presents the student with their learner model, offering them the opportunity to compare, discuss and negotiate their own beliefs regarding their capabilities with those inferred by the system, using natural language [18]. Bringing the affective learning dimension back up, open learner modeling in conversational agents could be oriented beyond cognitive domain, by presenting students with their affective learner model, i.e. the representation of their affective states instead of their knowledge. Considering that the contents of reflection encompass cognitive, non-cognitive and affective aspects [19], engaging students in negotiating their affective representation could enable a more holistic reflective approach. On the other hand, conversational teachable agents facilitate reflection through learning-by-teaching, since students' ideas are more accessible to evaluation and refinement when they are being explained and verbalized [20]. Inspired by the Protégé effect, which states that *"learning for the sake of teaching others is more beneficial than learning for one's own self"*, authors in [21] introduced Curiosity Notebook, which enables students to take the role of an instructor who teaches an AI agent through natural language dialogues. Since reflection encompasses both meta-cognition (i.e., focus on one's own thinking) and sense making (i.e., focus on content itself) [22], conversational teachable agents may provoke student's reflective thinking on lower-order cognitive skills (such as understanding a topic, like in [21]) or higher-order cognitive skills (such as reasoning, like in [23]). Finally, studies have demonstrated that student's reflective knowledge-building can be further enhanced by teaching an agent that is designed to be metacognitive and self-regulated [20].

2.4 Conversational Virtual Patients

Virtual Patients (VPs) are interactive computer simulations used as learning activities in modern healthcare education, especially in training clinical decision-making skills [24]. VPs are a well-established problem-based learning practice in medical education, which allows students to consider different options as the scenario unfolds, take decisions and explore the consequences of their actions [25].

In contrast to typical VPs, which depend upon multiple-choice inputs and restrict medical students' decisions to a predefined set of options, CVPs enable free-form conversation to take place using natural language and allow students to take control of the interaction. Apart from the technological advancement in terms of Human-Computer Interaction, this type of VPs may also offer an added educational value, by increasing the realism of the learning experience and make it match as nearly as possible to the real-world tasks of health-care professionals in practice, aligned with the characteristics of authentic learning [26]. Since medical education should shift from engaging students in reciting the correct answers to engaging them in asking the right questions [27], two-way dialogue-based VPs may better address the need for medical students to undertake a more active role in problem-based learning.

Additionally, considering the relationship between medical dialogue structure and both patient centeredness and patients' evaluative judgments of a visit [28], CVPs offer new opportunities for studying and training communications skills in medical students. Through a turn-by-turn interaction in natural language, CVPs allow medical students to scaffold the doctor-patient dialogue and, thereby, influence the (virtual) patient's experience of care. Finally, the implementation of VPs for training empathetic communication skills could be further enhanced via CVPs that employ affect detection tools (like sentiment analysis) to support the *affective scaffolding* in doctor-patient exchanges.

3 Technological background

Before reviewing the existing frameworks and available systems for developing a conversational agent, it is useful to explicate some core terminology for building intelligent conversational systems, summarized in Table 1.

Table 1. Core terminology

Term	Definition
Natural Language Processing (NLP)	*NLP* refers to all systems and methods that work together to handle interactions between machines and humans in the preferred language of the human [29]
Natural Language Understanding (NLU)	*NLU* is a subset of NLP in the sense that it is only the process of taking pure unstructured text and transforming it into structured data that a chatbot or a conversational agent will be able to work with [30]
Entity	An *entitiy* refers to the type of information a chatbot needs to extract from the user
Intent	An *intent* is the process of categorizing the intention of a user for a conversation turn
Action	An a*ction* is all the things a chatbot runs in response to user input

4 Frameworks and Development Systems

Most frameworks and development systems have at their core a NLU implementation, in order to convert the (text or speech) input provided by a human to an output more meaningful and easier to work with, from a machine's perspective. Currently, conversational agents are used in many different aspects in our daily lives, from tech support to diagnosing and treating patients, so there are a plethora of systems for developing them. Most frameworks use open technologies, such as open source tools, open libraries, etc. Table 2 presents some of the most well-known frameworks. All major development systems provide more or less the same functionalities, such as support for many different channels, visual editors, many APIs and third party plugins.

Table 2. Overview of frameworks

Framework	Data Storage	Supported SDKs	Cost
Rasa Open Source[a]	On-premise, Private Cloud, Third party providers	Python	Free (offers paid Enterprise Edition)
Botpress[b]	On-premise, Private Cloud, Third party providers	Javascript	Free (offers paid Enterprise Edition)
Microsoft Bot Framework(Botkit)[c,d]	On-premise, Azure	Node.js	Paid service
DialogFlow[e]	Google's cloud infrastructure	Node.js, Python, Go, C#, Java, PHPO, Ruby	Free with limited amount of requests, Offers paid plans
IBM Watson Assistant[f]	IBM's cloud infrastructure	GO, Python, Ruby,.NET, Unity, Java	Free with limited amount of requests, Offers paid plans

[a]https://rasa.com.
[b]https://botpress.com/.
[c]https://dev.botframework.com/.
[d]https://github.com/howdyai/botkit.
[e]https://dialogflow.com/.
[f]https://www.ibm.com/cloud/watson-assistant/.

4.1 Rasa Open Source

After reviewing the aforementioned frameworks, our team decided to go with Rasa Open Source, due to its zero cost, on-permise data storage and its user-friendly GUI. Rasa Open Source is, as its name suggests, an open source development system for natural language understanding, dialogue management, and integrations. It, also, provides Rasa X, a free GUI toolset used to improve contextual assistants built using Rasa Open Source. Together, they include all the features to create text- and voice-based assistants and chatbots. One key feature of its machine learning capabilities is that it is language agnostic so the training and deployment of an assistant can be in several different languages. Another important feature of Rasa Open Source, is its privacy driven policy for data. It provides on premise or private cloud deployment, giving full control over data, although it supports third party cloud providers as well. It has a built-in, although still experimental, versioning control with git, supports many APIs and uses Python for developing custom actions. Finally, it offers many choices for the preferred channels on which the chatbot will reside.

5   The Proposed System

5.1   Project's Goals & Requirements

In trying to cover the gap on intelligent conversational agents in education, our approach in building an educational chatbot is based on three guidelines. First, the chatbot's initial design and development should be based on co-creation, bringing educators, medical students, healthcare professionals and developers together, in order to build a final product that meets the actual users' demands and needs. Second, the framework that will be used, should offer all the necessary tools for continuous training of the model and easy usability for non-technical users and lastly, on premise data storage. Finally, the need for a sound technological environment and the above parameters led into the option of Rasa Open Source as the framework of choice to develop and deploy our chatbot.

5.2   Implementation

Building a chatbot with Rasa Open Source with Rasa X on top, requires a server with a minimum of 2 CPUs, 8 GB of RAM and a recommended 50 GB of storage. The deployment of our chatbot will be in our institution's own infrastructure, on an Ubuntu 18.04 virtual machine with the aforementioned requirements. The development of the CVP prototype was based on a VP scenario in cardiology, aiming to train decision-making skills regarding thromboembolism. The VP scenario was originally created under the Deep-Raft research project[2], which aims at raising awareness, educating and affecting systemic change on diagnosis and treatment of Atrial Fibrillation and Venous thromboembolism.

5.3   Training Data and Natural Language Understanding

The initial training data were extracted from the virtual patient scenario discussed in the previous paragraph. The training data for Rasa NLU is structured into different parts: *common examples*, *synonyms*, *regex features* and *lookup tables.*

While common examples is the only part that is mandatory, including the others helps the NLU model learn the domain with fewer examples and also help it be more confident of its predictions.

Synonyms will map extracted *entities* to the same name, for example mapping "my savings account" to simply "savings". However, this only happens *after* the entities have been extracted, so it needs to be provided examples with the synonyms present so that Rasa can learn to pick them up.

Lookup tables may be specified as plain text files containing newline-separated words or phrases. Upon loading the training data, these files are used to generate case-insensitive regex patterns that are added to the regex features.

In the first phase, the training data were created only by common examples and synonyms.

---

[2] https://deepraft.com/.

5.4 Rasa Stories

In order to train a chatbot properly, Rasa uses the concept of *stories*. Rasa stories are a form of training data used to train Rasa's dialogue management models, where user inputs are expressed as corresponding *intents* (and *entities* where necessary), while the responses of an assistant are expressed as corresponding *action* names. It doesn't matter if a story ends to a desirable point or not, actually it is as useful to feed the algorithm with as many possible right stories, as wrong ones. In the first phase of our training we created eight different stories ranging from totally wrong conversational paths to the most direct right path, as shown in Fig. 1. Additionally, Fig. 1 demonstrates a visual representation of a story's flow provided by Rasa's GUI editor.

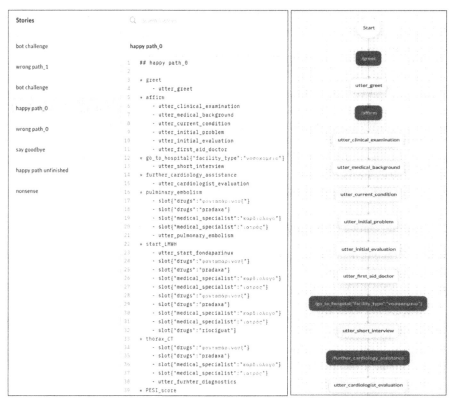

Fig. 1. An overview of the stories that were used to train our model (left) and a visual flowchart of a story (right)

6 Discussion

This work presented the development of a prototype CVP for training decision-making skills regarding thromboembolism in medical students. In contrast to typical VPs which rely on predefined multiple-choice input, the proposed CVP employs NLP and machine learning techniques to allow students to formulate their own utterances and interact with the VP in natural language.

The two-way dialogue-based interaction, that the proposed system enables, may enhance the authenticity of the learning experience in problem-based learning scenarios, by giving medical students a more active role in decision-making, simulating real-life healthcare settings, whilst maintaining a risk-free practice environment. Preliminary investigation of medical students' perceptions towards CVPs has demonstrated a high receptivity, with students perceiving the free-text input as a significant improvement, which provides a more personalized learning experience and a more effective training of clinical reasoning skills, over the conventional VPs [31].

The prototype system described in the present work will be further co-developed, inviting stakeholders to provide domain-knowledge and enrich the VP stories in RASA. Previous studies have highlighted the difficulties raised by the terminological needs of dialogue-based VPs [32]. In order to effectively handle term variants, healthcare professionals specializing in cardiology will contribute in accurately mapping related terms and expand vocabulary coverage. Additionally, medical students will interact with the CVPs in order to produce different scenario flows, corresponding to both correct and wrong branches.

Acknowledgements. This work was supported by the CEPEH project (Chatbots Enhance Personalised European Healthcare Curricula), funded by the European Commission through the Erasmus+ programme (Grant Number: 252583).

References

1. Malcolm, B., et al.: 2020 EDUCAUSE Horizon Report, Teaching and Learning Edition. EDUCAUSE, Louisville, CO (2020)
2. Shawar, B.A., Atwell, E.: Different measurement metrics to evaluate a chatbot system. In: Proceedings of the Workshop on Bridging the Gap: Academic and Industrial Research in Dialog Technologies, pp. 89–96. Association for Computational Linguistics, Rochester, NY (2007)
3. Io, H.N., Lee, C.B.: Chatbots and conversational agents: a bibliometric analysis. In: IEEE International Conference on Industrial Engineering and Engineering Management (IEEM), pp. 215–219. IEEE (2017)
4. Winkler, R., Söllner, M.: Unleashing the potential of chatbots in education: A state-of-the-art analysis. In: Academy of Management Annual Meeting (AOM). Chicago, USA (2018)
5. Hobert, S., von Wolff, R.M.: Say hello to your new automated tutor–a structured literature review on pedagogical conversational agents. In: 14th International Conference on Wirtschaftsinfor, pp. 301–314 (2019)
6. Krathwohl, D.R., Anderson, L.W.: A Taxonomy for Learning, Teaching, and Assessing: A Revision of Bloom's Taxonomy of Educational Objectives. Addison Wesley Longman, New York (2001)
7. Feng, D., Shaw, E., Kim, J., Hovy, E.: An intelligent discussion-bot for answering student queries in threaded discussions. In: Proceedings of the 11th International Conference on Intelligent User Interfaces, pp. 171–177 (2006)

8. Abbasi, S., Kazi, H.: Measuring effectiveness of learning chatbot systems on Student's learning outcome and memory retention. Asian J. Appl. Sci. Eng. **3**(2), 251–260 (2014)

9. Bayne, S.: Teacherbot: interventions in automated teaching. Teach. High. Educ. **20**(4), 455–467 (2015)

10. Bamidis, Panagiotis D.: Affective learning: principles, technologies, practice. In: Frasson, C., Kostopoulos, G. (eds.) BFAL 2017. LNCS (LNAI), vol. 10512, pp. 1–13. Springer, Cham (2017). https://doi.org/10.1007/978-3-319-67615-9_1

11. Latham, A., Crockett, K., McLean, D., Edmonds, B.: Adaptive tutoring in an intelligent conversational agent system. In: Nguyen, N.-T. (ed.) Transactions on Computational Collective Intelligence VIII. LNCS, vol. 7430, pp. 148–167. Springer, Heidelberg (2012). https://doi.org/10.1007/978-3-642-34645-3_7

12. Dias, S.B., Diniz, J.A.: FuzzyQoI model: A fuzzy logic-based modelling of users' quality of interaction with a learning management system under blended learning. Comput. Educ. **69**, 38–59 (2013)

13. Alepis, E., Virvou, M.: Automatic generation of emotions in tutoring agents for affective e-learning in medical education. Expert Syst. Appl. **38**(8), 9840–9847 (2011)

14. Dolianiti, F.S., et al.: Sentiment analysis on educational datasets: a comparative evaluation of commercial tools. Educ. J. Univ. Patras UNESCO Chair **6**(1), 262–273 (2019)

15. D'Mello, S., Graesser, A.: Dynamics of affective states during complex learning. Learn. Instr. **22**(2), 145–157 (2012)

16. Garrison, D.R., Anderson, T., Archer, W.: Critical inquiry in a text-based environment: Computer conferencing in higher education. Internet High. Educ. **2**(2–3), 87–105 (1999)

17. Dimitrova, V., Brna, P.: From interactive open learner modelling to intelligent mentoring: STyLE-OLM and Beyond. Int. J. Artif. Intell. Educ. **26**(1), 332–349 (2016)

18. Kerly, A., Ellis, R., Bull, S.: CALMsystem: a conversational agent for learner modelling. In: Ellis, R., Allen, T., Petridis, M. (eds.) Applications and Innovations in Intelligent Systems XV, pp. 89–102. Springer, London (2008). https://doi.org/10.1007/978-1-84800-086-5_7

19. Nguyen, Q.D., Fernandez, N., Karsenti, T., Charlin, B.: What is reflection? A conceptual analysis of major definitions and a proposal of a five-component model. Med. Educ. **48**(12), 1176–1189 (2014)

20. Roscoe, D., Wagster, J., Biswas, G.: Using teachable agent feedback to support effective learning by teaching. In: Proceedings of the Cognitive Science Conference (2008)

21. Chhibber, N., Law, E.: Using conversational agents to support learning by teaching. In: CHI 2019 (2019)

22. Davis, E.A.: Prompting middle school science students for productive reflection: generic and directed prompts. J. Learn. Sci. **12**(1), 91–142 (2003)

23. Pareto, L.: A teachable agent game engaging primary school children to learn arithmetic concepts and reasoning. Int. J. Artif. Intell. Educ. **24**(3), 251–283 (2014)

24. Dafli, E., Antoniou, P., Ioannidis, L., Dombros, N., Topps, D., Bamidis, P.D.: Virtual patients on the semantic Web: a proof-of-application study. J. Med. Internet Res. **17**(1), e16 (2015)

25. Poulton, T., Balasubramaniam, C.: Virtual patients: a year of change. Med. Teach. **33**(11), 933–937 (2011)

26. Reeves, T.C., Herrington, J., Oliver, R.: Authentic activities and online learning. In: HERDSA, pp. 562–567 (2002)

27. Dixon, A.: Problem-based learning: old wine in new bottles? In: Tan, O.S., Little, P., Hee, S.Y., Conway, J. (eds.) Problem-Based Learning: Educational Innovation Across Disciplines - A Collection of Selected Papers, pp. 34–45. Temasek Centre for Problem-Based Learning, Singapore (2000)

28. Roter, D.L., Larson, S.M., Beach, M.C., Cooper, L.A.: Interactive and evaluative correlates of dialogue sequence: a simulation study applying the RIAS to turn taking structures. Patient Educ. Couns. **71**(1), 26–33 (2008)

29. Eisenstein, J.: Introduction to Natural Language Processing. MIT Press, Cambridge (2019)
30. Bates, M.: Models of natural language understanding. Proc. Natl. Acad. Sci. **92**(22), 9977–9982 (1995)
31. Persad, A., Stroulia, E., Forgie, S.: A novel approach to virtual patient simulation using natural language processing. Med. Educ. **50**(11), 1162–1163 (2016)
32. Campillos-Llanos, L., Thomas, C., Bilinski, É., Zweigenbaum, P., Rosset, S.: Designing a virtual patient dialogue system based on terminology-rich resources: challenges and evaluation. Nat. Lang. Eng. **26**, 1–38 (2019)

Exploiting Assistive Technologies for People with Down Syndrome: A Multi-dimensional Impact Evaluation Analysis of Educational Feasibility and Usability

Ioanna Dratsiou, Maria Metaxa, Evangelia Romanopoulou, and Panagiotis Bamidis[✉]

Laboratory of Medical Physics, School of Medicine, Aristotle University of Thessaloniki,
PO Box 376, 54124 Thessaloniki, Greece
`idratsiou@gmail.com, metaxaem@gmail.com,`
`evangeliaromanopoulou@gmail.com, pdbamidis@gmail.com`

Abstract. Despite the potential benefits that Assistive Technologies (AT) could provide for People with Down Syndrome (PDS) and Intellectual Disabilities (PID), research and implementation of emerging AT for learning has mainly focused on developing adaptive accessible solutions and evaluating cognitive function. Unlike the parallel, but equally important role, of all stakeholders and factors involved in PDS and PID support and learning including medical practitioners, families and professionals, have not received adequate attention. This paper describes an interdisciplinary collaboration and multilevel evaluation focusing both on investigating the potential improvement of PDS memory performance after participating in cognitive training sessions. Cognitive assessment in 20 PDS working memory performance was conducted, whereas questionnaires were distributed to 29 relevant stakeholders evaluating the possible correlation between educational feasibility and usability of the AT introduced. Overall, the results showed that there was a significant improvement on PDS memory performance and significant positive correlation in between different variables of AT educational feasibility and usability.

Keywords: Assistive Technologies · Down syndrome · Intellectual disabilities · Educational feasibility · Usability

1 Introduction

1.1 Intellectual Disabilities and Down Syndrome

According to the United Nations Development Programme (UNDP), "Intellectual Disability" (ID) affects between one and three percent of the world population and is mainly associated with multiple conditions that impair brain's development before birth, during birth or in early childhood years. The major related conditions to ID are Down Syndrome, Fetal Alcohol Spectrum Disorder and Fragile X Syndrome [1]. Down syndrome

© Springer Nature Switzerland AG 2020
C. Frasson et al. (Eds.): BFAL 2020, LNAI 12462, pp. 148–159, 2020.
https://doi.org/10.1007/978-3-030-60735-7_16

(DS) or else Trisomy 21, is the most common one, since it estimated that about 1000 live births [2] and affects more than five million people worldwide [3]. DS is a genetic disorder caused by an additional chromosome in some or all the cells of the body, due to nondisjunction during cell division [4]. This extra chromosome (chromosome 21) is related to developmental delays to one's physical and mental condition [5] that become discernible in the areas of cognitive, linguistic, speech-motor and social development [6]. Consequently, Persons with DS (PDS) have different capacities and skills for under-standing and learning [7] and thus, each one of them demonstrates individual abilities, strengths and weaknesses, and has their own learning profile. In this vein, there is a consensus need for ongoing support and stimulation to Persons with ID (PID) aiming at developing and enhancing their skills in order to effectively facilitate their full social inclusion [8]. In addition to this attempt, Information and Communication Technology (ICT) and Assistive Technologies (AT) present new possibilities and efficient solutions that play a crucial role to the promotion of social inclusion and thereby, the improvement of quality of life for people dealing with intellectual disabilities in their different levels of affection [9, 10].

1.2 Assistive Technologies for PID and PDS in Learning

ICT and AT are recognized as valuable effective training and learning tools when consid-ering the improvement of quality of life for PID [10]. In educational processes, motivation is considered to be a key aspect to the acquisition of knowledge for children with learning difficulties [11]. Several studies have found that computer assisted instruction promotes greater enthusiasm than traditional paper and pen methods to students facing learning disabilities [11–13]. In addition, AT provides both visual and acoustic stimuli through the use of multimedia such as images, animations and videos facilitate understanding of the information provided. Besides that, provision of feedback gives a continuous stim-ulus to PID for continuing and successfully completing any task [14]. Although, when designing ICT Tools and AT for PDS, it is important to previously investigate their needs and abilities. Based on the unique characteristics, strength and weaknesses will enable the decision makers in selecting the most appropriate AT to be adopted with the purpose of more effective results [15].

1.3 Related Work

In this section related AT and ICT tools tailored to provide assistance and support to a generic or specific learning goal for PID and PDS are presented in accordance with classification introduced by [16].

Adaptivity refers to the interface or the content can be adapted (automatically or manually) for a specific user [16]. For instance, the project Poseidon aims at enabling PDS to be more independent and trigger their inclusion into society by using AT and developing apps focusing on different areas of daily living like navigation, daily planning and money handling [17]. A series of systems that use game elements and gamification tools including the HATLE, a computer aided tool on an Android platform that provides a multimedia playful learning environment [18]. Tools that provide accessible content for education or rehabilitation of specific skills such as SynMax, a mathematics computer application software that is developed to assist PDS to learn the number concepts [19]. Moreover, "Stella Software" [20] an online application adapted to PDS adults aiming at enhancing their cognitive and mental functions, including various types of exercises that use images, text and sound, creating an enriched training environment.

Meaningful collaborations and joint-ventures between family and school are highlighted as essential factors in enhancing students' social and behavioural outcomes addressed to inclusion [21–23], while the success of these partnerships depends on fostering positive attitudes, sharing common ideas and expectations as well as clear communication and trust among all involved stakeholders [24]. Additionally, a bodily conjunction between a cohesive, deliberate and collaborative focus and targeted training for teachers in working and collaborating with parents is promoted as beneficial practice for all parties involved [25].

Special interest presents an inter-organizational partnership between a local advocacy group for Down's syndrome, the public school system and a university professor in the United States, where through sharing common principles and resources, an inclusive training was developed tailored to students' with Down syndrome physical and emotional needs and individual learning goals [26].

With the ever-increasing availability of AT and ICT for PDS it is highlighted as of utmost importance the existence of a direct link between designers and researchers in order to develop innovative learning strategies and solutions addressed to users' needs and learning experiences [16]. The literature shows a great number of AT initiatives, specially designed for PDS and PID, by incorporating accessibility and usability features. Despite the fact that these are essential components for examining any benefits of a specific solution, they rarely evaluate the positive effects in terms of learning processes (acquisition, storage and progression, etc.). There is a lack of research into the potential relation between the educational feasibility and usability of the various AT developed.

2   Purpose of This Study

The aim of this study is to present a multi-dimensional evaluation of the educational feasibility and usability of a series of AT aiming at the cognitive training of PDS and PID. In particular, the novelty of this study lies in the interdisciplinary collaboration and engagement of all the relevant stakeholders involved in PDS and PID support and learning including PDS, medical practitioners, families and professionals.

More specifically, this research focuses in the investigation of the potential improvement of PDS working memory performance after their interaction with the system of AT and their participation in cognitive training sessions. While subsequently based on the evaluation of all the involved stakeholders, it is examined the correlation between the educational feasibility and usability of the aforementioned system of AT.

3   Proposed Framework of AT

3.1   Design and Learning Principles of Proposed AT

Guided by the multisensory principle, it is supported the idea that memory can be reinforced if interaction with learning is conducted by involving and activating simultaneously multiple senses, such as visual, auditory, tactile-kinesthetic and articulatory motor [27], while the essential learning construction is achieved through personalization of intervention in accordance with students' performance [28]. Additionally, *IMS Guidelines for Developing Accessible Learning Applications* [29] and *World Wide Web Consortium (W3C) Web Accessibility Initiative (WAI)* [30] provide essential guidance in designing accessible learning applications. In this regard, priority was given in taking into account these learning and design principles in order to adapt strategies, standards, and practices addressed to PDS and PID needs. In particular, the design and development of the proposed AT included accessibility features, continuous provision of motivation as well as maintenance of interest and engagement in the activities.

3.2 Proposed AT Addressed to PDS and PID

Integrated Healthcare System Long Lasting Memories Care - LLM Care
The "Integrated Health and Social Care System-LLM Care" [31] is an ICT platform that combines state-of-the-art cognitive exercises [32] with physical activity [33] and offers an integrated solution for cognitive and physical health, providing effective protection against cognitive decline [34]. It is a non-pharmaceutical intervention against cognitive deterioration, which substantiated qualitative results in both the specific brain functions, affected by ageing, and the psychological state of the participants. It also provides a comprehensive solution that prolongs the time of independent and autonomous living and has a direct impact on older adults [34], whereas there is potential for improving the quality of life of persons belonging to other vulnerable groups [35, 36]. On the basis of this prospect, this research aims at laying the ground for the development of an integrated platform including components predominantly geared towards PDS. More specifically, the memory game "Memorize-Image it!" and the interactive educational games and virtual scenarios are thoroughly described below.

Memorize-Image it!
The "Memorize-Image it!" application is a simple memory game specially developed for the needs of PDS [37]. The scope of the game is to choose correctly and in the proper order a series of images representing daily objects that are previously displayed on the screen in verbal and auditory form. It consists of six difficulty levels, starting with two words/objects and reaching up the upper limit of nine words/objects. The number of words/objects was based on the consensus view that even highly intelligent adults have a usual memory capacity of seven items in their working memory [38]. In order for the game to be both educationally appropriate and technically simple, the design guidelines were kept simple.

Interactive Educational Games and Virtual Scenarios
A series of seven (7) Games and ten (10) Virtual Scenarios tailored to PDS/PID routine operations and inclusive leisure activities were developed within the context of a funded by the European Commission project within the ERASMUS+ 2017 Programme, Key Action 2 - Strategic Partnerships for Adult Education aiming at promoting the inclusion of PDS [39, 40]. In particular, Games focused in training PDS and PID in designing their personal leisure plan and participating in various leisure activities, while Virtual

Scenarios were basically problem-based learning activities, that supported PDS and PID in making real-life decisions related to daily living leisure activities. They aimed at promoting autonomy and inclusion of PDS, developing digital skills, as well as enhancing self-decision and transversal skills (planning activities, make appointments, budget management, and communication).

4   Methods

4.1   Participants

A multi-dimensional assessment of the proposed AT solutions is introduced including the data collected as shown in Table 1. A total of 91 stakeholders participated in the survey, belonging in four distinct groups: (a) PDS, (b) medical practitioners, (c) families and (d) professionals. More specifically, 20 *PDS* aged from 10 to 49 years old took part in cognitive training sessions, whereas 20 *medical practitioners* in semesters 3th to 5th and 22 PDS *family members* with mean age 52,59 years old, coming from a range of occupational fields, were asked to assess the AT solutions. Moreover, 29 *professionals* aged from 25 to more than 50 years old provided their feedback after implementing the training sessions with PDS.

Table 1. Descriptive information of participants.

	PDS		Facilitators		Families	
	Group1	Group2	Medical Practitioners	Professionals		
Age (years)	10-20 70% 21-30 20% 31-40 10%	10-20 40% 21-30 30% 31-40 20% More than 40 10%	**Semester** 5th-6th 45% 7th-8th 40% 9th-10th 10% More than 11 5%	**Age (years)** 25-35 41,38% 36-45 31,03% More than 50 27,58%	**Age (years)** 30-40 4.54% 41-50 31.82% 51-60 59.10% More than 60 4.54%	
Gender F	40%	30%	80%	72,41%	95.46%	
Gender M	60%	70%	20%	27,59%	4.54%	
Related to the DS					Mother Father Brother/Sister	86.36% 9.10% 4.54%
Occupation					Retired Housekeeping Office worker Teacher Pharmacist	27.28% 27.27% 22.72% 13.64% 9.09%

4.2   Procedure, Instrumentation and Assessment

Following ethical approval, informed written consents were distributed to all *PDS* in order to participate in the cognitive training sessions. The participants were randomly allocated either to Group 1 ($N = 10$) or Group 2 ($N = 10$). Participants of Group 1 involved in cognitive training by interacting with the memory game Memorize-Image it!, whereas participants of Group 2 in cognitive exercises interacting with the ICT platform of the Integrated Healthcare System Long Lasting Memories Care-LLM Care. Cognitive assessments were conducted before and after the training sessions, including Digit Span [41] that was administered to both groups in order to assess their working memory performance, which is related to mental functions used in registering, storing and retrieving information [42]. PDS are highly related to lower performance in exercises that require recalling of digits, words or even non-words [43].

Regarding the facilitators involved in the cognitive training sessions, medical practitioners conducted the implementation of LLM Care to PDS for approximately 7–8 weeks, whilst professionals supported the interaction of PDS with the Games and Virtual Scenarios for 6 weeks. After the completion of the cognitive training sessions all facilitators were asked to assess the educational feasibility (ensure the intellectualization of information interaction between the subjects of the educational process) and usability (understand and identify user requirements) of the aforementioned AT utilized in the cognitive training. In particular, a 24-item questionnaire was developed aiming at evaluating a comprehensive set of categories of heuristics for playability (i.e., Game Play, Coolness/Entertainment/Humour/Emotional Immersion, and Usability & Game Mechanics), usability and educational feasibility in terms of training adequacy, training strategies making and other competencies, as well as the overall learning experience. Similarly, a questionnaire was developed and distributed to participants' families aiming at evaluating the positive effect and usability of the proposed AT in PDS.

5 Results

5.1 PDS Cognitive Assessment

This subsection presents the data extracted from the Digit Span test which was applied to PDS in order to assess the working memory performance between Group 1 and Group 2. In total, 20 PDS participated in the pilot activities and were evaluated before and after the cognitive training sessions. As shown in Table 2, the initial performance on Digit Span of the participants of Group 1 and Group 2 improved significantly after cognitive training with the memory game Memorize-Image it! and LLM Care.

Table 2. Cognitive assessment of PDS before and after training sessions.

Mean Performance (±S.D)		t(df)	p-value
	Pre	Post		
Group 1	10.00 (±3.91)	11.50 (±3.71)	−2.57 (9)	**.03**
Group 2	9.30 (±1.76)	10.70 (±2.05)	−3.09 (9)	**.01**

5.2 Correlation Analysis

Data obtained from the questionnaires completed by all stakeholders were analyzed by a Spearman correlation coefficient that was used to identify the relationship between the variables related to AT educational feasibility and usability. Particularly, three correlations were conducted; (i) within different variables regarding AT educational feasibility (Table 3), (ii) within different variables regarding AT usability (Table 4), (iii) within different variables between AT educational feasibility and AT usability (Table 5).

Table 3 shows the variables indicated a significant positive effect of AT educational feasibility. In specific, there is a significant relationship between training adequacy and PDS satisfaction of using AT, training strategies, PDS sense of creativity, AT content adhesion with real life and provision of proper information to PDS. Similarly, significant correlation was noticed between the training strategies adopted by the trainers and PDS sense of interest, engagement, social and communication skills, and their overall benefit gained by AT provided, as well as on the provision of proper information and absence

Table 3. Correlation analysis regarding educational feasibility.

Variable 1	Variable 2	r_s	p value
Training Adequacy	Satisfaction of using AT	.64	.010
	Training Strategies	.58	.003
	Sense of creativity	.43	.033
	Content adhesion with real life	.44	.029
	Provision of proper information	.42	.037
Training Strategies	User's optimum benefit by AT	.79	.000
	User's sense of interest	.45	.027
	User's engagement	.47	.019
	User's development/enhancement of social skills and communication	.53	.007
	Absence of burden during interaction	.44	.028
	Provision of proper information	.52	.009
User's optimum benefit by AT	User's development/enhancement of social skills and communication	.64	.001

Table 4. Correlation analysis regarding usability.

Variable 1	Variable 2	r_s	p value
Proper audio and visual content	No-necessity of manual or documentation guidance	.45	.014
	Provision of appropriate audio/visual feedback	.68	.000
	User friendly interface	.52	.004
No-necessity of manual or documentation guidance	Provision of appropriate audio/visual feedback	.64	.000
User friendly interface	Provision of appropriate audio/visual feedback	.72	.000
	No-necessity of manual or documentation guidance	.39	.036

Table 5. Correlation analysis between education feasibility and usability.

Variable 1	Variable 2	r_s	p value
Proper audio and visual content	Training Strategies	.52	.009
	User's optimum benefit by AT	.59	.002
User's engagement	Proper audio and visual content	.60	.000
	No-necessity of manual or documentation guidance	.43	.020
	Provision of appropriate audio/visual feedback	.69	.000
	User friendly interface	.64	.000
User's sense of interest	Proper audio and visual content	.73	.000
	No-necessity of manual or documentation guidance	.58	.001
	Provision of appropriate audio/visual feedback	.65	.000
	User friendly interface	.66	.000

of cognitive burden during interaction with AT. Equivalent results were found between PDS optimum benefit by AT and the enhancement of their social and communication skills.

Concerning usability, Spearman's correlation analysis shows significant relationship between proper audio and visual content and no-necessity of manual or documentation guidance, provision of appropriate audio/visual feedback, and user friendly interface. Furthermore, provision of appropriate audio/visual feedback is significantly related to no-necessity of manual guidance and user friendly interface (Table 4).

Table 5 shows the variables that indicated a significant positive effect between educational feasibility and usability of AT. More specifically, there is a significant relationship between proper audio and visual content and training strategies implemented by trainers as well as with PDS optimum benefit by AT. Regarding PDS engagement there is a significant relationship between proper audio and visual content, no-necessity of manual or documentation guidance through their interaction with AT, provision of appropriate audio/visual feedback and user friendly interface. Additionally, significant relationship is shown between PDS sense of interest and proper audio and visual content, provision of appropriate audio/visual feedback, no-necessity of manual or documentation guidance through their interaction with AT and user friendly interface.

6   Discussion

This study aimed to provide an overview of the importance of the interdisciplinary collaboration of all stakeholders involved in PDS support and learning, as medical practitioners, families and professionals, and contribute to laying the groundwork for a better understanding of a multi-level evaluation of the AT introduced. Specifically, three AT solutions were described, (a) the *Integrated Healthcare System Long Lasting Memories Care-LLM Care*, (b) the memory game *Memorize-Image it!* and (c) the *Educational Games and Virtual Scenarios*. PDS participated in cognitive training sessions by interacting with the above AT and subsequently a multidimensional evaluation was conducted focusing both on investigating the potential improvement of PDS working memory performance and the correlation between educational feasibility and usability of the AT introduced, as emerged from the stakeholders' evaluation.

Digit Span [41] was distributed in PDS participants before and after their participation in cognitive training sessions aiming to assess their working memory performance, which is related to mental functions used in registering, storing and retrieving information. More specifically, PDS participation in cognitive training sessions actualizing Memorize-Image it! showed a significant improvement on their working memory performance equivalent with those who participated in the training sessions of the LLM Care. In addition, Spearman's correlation analysis was conducted to identify the correlation between variables related to educational feasibility and usability of AT proposed. The results showed significant positive correlation within variables of educational feasibility, within variables of usability as well as in between variables of educational feasibility and usability.

As with the majority of studies, the design of the current study is subject to some possible limitations. Although the number of PDS participated in this study could be considered sufficient, time and sample-related limitations remain as an inevitable issue. With regards to the implementation of the proposed AT solutions in a specific sample of stakeholders the inclusion of a larger and broader range of sample is considered essential for the generalization of the results.

Despite its limitations the procedure followed in this study was tailored in that way in order to also involve relevant stakeholders, including medical practitioners, families and professionals in a multi-dimensional evaluation. The findings of this study are in concordance with existing literature where the enactment of cohesive, deliberate and collaborative partnerships among all involved stakeholders including individuals, families, service providers and policy developers is aiming at designing/developing of policies and practices addressed to PDS inclusion [21, 22, 25]. Finally, for the successful implementation and interaction with the proposed AT solutions it is necessary to consider their acceptance by all the related stakeholders and highlight certain barriers to their effective use, like digital skills deficits or reluctance to change. To this end, a baseline phase for familiarization with the proposed learning framework and AT solutions is fundamental.

In summary, all three AT solutions proposed have a positive and added effect to PDS, however it should be noted that this is only one step in a greater research endeavor of the overall impact of these AT solutions. Future steps include the development of an Integrated Health and Social Care platform addressed to PDS by also including the memory game Memorize-Image it! as well as the interactive educational games and virtual scenarios. In this perspective, further analysis and research should be conducted by recruiting a larger sample of PDS, in order to investigate the potential long-term effects on learning processes (acquisition, storage and progression, etc.) and on the promotion of PDS inclusion in general.

Disclosure Statement. The authors declare that the research was conducted in the absence of any commercial or financial relationships that could be construed as a potential conflict of interest.

References

1. United Nations Development Program. United Nations: Disability Inclusive Development in UNDP. Guidance and entry point (2018)
2. Weijerman, M.E., de Winter, J.P.: Clinical practice the care of children with Down syndrome. Conseq. Down Syndrome Patient Family **169**, 11 (2011)
3. ECNP: Down Syndrome and other genetic developmental disorders network (n.d.). Accessed 1 June 2019. https://www.ecnp.eu/research-innovation/ECNP-networks/List-ECNP-Networks/Down-syndrome
4. Jacobs, P., Baikie, A.G., Strong, J.A.: The somatic chromosomes in mongolism. Lancet **273**(7075), 710 (1959)
5. Nadel, L. (ed.): The Psychobiology of DS. Issues in the Biology of Language and Cognition. The MIT Press, Cambridge (1988)
6. Chapman, R., Hesketh, L.: Behavioral phenotype of individuals with DS. Ment. Retard. Dev. Disabil. Res. Rev. **6**(2), 84–95 (2000)
7. Daunhauer, L.A., Fidler, D.J., Will, E.: School function in students with down syndrome. Am. J. Occup. Ther. **68**(2), 167–176 (2014)
8. Buttimer, J., Tierney, E.: Patterns of leisure participation among adolescents with a mild intellectual disability. J. Intellect. Disabil. **9**(1), 25–42 (2005)
9. Gates, B., Atherton, H.: Learning Disabilities: Toward Inclusion. Elsevier Health Sciences, London (2007)
10. Acedo, M.T., Herrera, S.S., Traver, M.T.: Las TIC como herramienta de apoyo para personas con Trastorno del Espectro Autista (TEA). Revista de Educación Inclusiva **9**(2-bis), 102–136 (2017)
11. Chen, S.S., Bernard-Opitz, V.: Comparison of personal and computer-assisted instruction for children with autism. Ment. Retard. **31**(6), 368 (1993)
12. Ahmad, W.F.W., Muddin, H.N.B.I., Shafie, A.: Number skills mobile application for Down syndrome children. In: International Conference on Computer and Information Sciences on Proceedings, pp. 1–6. Convention Center, Kuala Lumpur, Malaysia (2014)
13. Ortega-Tudela, J.M., Gómez-Ariza, C.J.: Computer-assisted teaching and mathematical learning in down syndrome children. J. Comput. Assist. Learn. **22**(4), 298–307 (2006)
14. Black, B., Wood, A.: Utilising information communication technology to assist the education of individuals with DS. Technical Report: The DS Educational Trust, Portmouth, UK (2003). Accessed https://scinapse.io/papers/2167202491
15. Cano, A.R., Fernández-Manjón, B., García-Tejedor, Á.J.: Using game learning analytics for validating the design of a learning game for adults with intellectual disabilities. Br. J. Educ. Technol. **49**(4), 659–672 (2018)
16. Cinquin, P., Guitton, P., Sauzéon, H.: Online e-learning and cognitive disabilities: a systematic review. Comput. Educ. Elsevier **130**, 152–167 (2019)
17. Rus, S., Braun, A.: Money handling training-applications for persons with down syndrome. In: 12th International Conference on Intelligent Environments (IE) on Proceedings, London, 2016, pp. 214–217 (2016)
18. Felix, G.V., Mena, J.L., Ostos, R., Maestre, E.: A pilot study of the use of emerging computer technologies to improve the effectiveness of reading and writing therapies in children with Down syndrome. Br. J. Edu. Technol. **48**(2), 611–624 (2016)

19. Shafie, A., et al.: "SynMax": a mathematics application tool for down syndrome children. In: Zaman, H.B., Robinson, P., Olivier, P., Shih, Timothy K., Velastin, S. (eds.) IVIC 2013. LNCS, vol. 8237, pp. 615–626. Springer, Cham (2013). https://doi.org/10.1007/978-3-319-02958-0_56

20. Bargagna, S., et al.: Computer-based cognitive training in adults with down's syndrome. In: Stephanidis, C., Antona, M. (eds.) UAHCI 2014. LNCS, vol. 8514, pp. 197–208. Springer, Cham (2014). https://doi.org/10.1007/978-3-319-07440-5_19

21. Buchner, T., et al.: Paving the way through mainstream education: the interplay of families, schools and disabled students. Res. Pap. Educ. 30(4), 411–426 (2015)

22. Lendrum, A., Barlow, A., Humphrey, N.: Developing positive school–home relationships through structured conversations with parents of learners with special educational needs and disabilities (SEND). J. Res. Spec. Educ. Needs 15(2), 87–96 (2015)

23. West, E., Pirtle, J.: Mothers' and fathers' perspectives on quality special educators and the attributes that influence effective inclusive practices. Educ. Train. Autism Dev. Disabil. 49(2), 290–300 (2014)

24. Falkmer, M., Anderson, K., Joosten, A., Falkmer, T.: Parents' perspectives on inclusive schools for children with autism spectrum conditions. Int. J. Disabil. Dev. Educ. 62(1), 1–23 (2015)

25. Bysterveldt, V.A., Westerveld, M., Garvis, S.: Parents' and teacher aides' perceptions and expectations of the language and communication abilities of children with Down syndrome. Speech Lang. Hear. 22, 1–12 (2018)

26. Vaughan, M., Henderson, A.: Exceptional educators: a collaborative training partnership for the inclusion of students with Down's syndrome. Support Learn. 31(1), 46–58 (2016)

27. Moats, L.C., Farrell, M.L.: Multisensory structured language education. In: Birsh, J.R. (ed.) Multisensory Teaching of Basic Language Skills, pp. 23–41. Paul Brookes Publishing, Baltimore (2005)

28. Sorden, S.: A cognitive approach to instructional design for multimedia learning. Inform. Sci. Int. J. Emerg. Transdiscipl. 8, 263–279 (2005)

29. IMS Global Homepage. https://www.imsglobal.org/accessibility/accessiblevers/sec3.html. Accessed 29 Mar 2020

30. Web Accessibility Initiatives Homepage. https://www.w3.org/WAI/. Accessed 29 Mar 2020

31. LLM Care Homepage. www.llmcare.gr/en. Accessed 29 Mar 2020

32. BrainHQ Homepage. www.brainhq.com. Accessed 29 Mar 2020

33. wFitForAll Homepage. www.fitforall.gr. Accessed 29 Mar 2020

34. Bamidis, P.D., et al.: Gains in cognition through combined cognitive and physical training: the role of training dosage and severity of neurocognitive disorder. Front. Aging Neurosci. 7, 152 (2015)

35. Romanopoulou, E., Zilidou, V., Savvidis, T., Chatzisevastou-Loukidou, C., Bamidis, P.: Unmet needs of persons with down syndrome: how assistive technology and game- based training may fill the gap. Stud. Health Technol. Inform. 251, 15–18 (2018)

36. O'Neill, B., Gillespie, A.: Simulating naturalistic instruction: the case for a voice mediated interface for assistive technology for cognition. J. Assist. Technol. 2(2), 22–31 (2008)

37. Metaxa, M., et al.: Enhancing verbal working memory of persons with down syndrome through a digital game: an experimental approach. In: 8th Hellenic Society for Biomedical Technology on Proceedings, p. 69, Athens, Greece (2019)

38. Miller, G.A.: The magical number seven, plus or minus two: some limits on our capacity for processing information. Psychol. Rev. 63(2), 81 (1956)

39. DS Leisure Homepage. www.dsleisure.eu. Accessed 29 Mar 2020

40. Metaxa, M., et al.: Co-creating innovative tools with and for people with intellectual disabilities: the case of DS leisure e-training platform. In: OpenLivingLab Days Conference "Co-creating Innovation: Scaling-up from Local to Global" on Proceedings, Thessaloniki, Greece, pp. 115–126 (2019)

41. Wechsler, D.: Manual for the Wechsler Adult Intelligence Scale. Psychological Corporation, New York (1955)
42. Gillespie, A., Best, C., O'Neill, B.: Cognitive function and assistive technology for cognition: a systematic review. J. Int. Neuropsychol. Soc. **18**(1), 1–19 (2012)
43. Rowe, J., Lavender, A., Turk, V.: Cognitive executive function in down's syndrome. Br. J. Clin. Psychol. **45**(1), 5–17 (2006)

Distance Learning for Secondary Education Students. The Role of Educational Neuroscience

Spyridon Doukakis[1](✉) and Evita C. Alexopoulos[2]

[1] Department of Informatics, Ionian University, 7 Tsirigoti Square, 49132 Corfu, Greece
sdoukakis@ionio.gr
[2] Pierce-the American College of Greece, 6 Gravias Str., 15342 Agia Paraskevi, Athens, Greece
evitaalexopoulos@acg.edu

Abstract. Distance education has been an alternative to traditional education for several decades. However, during the pandemic, distance education was the only solution that could be applied, in order to continue the educational process and at the same time to protect the health of students and their families. This form is described as Emergency Remote Teaching, because although it is based on online teaching practices, it does not fully use the principles of distance education and does not include educational design and operation models developed in the context of distance education. Despite the limited integration of the principles of distance education, efforts are made to enhance learning, develop knowledge and skills, and modify students' attitudes through the educational process. In this context, the role of educational neuroscience is important and the use of the results of relevant research is crucial in order to enhance learning. After a brief description of the framework of implementation of Emergency Remote Teaching, this article presents difficulties that arise from this implementation and describes ways in which these difficulties can be reduced, according to findings in the field of educational neuroscience research.

Keywords: Educational neuroscience · Emergency remote teaching · Educational practices

1 Introduction

In recent decades, distance education has witnessed an increase as it is offered in many different educational contexts (school education, university education, training). This increase has led a significant number of educators to be trained in its principles, to develop appropriate educational material so as to knowledgeably engage in distance education. At the same time, the development of new digital tools has provided significant opportunities to improve the online user experience. These tools are used to a high degree to offer successful learning experiences to participants (educators and learners) [1].

Thus, school structures, universities, and educational institutions offered education and training, using successful models, exclusively from a distance. In this context, the COVID-19 pandemic did not affect the operation of these structures, as the educational process had already been conducted remotely [2]. However, educational structures using

© Springer Nature Switzerland AG 2020
C. Frasson et al. (Eds.): BFAL 2020, LNAI 12462, pp. 160–168, 2020.
https://doi.org/10.1007/978-3-030-60735-7_17

physical spaces (e.g. school buildings, university amphitheaters) were forced to suspend the provision of educational services in these spaces and to use a distance education model so as to continue the educational process smoothly.

Despite the intensive effort of these educational structures, continued smooth operation was not an easy task due to: (a) the necessity of immediate implementation of distance education, (b) the inexperience of educators, (c) the absence of an implementation plan, and (d) the lack of students' experience in the new model of education. The above circumstances led to the implementation of a varied model, that of Emergency Remote Teaching (ERT). ERT is unquestionably distance learning, but with several differences.

In this article, ERT is introduced and distinguished from distance learning not only because of the possible lack of training and experience of educators called upon to practice ERT, but also due to the impossibility of applying the design and implementation principles of distance education. It is due to these differences, that questions arose related to the possible difficulties faced by both educators and students, the pedagogical potentiality of digital tools to achieve learning, and, ultimately, the success of the distance education project.

In this context, the researchers' contribution from the fields of cognitive science, psychology, and education is crucial. At the same time, the research findings from the field of educational neuroscience can be a guide for both the improvement of educational practices and the training of educators. Therefore, educational neuroscience plays a key role in reducing pedagogical problems and increasing learning opportunities. For this purpose, after defining ERT, a discussion on educational neuroscience follows, where research results are presented and their connection with distance education is attempted. The work concludes with suggestions for educational practices and suggestions for further research in distance education, which can transform the knowledge of educators and students with the ultimate goal of improving the educational process.

2   Distance Learning and Emergency Remote Teaching

The development of computer tools and software that support distance education, facilitated people, so that with a computer machine (computer, tablet, mobile phone) and an internet connection they can participate in online teaching courses. Distance learning can be done synchronously or asynchronously. Furthermore, a sturdy online educational program does not limit itself to a linear transmission of knowledge as online education recognizes learning as a social and cognitive process. Therefore, it capitalizes on building into the educational process different types of learner interaction (with content, with educator, with other learners) [2].

According to researchers, successful participation in online teaching structures occurs within an "ecosystem of learner supports" that is built over time and includes similar mechanisms, such as library resources, career services, university social networks, etc., to those offered in face to face (F2F) education and which, of course, require time and funding. Therefore, "effective online learning results from careful instructional design and planning, using a systematic model for design and development" [2].

The urgency of dealing with the pandemic did not allow educational structures that used primarily physical spaces (e.g. school buildings, university amphitheaters) to develop an "ecosystem of learner supports" with similar characteristics and mechanisms to those available in distance education structures. On the contrary, what must be assumed is that the pandemic and the requirement for social isolation it enforced obliged educators around the world to switch teaching modes almost overnight. The educational planning for the integrated application of distance education was not possible and, therefore, an attempt was made to either implement or adapt the lesson plans to the new educational environment. Thus, the educator had to adapt and come up with solutions to engage and connect with a physically absent class and, finally, to use less familiar or even entirely novel technology. As a result, it can be safely argued that what is currently happening in virtual classrooms and schools around the world is not online teaching, but teaching that is in many ways reactive to the extreme and unprecedented circumstances of the pandemic. Despite educators' "best intentions to serve their learners" needs, the quality of service resulted in "suboptimal" teaching [2, 3]. Consequently, this form of teaching should not be described as online teaching but rather should be recognized as Emergency Remote Teaching (ERT), distinguished from the former and evaluated accordingly.

Taking into account the above and adding (a) the need to modify the profile of the educational unit due to the new conditions and (b) the different needs of educators and students, the implementation framework becomes complex and, as a result, the outcome might often be a "pick and mix" approach for instructional methods, implementation tools, as well as learners' needs. ERT will operate in an idiosyncratic context where faculty is learning and /or training in new technologies, in new lesson designs, while teaching at the same time since schools are still in operation. Therefore, ERT faces a lot of challenges that online education has resolved.

At the same time, the choice of emergency solutions may result in a disregard of pedagogy and of a systematic model for lesson design and execution, and in the conducting of weak lessons or lessons relying partly on chance and /or practical solutions, which, even if they work, will cause heightened stress levels in instructors. Finally, it is important to point out that these idiosyncratic, largely random, choices that are not based on the principles of distance education pedagogy can lead to negative attitudes towards distance education, as both educators and students may confuse what is ERT with structured and well-defined distance education [2].

In recent years, educational neuroscience has made a significant contribution to the development of new perspectives on the educational process, based on research results which can contribute to the improvement of learning. These findings can be applied both in the school environment and in the environment where the learner works and prepares for learning, such as his /her home. In this context, the next chapter will attempt to present research findings in the field of educational neuroscience and connect these with distance education, in general, and ERT, in particular, findings that can translate into successful teaching practices.

3 Educational Neuroscience

Through neuroscience, attempts are made to explain the working of the brain and the connected nervous system, the functional architecture of the mind, and how the brain and mind work together. With their research in the field, scientists enhance their knowledge of the neural mechanisms underlying human development and learning. The use of brain imaging techniques, such as functional magnetic resonance imaging (fMRI), electroencephalography (EEG), and positron emission topography (PET), provide data that helps to explore the functional organization of the human brain. In recent years, there has been a rapid development of the neuroscience industry, which has led to several collaborations with other areas of human activity. Education is one such discipline since the incorporation of neuroscience can enhance our understanding of the mental and physiological processes involved in learning. The extensive attempts to connect neuroscience, cognitive science, psychology, and education have resulted in a fast-growing interdisciplinary field of study which has been labeled as "Educational Neuroscience," "Mind, Brain, and Education Science," "Neuroeducation" (see Fig. 1).

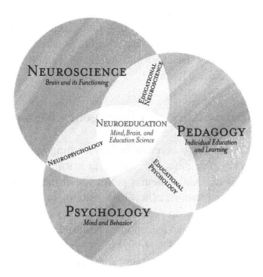

Fig. 1. The Emergence of Neuroeducation Source: Interpretation of Tokuhama-Espinosa's Transdisciplinary Field by Nakagawa, (2008), redrawn by Bramwell 2010.

In this new area, professionals in the field of education, cognitive scientists, and neuroscientists collaborate to use the results of neuroscience research in educational contexts [4, 5]. Educational Neuroscience or Neuroeducation "better reflects a field with education at its core, uniquely characterized by its own methods and techniques, and which constructs knowledge based on experiential, social and biological evidence" [6]. Some research groups have argued the existence of a gulf between the findings in neuroscience and educational practice while others have developed models and frameworks for applying the findings to everyday teaching practice [7, 8].

Educational practice is a complex matter. Educators have at their disposal a variety of tools from which they must choose the most appropriate to enhance their pedagogical approaches and their approaches to subject matter. However, the complexity of the brain and its role in achieving learning is crucial. Given that the achievement of the desired learning outcomes is not significantly affected by the quality of educators [9], but by the way the educator will "influence" the context of the learner's brain, educator training in educational neuroscience is a necessity. With this training, educators will be enabled to evaluate teaching practices, will be able to add and remove teaching tools and techniques, thus offering strategies and models, which, according to educational neuroscience research, contribute to learning. In addition, it is possible to see that the teaching and learning practices that follow are validated by the results of research in the field of educational neuroscience. However, the ultimate gain from training educators in educational neuroscience is the transformation of their knowledge which will eventually result in improving student knowledge and learning.

It is particularly interesting that educators with knowledge of how the brain works claim that they are highly capable of influencing their students' learning in relation to the untrained educators [10, 11]. What is more, it seems that educators who know how the brain learns, differentiate their educational practice, recognizing multiple teaching and learning pathways, and, therefore, rejecting the educational model that provides "the same recipe" for all students. In the next section, an attempt will be made, based on research findings, to identify strategies and actions that can improve the educational process in both ERT and distance learning.

4   Educational Neuroscience and Emergency Remote Teaching

The flexibility of the brain and the acceptance that learning ability is neither predetermined nor constant is a key parameter for improving learning [12]. Plasticity describes how different experiences reorganize neural pathways in the brain. In this way, when someone learns new things or memorizes new information, long-term functional changes take place in the brain. In addition to genetic factors, a person's brain is shaped by the characteristics of the environment and its actions. Therefore, when someone learns something, s/he develops the brain in one of the following ways: (a) by creating a new pathway, which is initially subtle, but is fortified the more s/he delves into the concept under study; (b) by further strengthening an existing pathway; and (c) by forming a new connection between two previously disconnected pathways. In addition, when these pathways are no longer needed, they gradually disappear [13]. As a result, people need to be trained so that when they encounter a difficult subject, they make a conscious effort to strengthen the brain areas needed in order to persist more on the subject rather than to decide that they are not capable of dealing with it [14].

In the context of distance education, the integration of multiple and different activities is necessary to enhance learning. In addition, due to the multiple tools, such as the private chat, the group chat, teamwork opportunities, optional digital tools, the shared whiteboard, etc., available in distance education, the development of neural pathways and connections can be enhanced and, as a result, opportunities for the learner to gain experience and acquire new learning become unlimited.

Furthermore, assessment for learning and assessment of learning have been shown to play a key role in determining a person's knowledge, as well as in shaping his/her knowledge [15]. Providing frequent and non-threatening assessment of an idea or concept, along with appropriate feedback, plays an important role in memory consolidation.

In the context of distance education, digital environments include a variety of tools that can enhance memory consolidation (creating online assignments, quizzes, gamification of activities, etc.) [15]. The use of formative assessment during distance learning is necessary so that the student can see what s/he knows and the educator can evaluate which of the expected learning outcomes have been achieved by the student and to what extent. This assessment helps and strengthens the student while, at the same time, improving the way the educator works.

Any form of assessment is very likely to highlight difficulties and obstacles for students. Exploiting the obstacles and misunderstandings of students can play a crucial role in distance education. Although in an educational context mistakes have been associated with consequences such as punishment or grade reduction, their utilization in distance education provides opportunities for brain development. As part of the learning process, dealing with obstacles and correcting mistakes enhances neural connections, speeding up and enriching the learning experience. Research highlights the positive effects of exploiting students' mistakes, as this enhances the transformation of one's knowledge [16].

Designing educational scenarios with open-ended questions that have more than one correct answer is important for educators in order to work on misunderstandings and to help students to overcome the obstacles they encounter. By using appropriate digital tools in distance education, students can experiment, overcome obstacles, highlight, and reduce mistakes in order to develop their brain. With the ability to make immediate use of different resources, students can work in groups creatively. Error detection activities, progressive error reduction strategies, and practices that will encourage experimentation without being associated with negative consequences in the event of an error can lead to an ideal learning experience [17]. In addition, the ability for each student to answer a question using the personal chat or send an answer to the educator without being able to see the answers of other students, gives the educator the opportunity to observe and record potential problems and to work with them, thus enhancing learning in remote environments.

Neural pathways and learning are optimized when the student has the opportunity to consider a concept or idea using a multidimensional approach. According to the literature, the multidimensional approach plays a crucial role in student involvement [18]. The educator has the obligation to offer multiple opportunities for the development and reorganization of the neural pathways in the brain of his/her students. To do this, educators must design lessons that allow students to try new strategies and to seek information using activities that explore open-ended topics or by giving students the opportunity to work in different ways and exploiting different pathways that lead to the same answer. At the same time, it is important for educators to maximize the strategies that promote positive emotion [19]. Research has shown that while threats hinder learning, positive emotional experiences, in which the brain produces certain chemicals or neurotransmitters, can contribute to long-term memory. Moreover, research shows that different areas of the brain are activated depending on the activity one engages in. Therefore, in the context of distance learning, it is useful for students to work on activities that can be approached in different ways, instead of being assigned identical or similar questions /exercises. For example, it is interesting to try to work on problems that can be solved (a) with operations, (b) diagrammatically, (c) algorithmically (coding) and (d) by developing a story about the problem, creating an image or constructing an object [20].

Two more issues that arise from the field of educational neuroscience and are related to distance education are (a) the value of speed in relation to creativity and flexibility and (b) student collaboration. More specifically, when students approach concepts and ideas with creativity and flexibility, they seem to optimize their learning [21]. Conversely, when people generally work under pressure, their working memory decreases and, consequently, at first they become anxious and then they feel that "their mind has stopped" [22]. For this reason, working time needs to be granted without a request for information reproduction or speed of action since the development of neural pathways and synapses is a slow process.

The importance of working with other people to strengthen neural pathways and learning is also a good practice in distance learning [23]. This last dimension comes to highlight the value of the sociocultural approach to learning [24] and the need to provide students with such opportunities in multiple ways.

5   Conclusion

In this paper, an attempt was made to approach distance education through the context of Emergency Remote Teaching (ERT) and based on the results from the field of educational neuroscience. The findings of educational neuroscience related to brain plasticity, methods of student assessment, instruction through the use of multiple representations, creativity, flexibility, collaboration, and positive emotional experiences can be applied and can enhance distance learning. In this way, educators who want to implement strategies based on educational neuroscience research can transform their practices, assess the impact of what they are trying to modify, and, eventually, be led to sustainable long-term solutions that can be used in the classical frameworks.

It is important to evaluate these options with further research and targeted activities that follow the principles and methodologies described. The proposals could be implemented by simultaneously monitoring the student's brain during the lesson in order to identify the activated brain areas and creating a trigger that will warn the educator when a student is distracted or does not understand a concept. Neurofeedback [25] and the recording and measurement of digital biomarkers could play a key role in (a) measuring brain activity according to the tasks, (b) recording how knowledge acquisition can be supported by neuroscience tools, and (c) suggesting how content can be adapted according to biofeedback measures. In this way, the personalized and differentiated learning that can easily be offered in distance education through learning management systems can become a reality and can help students to maximize their knowledge. The aforementioned approach is crucial as the educational process is all the more required to strengthen skills, to change attitudes, and to enhance learning.

References

1. Moore, M.G., Resta, P., Rumble, G., Tait, A., Zaparovanny, Y.: Open and distance learning: trends, policy and strategy considerations. UNESCO (2002)

2. Hodges, C., Moore, S., Lockee, B., Trust, T., Bond, A.: The difference between emergency remote teaching and online learning. https://er.educause.edu/articles/2020/3/the-difference-between-emergency-remote-teaching-and-online-learning. Accessed 27 Mar 2020

3. Czerniewicz, L., Walji, S.: Issues for Universities Using Private Companies for Online Education. University of Cape Town, Cape Town (2019)

4. Ansari, D., Coch, D., De Smedt, B.: Connecting education and cognitive neuroscience: where will the journey take us? Educ. Philos. Theory **43**(1), 37–42 (2011)

5. Nouri, A.: The basic principles of research in neuroeducation studies. Int. J. Cogn. Res. Sci. Eng. Educ. **4**(1), 59 (2016)

6. Howard-Jones, P.A.: A multiperspective approach to neuroeducational research. Educ. Philos. Theory **43**(1), 24–30 (2011)

7. Horvath, J.C., Donoghue, G.M.: A bridge too far–revisited: reframing Bruer's neuroeducation argument for modern science of learning practitioners. Front. Psychol. **7**, 377 (2016)

8. Brookman-Byrne, A., Commissar, L.: Future avenues for educational neuroscience from the perspective of EARLI SIG 22 conference attendees. Mind Brain Educ. **13**(3), 176–183 (2019)

9. Leithwood, K., Sun, J., Schumacker, R.: How school leadership influences student learning: a test of "The Four Paths Model". Educ. Adm. Q. https://doi.org/10.1177/0013161X19878772 (2017)

10. JohnBull, R.M., Hardiman, M., Rinne, L.: Professional development effects on teacher efficacy: exploring how knowledge of neuro-and cognitive sciences changes beliefs and practices. In: Annual Meeting of the American Educational Research Association, San Francisco, CA (2013)

11. Whitman, G., Kelleher, I.: Neuroteach: Brain Science and the Future of Education. Rowman and Littlefield, Maryland (2016)

12. Rees, P., Booth, R., Jones, A.: The emergence of neuroscientific evidence on brain plasticity: implications for educational practice. Educ. Child Psychol. **33**(1), 8–19 (2016)

13. Anderson, R.K., Boaler, J., Dieckmann, J.A.: Achieving elusive teacher change through challenging myths about learning: a blended approach. Educ. Sci. **8**(3), 98 (2018)

14. Darling-Hammond, L., Flook, L., Cook-Harvey, C., Barron, B., Osher, D.: Implications for educational practice of the science of learning and development. Appl. Dev. Sci. **24**(2), 97–140 (2020)

15. Hwang, G.J., Chang, H.F.: A formative assessment-based mobile learning approach to improving the learning attitudes and achievements of students. Comput. Educ. **56**(4), 1023–1031 (2011)

16. Moser, J.S., Schroder, H.S., Heeter, C., Moran, T.P., Lee, Y.H.: Mind your errors: Evidence for a neural mechanism linking growth mind-set to adaptive posterror adjustments. Psychol. Sci. **22**(12), 1484–1489 (2011)

17. Nottingham, J.: The Learning Challenge: How to Guide Your Students Through the Learning Pit to Achieve Deeper Understanding. Sage Publications, London (2017)

18. Niiya, Y., Brook, A.T., Crocker, J.: Contingent self-worth and self-handicapping: do incremental theorists protect self-esteem? Self Identity **9**(3), 276–297 (2010)

19. Hardiman, M.M.: The Brain-Targeted Teaching Model for 21st-Century Schools. Corwin Press, Thousand Oaks (2012)

20. Boaler, J.: Urban success: a multidimensional mathematics approach with equitable outcomes. Phi Delta Kappan **87**(5), 364–369 (2006)

21. Novick, J.M., Bunting, M.F., Engle, R.W., Dougherty, M.R. (eds.): Cognitive and Working Memory Training: Perspectives from Psychology, Neuroscience, and Human Development. Oxford University Press, Oxford (2019)

22. Beilock, S.: Back to school: dealing with academic stress. Psychol. Sci. Agenda **25**(9), 1–5 (2011)

23. Decety, J., Jackson, P.L., Sommerville, J.A., Chaminade, T., Meltzoff, A.N.: The neural bases of cooperation and competition: an fMRI investigation. Neuroimage **23**(2), 744–751 (2004)
24. Wertsch, J.V., Toma, C.: Discourse and learning in the classroom: a sociocultural approach. In: Steffe, L.P., Gale, J. (eds.) Constructivism in Education, pp. 177–192. Routledge, London (2012)
25. Marsel, M., et al.: How to build a hybrid neurofeedback platform combining EEG and fMRI. Frontiers in Neuroscience **11**, 140 (2017)

Towards a Reference Model to Ensure the Quality of Massive Open Online Courses and E-Learning

Christos Troussas[✉], Akrivi Krouska, and Cleo Sgouropoulou

Department of Informatics and Computer Engineering, University of West Attica, Egaleo, Greece
{ctrouss,akrouska,csgouro}@uniwa.gr

Abstract. The proliferation of Internet has introduced new technological advances into digital education. One of them is the Massive Open Online Courses (MOOCs). MOOCs are online learning environments offering educational programs to large numbers of geographically dispersed students, free of charge. The rapid development of MOOCs leads to investigate their provided quality of learning, consisting of a combination of factors such as the development life cycle of MOOCs, the quality criteria and the involved members. In view of the above, this paper presents QUMMEL (Quality Model for MOOCs and E-Learning) which is a novel reference model for assessing the quality in e-learning and MOOCs. QUMMEL is a three-dimensional model, being consisted of distinct phases, perspectives and roles. It represents a holistic approach for ensuring quality in either a MOOC or an e-learning environment in terms of pedagogical, technological and strategic perspectives. The evaluation results of applying the QUMMEL in the development of a MOOC are very promising and can offer a fertile ground to foster quality in e-learning.

Keywords: E-Learning · Reference model · MOOCs · Quality assurance in e-learning

1 Introduction

During the last years, the rapid development of technology has reformed and modernized the field of education. Such technological advancements gave birth to Massive Open Online Courses (MOOCs). MOOCs are online courses aimed at unlimited participation and open access via the web [1]. In addition to traditional course materials such as filmed lectures, readings, and problem sets, many MOOCs provide interactive courses with user forums to support community interactions among students, professors, and teaching assistants (TAs), as well as, immediate feedback to quick quizzes and assignments [2]. Hence, many researchers worldwide design and build MOOCs in order to provide an integrated learning experience to students and offer a student-centric learning environment. However, there is an increasingly arising challenge concerning the existing available options to deliver more coherent learning applications based on

© Springer Nature Switzerland AG 2020
C. Frasson et al. (Eds.): BFAL 2020, LNAI 12462, pp. 169–175, 2020.
https://doi.org/10.1007/978-3-030-60735-7_18

students' needs and preferences. As such, a clear understanding of the preferred style of instruction, individual preferences and social needs is the cornerstone to provide quality in e-learning [3].

There are several factors in designing effective e-learning applications [4, 5]. The organization and delivery of the learning material is an important factor reflecting quality in e-learning since learners can be offered best practices and enhance their performance. Sufficient chances for synchronous or asynchronous communication along with manners of collaboration can provide a fertile ground in long-time instruction with respect to the delivery methods of the educational material [6]. Moreover, the design of the learning environment plays a leading role in the quality of e-learning; an effective learning environment can on the one hand offer data and information with regard to the educational process and on the other hand keep learners engaged throughout their effort [3, 7]. Furthermore, the content of the course should be concise and consistent in order to advance the knowledge levels of the students [8]. This factor should encompass modeling of students in order to provide a personalized and self-paced way in digital instruction [9]. As such, grain-size learning involving learning objects split into smaller nuggets can serve for an efficient learning content. Interactions between students and computers are very crucial since they involve issues such as tailored assessment opportunities and types, adaptation of the learning activity based on learners' misconception or even individualized advice to them [10, 11].

In view of the above, it is inferred that quality in the educational process cannot be simply delivered by an e-learning platform. Indeed, it should be incorporated as a main framework which will be applied at the design of the platform and will involve all the stakeholders (e.g. learners, instructors, software designers) and their interaction with the environment. Moreover, quality in e-learning cannot be measured solely by the achievement of the leaning outcomes; it involves every method and technique that is utilized to offer the learner an environment full of opportunities and to serve as modules servicing the instructional aspects.

The necessity of providing quality in e-learning is further accentuated by universities and educational organizations [12]. Given that their main activity is education, they perceive quality as a unidirectional future perspective. Hence, they seek to establish quality standards in all the educational services provided to students in terms of flexibility, learning material delivery, dynamicness and ubiquitousness. However, there is lack of and generally accepted qualifiers of quality [13]. There is an emerging need to implement such an education model, which substantially contributes to the enhancement of the quality of universities and educational organizations [13].

This paper presents QUMMEL (Quality Model for MOOCs and E-Learning) which is a novel reference model for assessing the quality in e-learning and MOOCs. QUMMEL is a three-dimensional model, being consisted of distinct phases, perspectives and roles. It presents a holistic approach for ensuring quality in either a MOOC or an e-learning environment in terms of pedagogical, technological and strategic perspectives. QUMMEL was fully evaluated and the experimental results show that it can serve for building qualitative and effective learning technology systems. The main benefits of QUMMEL are:

- It provides a generic framework that can be adapted to each specific context.

- It identifies key quality criteria for better orientation on the MOOC design.
- It presents a checklist for the quality development and evaluation of MOOCs.
- It enables a continuous improvement cycle for MOOC design and provision.

The remainder of this paper is structured as follows. Firstly, the related work is presented. In Sect. 3, the overview of QUMMEL is described. Following, the evaluation of QUMMEL is conducted using a system developed based on this model and an established framework for evaluating it, and its results are discussed. Finally, the conclusions are drawn and the future plans are shown.

2 Related Work

Many research efforts regarding the measurement of the quality in e-learning and MOOCS have been presented. For example, in [14], the authors provided a roadmap in terms of the meanings, uses, evolution, and applicability of the variables in assessing the quality in e-learning.

Another work, by [15], presents a framework which involves both internal and external learner factors having impact on the educational procedure. More specifically, the authors mention that the learners' state of mind and the technology experience can affect the quality of the learning process.

In [16], the authors present an e-quality framework, oriented in socio-cultural thinking. It involves practical and theoretical knowledge and focuses solely on virtual institutions.

In [17], the author presents a framework which includes several quality criteria and standards. These criteria mainly focus on specific modalities of e-learning systems such as the design, the structure and the delivery of the learning material, the ways of assistance provided to learners, the assessment tool and the teaching strategies.

In [18], a quality framework is also presented. This framework lies in the determination of several aspects such as accessibility, flexibility, interactiveness, personalization and productivity within the field of e-learning in higher education.

In [19], the authors present a model for quality evaluation. This model mainly focuses on the course material design, the flexibility, the learning support and the learner-computer interaction.

However, after a thorough investigation in the related scientific literature, we came up with the result that the quality measurements mainly focus on the resources and the processes pertaining the open and distance learning. There is a research gap on the identification and measurement of output and outcome of the learning process which are also taken into consideration in this research.

3 Overview of QUMMEL

QUMMEL consists of three dimensions including quality criteria and instruments:

- Dimension 1 – Phases: Analysis, Design, Implementation, Realization, Evaluation. The phases are dependent of each other, but are processed in parallel, corresponding to the development life cycle of the MOOC. In particular, the evaluation phase starts at the beginning of the planning and designing of the MOOC allowing a formative evaluation of all processes. Therefore, the evaluation can ensure a continuous improvement cycle during all phases and the whole development of the MOOC.

- Dimension 2 – Perspectives: Pedagogical, Technological, and Strategic. Each perspective has to be considered and addressed in the five aforementioned phases. They refer to the quality criteria/requirements that should be achieved by each process of the phases in order to develop an effective MOOC.
- Dimension 3 – Roles: Designer, Facilitator, and Provider. It refers to the members involved into the development life cycle of the MOOC.

QUMMEL is based on the International ISO standard ISO/IEC 40180 (former ISO/IEC 19796-1), which ensures quality for learning, education and training. It is also based on results from mixed methods research survey in MOOQs and semi-structured interviews as well as the feedback from the MOOQ Workshops [20].

QUMMEL defines the processes of which each phase consists, as well as their quality criteria and the roles that are responsible for them or involved into them [20]. Therefore, MOOC designers, facilitators and providers have to select the appropriate and relevant phases and processes according to their situation, the learning objectives, target groups, context and conditions. Some processes are pre-specified and (partly or completely) defined by pre-conditions and requirements (e.g. the available resources, budget and staff). Nevertheless, it is recommended to document also these processes defined by pre-conditions and requirements to ensure all involved stakeholders are duly informed.

4   Evaluation of System Designed Based QUMMEL

QUMMEL was evaluated as presented in this section. An adaptive e-learning system for tutoring the programming language C# was designed and implemented, aligning to the dimensions of QUMMEL. More specifically, the e-learning system for C# programming was used by university students and delivered ten different chapters and quizzes for assessment. This adaptive e-learning system, using QUMMEL, was evaluated by learners and experts in the field of computer science and engineering. For the purposes of the evaluation, the framework of Scheerens [21] was used. It is comprised of the following indicators:

- Output indicators
- Outcome indicators
- Impact indicators

The Output indicators involve achievement measures, subject matter-based literacy and competencies (e.g., learning to learn). The Outcome indicators involve attainment measures, graduation rates, proportion of students, graduated without delay, drop-out rates and class repetition rates. Finally, the impact indicators involve quality issues, social participation rates, degree of social participation and skills shortages and surpluses.

In the evaluation study, the population was consisted of 10 experts who are faculty members in Greek universities, 2 instructors who also serve as faculty members with a cognitive subject of programming languages and 70 university students. The students were presented the learning platform and they used it for the scope of learning the programming language C# for an academic semester. Special reference was given to QUMMEL and the population (both learners and experts) was explained in depth the quality dimensions followed in the e-learning platform. After the interaction with the learning environment for the academic semester, the learners were given self-supplemented scale questionnaires pertaining to their learning experience and QUMMEL. Indeed, they paid attention thoroughly during their interaction with the system. The questionnaires included 35 closed questions, as follows:

- 11 questions concerning the Output indicators
- 14 questions concerning the Outcome indicators
- 10 questions concerning the Impact indicators

The above questions were aligned to the Scheerens framework [21] and followed a ranking from 0–5 (0 is negative and 5 is positive). Following, Table 1 depicts a small sample of questions that were asked to learners and instructors.

Table 1. Sample of evaluation's questionnaire.

N	Questions
1	Rate your competencies in C# programming after the interaction with the system
2	Rate the assessment tool of the e-learning platform
3	Did you think to drop out (quit learning) during the interaction with the system?
4	Rate your social participation (collaboration with peers)
5	Rate your learning outcomes
6	Rate your acquired skills in C# programming
7	Rate the degree of personalization offered by the system
8	Rate your overall experience
9	Rate the quality of instruction

The evaluation results are very promising, generating a fertile ground for the incorporation of QUMMEL for MOOCs and e-learning quality enhancement. The results show a high acceptance degree of QUMMEL which tends to fortify e-learning environments and offer a more effective and qualitative learning experience to students. Students declared that their learning outcome was achieved using the e-learning platform in a percentage of 82%. 88% of them stated that the assessment tool of the system was well-structured and effective and 84% of them declared that their skills in C# programming were improved. Their overall experience was very good as stated by 90% of them. Finally, 94% students declared that quality was assured using QUMMEL and it is an integral framework for promoting quality in e-learning.

Furthermore, the two instructors (faculty members in the field of programming languages) were posed several questions, such as: "Assess the drop-out rates of students",

"Assess the class repetition rates" and "Rate the quality of instructors". Since the evaluation study seeks to assess QUMMEL, their answers in the third question need to be underlined. Specifically, both instructors declared the high degree in quality of the e-learning platform and accentuated the fact that QUMMEL can enhance the quality in MOOCs and generally in e-learning.

Finally, the ten experts (faculty members in Greek universities) were asked to rate QUMMEL. All of them declared that QUMMEL can indeed enhance the quality of e-learning systems and proposed that it can serve as a guideline for future research efforts pertaining to the design and implementation of MOOCs and e-learning systems.

5   Conclusions

This paper presents QUMMEL which is a model for ensuring quality in MOOCs and e-learning in general. QUMMEL serves for better design of MOOCs, provides guidelines for quality development and evaluation while identifying key quality criteria for better organization of e-learning. QUMMEL is based on the International ISO standard ISO/IEC 40180 (former ISO/IEC 19796-1), the results from mixed methods research quality surveys for MOOQs and semi-structured interviews, as well as the feedback from MOOQ Workshops.

The evaluation results focusing mainly on the quality of MOOCs and e-learning arose from the incorporation of QUMMEL in an e-learning platform for C# programming tutoring. They are very promising and can offer a fertile ground to foster quality in e-learning. As such, future researchers can use the checklist of QUMMEL for designing and building qualitative personalized and adaptive e-learning systems.

Future plans include the evaluation of QUMMEL by learners, computer experts, facilitators and providers worldwide to the direction of creating an international standard for ensuring quality in MOOCs and e-learning.

References

1. Salamah, U., Helmi, R.A.A.: MOOC platforms: a review and comparison. Int. J. Eng. Technol. (UAE) **7**(4), 70–74 (2018)
2. Rasheed, R.A., Kamsin, A., Abdullah, N.A., Zakari, A., Haruna, K.: A systematic mapping study of the empirical MOOC literature. IEEE Access **7**, 124809–124827 (2019)
3. Littenberg-Tobias, J., Reich, J.: Evaluating access, quality, and equity in online learning: a case study of a MOOC-based blended professional degree program. Internet High. Educ. **47**, 100759 (2020)
4. Krouska, A., Troussas, C., Virvou, M.: SN-learning: an exploratory study beyond e-learning and evaluation of its applications using EV-SNL framework. J. Comput. Assist. Learn. **35**(2), 168–177 (2019)
5. Krouska, A., Troussas, C., Virvou, M.: A literature review of Social Networking-based Learning Systems using a novel ISO-based framework. Intell. Decis. Technol. **13**(1), 23–39 (2019)
6. Krouska, A., Troussas, C., Virvou, M.: Social networks as a learning environment: Developed applications and comparative analysis. In: 2017 8th International Conference on Information, Intelligence, Systems & Applications (IISA), pp. 1–6. IEEE (2017)

7. Deng, R., Benckendorff, P., Gannaway, D.: Linking learner factors, teaching context, and engagement patterns with MOOC learning outcomes. J. Comput. Assist. Learn. **36**, 688–708 (2020)

8. Troussas, C., Krouska, A., Virvou, M., Sougela, E.: Using hierarchical modeling of thinking skills to lead students to higher order cognition and enhance social e-learning. In: 2018 9th International Conference on Information, Intelligence, Systems and Applications (IISA), pp. 1–5. IEEE (2018)

9. Troussas, C., Krouska, A., Virvou, M.: Using a multi module model for learning analytics to predict learners' cognitive states and provide tailored learning pathways and assessment. In: Virvou, M., Alepis, E., Tsihrintzis, George A., Jain, Lakhmi C. (eds.) Machine Learning Paradigms. ISRL, vol. 158, pp. 9–22. Springer, Cham (2020). https://doi.org/10.1007/978-3-030-13743-4_2

10. Krouska, A., Troussas, C., Virvou, M.: Computerized adaptive assessment using accumulative learning activities based on revised bloom's taxonomy. In: Virvou, M., Kumeno, F., Oikonomou, K. (eds.) JCKBSE 2018. SIST, vol. 108, pp. 252–258. Springer, Cham (2019). https://doi.org/10.1007/978-3-319-97679-2_26

11. Troussas, C., Krouska, A., Virvou, M.: Adaptive e-learning interactions using dynamic clustering of learners' characteristics. In: 2019 10th International Conference on Information, Intelligence, Systems and Applications (IISA), pp. 1–7. IEEE (2019)

12. Torres-Coronas, T., Vidal-Blasco, M.A.: MOOC and blended learning models: analysis from a stakeholders' perspective. In: Online Course Management: Concepts, Methodologies, Tools, and Applications, pp. 276–288. IGI Global (2018)

13. Misut, M., Pribilova, K.: Measuring of quality in the context of e-learning. Procedia Soc. Behav. Sci. **177**, 312–319 (2015)

14. Vlachopoulos, D.: Assuring quality in e-learning course design: the roadmap. Int. Rev. Res. Open Distrib. Learn. IRRODL **17**(6), 183–205 (2016)

15. Pedram, S., Perez, P., Palmisano, S., Farrelly, M.: The factors affecting the quality of learning process and outcome in virtual reality environment for safety training in the context of mining industry. In: Cassenti, Daniel N. (ed.) AHFE 2018. AISC, vol. 780, pp. 404–411. Springer, Cham (2019). https://doi.org/10.1007/978-3-319-94223-0_38

16. Masoumi, D., Lindström, B.: Quality in e-learning: a framework for promoting and assuring quality in virtual institutions. J. Comput. Assist. Learn. **28**(1), 27–41 (2012)

17. Esfijani, A.: Measuring quality in online education: A meta-synthesis. Am. J. Distance Educ. **32**(1), 57–73 (2018)

18. Ossiannilsson, E., Landgren, L.: Quality in e-learning–a conceptual framework based on experiences from three international benchmarking projects. J. Comput. Assist. Learn. **28**(1), 42–51 (2012)

19. Hadullo, K., Oboko, R., Omwenga, E.: A model for evaluating e-learning systems quality in higher education in developing countries. Int. J. Educ. Dev. Using ICT **13**(2), 185–204 (2017)

20. Stracke, C.M., Tan, E.: The quality of open online learning and education: towards a quality reference framework for MOOCs. In: 13th International Conference of the Learning Sciences: Rethinking learning in the Digital Age: Making the Learning Sciences Count, pp. 1029–1032. International Society of the Learning Sciences (2018)

21. Scheerens, J., Luyten, H., van Ravens, J.: Measuring educational quality by means of indicators. In: Perspectives on Educational Quality, pp. 35–50. Springer, Dordrecht (2011)

Technology Contribution to Improve Autistic Children Life Quality

Zhoe Comas-González[1](✉), Andrés Sánchez-Comas[1], Emiro De-La-Hoz-Franco[1],
Kåre Synnes[2], Joaquín F. Sánchez[3], and Carlos Collazos-Morales[3](✉)

[1] Universidad de la Costa, Barranquilla, Colombia
zcomas1@cuc.edu.co
[2] Luleå Tekniska Universitet, Luleå, Sweden
[3] Universidad Manuela Beltrán, Bogotá, Colombia
carlos.collazos@docentes.umb.edu.co

Abstract. To review published literature on the use of technology and how it has improved autistic children life style. A systematic review of the English literature was performed using the PRISMA guideline. Papers indexed in WOS and Scopus databases were included, adjusted to a timeline between 2016 and 2020 and focused on mobile technology, interventions, improvement of social behavior and communication and autism, aimed to describe the most used mechanism to improve autistic life style. Thirty two (32) papers were included in the review. We obtained 14 papers on the Scopus database and 18 on the WOS database. The majority of studies evidenced the use of virtual reality, mobile devices, video modelling and robots as the most common applications for autism therapies. Technology has caused an improvement in autistic children life quality. The development of mobile applications, virtual reality applications and robots have showed a positive impact reflected in the performance of daily activities and a better understanding of how they feel, how to behave, how to express themselves and interact with others. Technology gives the opportunity to monitor children status; and offers adaptability, safety, and accuracy of the information.

Keywords: Autism spectrum disorder · Autism therapies · Technology intervention · Review of the literature

1 Introduction

Autism Spectrum Disorder (ASD) is a neurodevelopmental condition characterized by difficulties in social interaction and communication [1]. Repetitive and stereotyped behavior, visual fascination, adverse response to specific sounds, excessive smelling and verbal and non-verbal communication are some features that characterize autism [2]. Technology as an important tool, provides solution in any area. Health field has received relevant contribution from technology [3]. Along the years, scientist around the world have conducted researches which results have break paradigms in society, introduced new concepts and developed devices that have improved life quality of individuals. Technology has also generated changes in social schemes [4]. It allows to study

© Springer Nature Switzerland AG 2020
C. Frasson et al. (Eds.): BFAL 2020, LNAI 12462, pp. 176–185, 2020.
https://doi.org/10.1007/978-3-030-60735-7_19

the human body trough sensing, scanning, and some other techniques, enabling to make a deep search and obtain reliable results in a short time.

Related to the autism disorder, the literature shows how technology applications have been used to improve the life quality of children with autism. For example, with the use of collaborative virtual environments [5]. By the other hand, considering they avoid face to face communication, interact with animated dolls like avatars or robots help them to lose fear and gain security [2]. It promotes the concentration, the identification of patterns and confidence [2, 6]. This is a reason why this type of applications has been incorporated in the education field [7–9]. This study has the objective to review published literature on the use of technology and how it has improved the life quality of children with autism, based on the prism methodology. Video modelling, virtual environment, robots and mobile technology are the most used technological intervention with a positive impact.

The main objective of this study was to review published literature on the use of technology and how it has improved autistic children life quality. Specific research questions were: a) What type of technology has been used as therapies in autistic children? b) What type of technology is commonly used and is the most appropriate in therapies for autistic children? c) What are the challenges of technology in autistic children life quality? The paper is divided in four sections: the first one corresponds to the introduction. The second section describes the methodology and results. The third one describes the conceptual development and the fourth one the conclusions.

2 Methodology

We followed the Preferred Reporting Items for Systematic Reviews and Meta-Analyses (PRISMA) guidelines to perform a systematic review of the literature on technology and its main contribution to the autistic children life style [10, 11]. Studies were included if they: (1) were primarily focused on technology and/or autism life quality; (2) involved technological and some non-technological therapies or interventions (3) described the improvement in children dailies activities; (4) studies that required participants that used mobile devices, wearables, video game consoles and/or robotic toys; (5) were published in English language between 2016 and 2020; (6) were published as journals papers or proceeding papers [12].

Studies were excluded if a) they were related to autism in teenagers, young adults or adults; b) they were not related to autism; c) they were not related to therapies for autism; d) results published previous 2015; e) not written in English. We performed two deep searches in the cross-domain databases Scopus and Web of Science using the query defined for this study. In the first search we obtained 599 results. Then we filtered applying the exclusion criteria briefly mentioned below, eliminating the duplicated documents and obtaining 172 papers.

We included in the review a total of 32 publications. These were selected from 599 results (Fig. 1) with references discarded for not being related to autism or therapies for autism; for irrelevance of subject area and source (e.g., procedia computer science, cell) and to the source type. Virtual reality, mobile devices, video modelling and robots are the most common applications for autism therapies (Figs. 2, 3, 4 and Table 1).

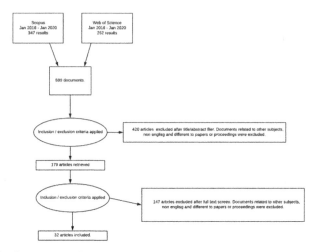

Fig. 1. PRISMA diagram of the literature review process. Own source.

Table 1. Queries performed in two research databases.

Database	Query	Results	Papers retained
Scopus	(Autism) AND (children) AND (technology) AND (Autism therapy)	347	14
Web of Science	(Autism) AND (children) AND (technology) AND (Autism therapy)	252	18

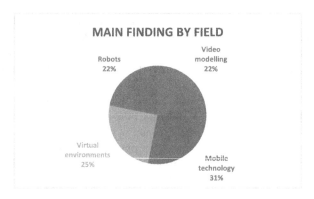

Fig. 2. Main finding by field. Own source.

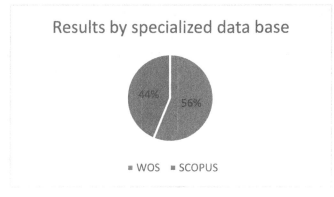

Fig. 3. Results by specialized data base. Own source.

Fig. 4. Typology of publication results. Own source.

3 Conceptual Development

Due the advances of technology, emerging solutions and trends are appearing in all fields [5]. Significant technological progress impact the life quality of individuals, which is reflected in a several factors like cultural, educative and economics [13, 14]. The authors [15] express in their job that "the technological evolution has created several convenient approaches to deal", which is true because nowadays we can find any kind of applications, solutions and contributions that impacts Health and Education. According to the review of the literature, technologies studies related to autism and life quality have emphasized on four types: video modelling based instruction, mobile technologies, virtual environments and robots [16–20]. The incursion of technology and ICT have generated new techniques which include mobile applications, wearables, Internet of Things or virtual environments [21–35]. Some studies have emphasized on four types of technologies, which are practical and usefull for autistic children, these ones are: video modelling based instruction, tactile devices, virtual environments, and robots [15].

3.1 Video Modelling Based Instructions and Tactile Devices

Video modeling (VM) is a good-practice used to teach social communication and daily living skills to students with autism [36–41]. Some studies have shown the effectiveness of this technique in the improvement of social capabilities [42] with Autism). VM consists in the imitation of patterns or situations recreated in a video, it helps to analyses the human behavior in children with autism [43].

Studies reveal the effectiveness in developing targeted skills and its achievement. Animated video modelling may contribute to a rapid acquisition of the attention and social engagement [42] (Fig. 5).

Fig. 5. Video modelling and tactile device [26].

Children with autism have a strong fascination for technology. The incursion of touch screen technologies have generated a transformative and positive effect in their lives.

Mobile applications promote the learning of abilities like the pronunciation and meaning of words, identification of colors and animals, numbers, clothes or seasons [44]. However, there is a large list of existing apps that can be downloaded from the App store or Google Play Store. These app are focused to help with a certain disability, there are ones for individuals with limitation of speak and deficiency of reading [26]. These type of technology has contributed positivity in the improvement of communicative abilities and learning. Some achievements are that ASD children can express themselves through simple sentences based on basic pictures; reread a phrase or write easy sentences [5]. This type of technological contributions help not only children with autism to have a better life, but also their parents, teachers and relatives to understand them better. The motivation plays an important role. The author [42] explain the use of an app to schedule dailies activities. Every task schedule corresponds to a goal for their children. The study [42] describe the functions of an app called TalNA. It is a touch screen learning based application designed to facilitate the learning of basic numeracy. Like other apps, they can be downloaded from the App Store or Google Play Store.

3.2 Virtual Environments

Virtual reality (VR) has been used for training autistic individuals since a long time. It has been proved a real effectiveness for the development of social skills, and how to perform daily activities [30]. The literature shows how it has been implemented to face several situations. Many serious games have been created to improve social interaction in autistic individuals [33]. The authors [34] uses virtual reality to teach autistic children how to cross the street and how to take a bus. The authors [35] developed a virtual environment to promote independent functioning among the autistic community. In this order, [36] developed a virtual environment called VR4VR System, for vocational training (Fig. 6).

Fig. 6. Virtual reality therapy [37].

The main contribution of virtual technology to the community is focused into teaching how behave and to interact with others. Being understood is an increasingly challenge nowadays, especially for them. Virtual reality gives them the possibility to express themselves and to be understood. It also facilitates learning process because its strong connection to a new and playful world, also due the lack of interaction with real people [37]. Furthermore, there are studies related to the use of technological accessories like virtual glasses or eye tracking. It helps to determine how engaged a children is with the virtual world by tracking the eye movement and their facial expressions [37].

3.3 Robots

Some interventions with technology are related to the interaction with robots. The idea of using robotic devices in autism therapies began in 1976 thanks to the study held by Weir and Emanuel [39] whom used a small wheeled robot with a seven years old autistic boy. Since then, there have been applications focused to improve social and cognitive skills. The emergent robotic and technological literature has demonstrated that individuals under the autism condition have preference for robotics toys over non-robotic ones [40], that is an explanation why this technology is used as a therapy too. The authors [41] explain that humanoid robots are used for therapies that involves social or learning aspects (Fig. 7).

Fig. 7. Autism therapy with robots [42].

Robots has less sensory and social cues than people, so children with autism feel confident and safe using them. Robots are considered as one of the most popular practical application, that grows dynamically and that is good for autistic therapies. However, there still work to do in the field.

4 Conclusion

The literature shows an extended work in studies related to technology and children with autism, which is evidenced in the 347 results found in Scopus and 252 found in Web of Science. Despite of the technological contribution that technologies like virtual environments, mobile technology, robots and video modeling have done to contribute into the autistic community, they have not been validated clinically by health professionals. The Gartner graphic shows that the autism and technology field will continue growing in future years, evidencing the importance to cooperate and work closely with health experts. The authors consider this is an increasingly field of application.

The most relevant documentation obtained from the review of the literature demonstrate important input in autism, reflected in the 100% work published in the highest impact factor journals and proceedings in WOS and Scopus. The 78% of the results highlight the contribution of technologies to improve learning, social and communicative abilities through video modeling, virtual environments and mobile technology. Only the 22% of the literature was related to robotics interventions for autism. However, since 2018 studies related to robots, virtual environments and mobile technologies have increased. The review of the literature evidenced that autism can be diagnosed at early stages. Also, that children and teenagers with autism have a strong fascination for technology. This is an important outcome because it demonstrates that technology can contribute in the field, improving social and educational learning, behavior and life quality. As a conclusion, technology does impact in children with autism life quality. The authors consider this is an increasingly field of application that will impact the easily adaptation of children with autism.

Acknowledgments. This research has been supported under the REMIND project Marie Sklodowska Curie EU Framework for Research and Innovation Horizon 2020, under grant agreement No. 734355 Project REMIND.

References

1. Dekhil, O., et al.: Using resting state functional MRI to build a personalized autism diagnosis system. no. Isbi, pp. 1381–1385 (2018)
2. Bekele, E., Wade, J., Bian, D., Fan, J., Swanson, A., Warren, Z.: Multimodal adaptive social interaction in virtual environment (MASI-VR) for children with autism spectrum disorders (ASD). In: 2016 IEEE Virtual Reality (VR), pp. 121–130 (2016)
3. Santamaria, A.F., De Rango, F., Serianni, A., Raimondo, P.: A real IoT device deployment for e-Health applications under lightweight communication protocols, activity classifier and edge data filtering. Comput. Commun. **128**, 60–73 (2018)
4. Rodrigues, J.J.P.C., et al.: Enabling technologies for the internet of health things. In: IEEE Access, vol. 6, pp. 13129–13141 (2018)

5. Comas-González, Z., Echeverri-Ocampo, I., Zamora-Musa, R., Velez, J., Sarmiento, R., Orellana, M.: Recent trends in virtual education and its strong connection with the immersive environments [Tendencias recientes de la educación virtual y su fuerte conexión con los entornos inmersivos]. Espacios, vol. 38, no. 15 (2017)
6. Pilotte, M.: Autism spectrum disorder and engineering education—needs and considerations. In: 2016 IEEE Frontiers in Education Conference (FIE) (2016)
7. Uzuegbunam, N., Wong, W.H., Ching, S., Cheung, S., Ruble, L.: MEBook: multimedia social greetings intervention for children with autism spectrum disorders. IEEE Trans. Learn. Technol. **XX** (January 2016), 1–17 (2017)
8. Beattie, M., Hallberg, J., Nugent, C., Synnes, K., Cleland, I., Lee, S.: A collaborative patient-carer interface for generating home based rules for self-management. In: Bodine, C., Helal, S., Gu, T., Mokhtari, M. (eds.) ICOST 2014. LNCS, vol. 8456, pp. 93–102. Springer, Cham (2015). https://doi.org/10.1007/978-3-319-14424-5_10
9. Ahmed, I.U., Hassan, N., Rashid, H.: Solar powered smart wearable health monitoring and tracking device based on GPS and GSM technology for children with autism. In: 2017 4th International Conference on Advances in Electrical Engineering (ICAEE), pp. 111–116 (2017)
10. Ogwulu, C.B., Jackson, L.J., Kinghorn, P., Roberts, T.E.: A systematic review of the techniques used to value temporary health states. Value Health **20**(8), 1180–1197 (2017)
11. De-La-Hoz-Franco, E., Ariza-Colpas, P., Quero, J.M., Espinilla, M.: Sensor-based datasets for human activity recognition—a systematic review of literature. IEEE Access **6**, 59192–59210 (2018)
12. Comas-González, Z., Simancas-García, J., Rueda Bernal, V., Vélez-Zapata, J., Percia, I.: Redes de sensores inalámbricos para la monitorización de sistemas de calefacción, ventilación y aire acondicionado. Rev. Espac. **39**(45), 13 (2018)
13. Bagdadli, S., Gianecchini, M.: Organizational career management practices and objective career success: a systematic review and framework. Hum. Resour. Manag. Rev. (September 2017), 1 (2018)
14. Briscoe, E., Appling, S., Schlosser, J.: Technology futures from passive crowdsourcing. IEEE Trans. Comput. Soc. Syst. **3**(1), 23–31 (2016)
15. Zaki, T., Islam, M.N., Uddin, S., Tumpa, S.N., Hossain, J.: Towards developing a learning tool for children with autism. In: 2017 6th International Conference on Informatics, Electronics and Vision & 2017 7th International Symposium in Computational Medical and Health Technology (ICIEV-ISCMHT) (2017)
16. Shi, Y., Das, S., Douglas, S., Biswas, S.: An experimental wearable IoT for data-driven management of autism. In: 2017 9th International Conference on Communication Systems and Networks, COMSNETS 2017, pp. 468–471 (2017)
17. Pasco, G.: The value of early intervention for children with autism. Paediatr. Child Health (Oxford) **28**(8), 364–367 (2018)
18. Moreno, J.C., Morales, E.M.S., Seller, E.P.: Case study of the vulnerabilities that children with autism spectrum disorder have in education: the importance of early detection. Procedia Soc. Behav. Sci. **237**, 661–666 (2017)
19. Grossard, C., Grynspan, O., Serret, S., Jouen, A.L., Bailly, K., Cohen, D.: Serious games to teach social interactions and emotions to individuals with autism spectrum disorders (ASD). Comput. Educ. **113**, 195–211 (2017)
20. Bozgeyikli, L., Raij, A., Katkoori, S., Alqasemi, R.: A survey on virtual reality for individuals with autism spectrum disorder: design considerations. IEEE Trans. Learn. Technol. **11**(2), 133–151 (2018)
21. Boyd, L.E., Hayes, G.R.: Wearable assistive technologies for autism opportunities and challenges. IEEE Pervasive Comput. **17**, 11–21 (2018)

22. Kumdee, O.: Repetitive motion detection for human behavior understanding from video images. In: 2015 IEEE International Symposium on Signal Processing and Information Technology (ISSPIT), pp. 484–489 (2015)
23. Zunino, A., et al.: Video gesture analysis for autism spectrum disorder detection. In: 2018 24th International Conference on Pattern Recognition (ICPR), pp. 3421–3426 (2018)
24. Min, C.-H.: Automatic detection and labeling of self-stimulatory behavioral patterns in children with autism spectrum disorder. In: 2017 39th Annual International Conference of the IEEE Engineering in Medicine and Biology Society (EMBC), pp. 279–282 (2017)
25. Calandra, D.M. Di Mauro, D., Cutugno, F., Di Martino, S.: Navigating wall-sized displays with the gaze: a proposal for cultural heritage. CEUR Workshop Proceeding, vol. 1621, no. January pp. 36–43 (2016)
26. Seshadri, S.: iPad gives voice to kids with autism. CNN (2012). https://edition.cnn.com/2012/05/14/tech/gaming-gadgets/ipad-autism/index.html
27. Al-khalifa, H.S., Alrajhi, W., Alhassan, S., Almotlag, M.: Requirement elicitation for a toilet training wearable watch to serve autistic children. In: 2017 6th International Conference on Information and Communication Technology and Accessibility (ICTA) (2018)
28. Technologies, R., Hollosy, W.O.N., Notenboom, T., Banos, O.: A study on the perceptions of autistic adolescents towards mainstream emotion. In: 12th International Conference on Ubiquitous Computing and Ambient Intelligence (UCAmI 2018), vol. 10, pp. 1–12 (2018)
29. Adolfo, J., Camargo, C., Augusto, C., Cortés, P., García, P.: Evaluación de las emociones de usuarios en tareas con realimentación háptica utilizado el dispositivo Emotiv Insight Assessment of the users emotions in haptic feedback tasks using the Emotiv Insight device. INGE CUC **15**(1), 9–16 (2019)
30. Chandler, D.: Opening new worlds for those with autism: technology is creating great new possibilities for those on every part of the spectrum. IEEE Pulse. **7**(4), 43–46 (2016)
31. Akbar, G.S.: User interface (UI) design of scheduling activity apps for autistic children. In: 2017 International Conference on Orange Technologies (ICOT), pp. 129–133 (2017)
32. Kamaruzaman, M.F., Noor, H., Hanapiah, F.A., Halabi, M., Azahari, H.: Efficacy of DTT by using touchscreen learning numeracy app for children with autism. In: 2016 IEEE 8th International Conference on Engineering Education (ICEED), pp. 198–201 (2016)
33. Papathomas, P., Goldschmidt, K.: Utilizing virtual reality and immersion video technology as a focused learning tool for children with autism spectrum disorder. J. Pediatr. Nurs. **35**, 8–9 (2017)
34. Didehbani, N., Allen, T., Kandalaft, M., Krawczyk, D., Chapman, S.: Virtual Reality Social Cognition Training for children with high functioning autism. Comput. Hum. Behav. **62**, 703–711 (2016)
35. Lamash, L., Klinger, E., Josman, N.: Using a virtual supermarket to promote independent functioning among adolescents with Autism Spectrum Disorder. In: International Conference on Virtual Rehabilitation, ICVR (2017)
36. Bozgeyikli, L., Bozgeyikli, E., Raij, A., Alqasemi, R., Katkoori, S., Dubey, R.: Vocational training with immersive virtual reality for individuals with autism: towards better design practices. In: 2016 IEEE 2nd Workshop on Everyday Virtual Reality, WEVR 2016, pp. 21–25 (2017)
37. Health Tech Digital: Floreo brings autism therapy into the home environment. https://www.healthtechdigital.com/floreo-brings-autism-therapy-into-the-home-environment/
38. Munoz, R., Barcelos, T.T.S., Villarroel, R., Silveira, I.F.: Game design workshop to develop computational thinking skills in teenagers with Autism Spectrum Disorders. In: 2016 11th Iberian Conference on Information Systems and Technologies (CISTI), pp. 1–4 (2016)

39. Salter, T., Davey, N., Francoise, M.: Designing & developing QueBall, a robotic device for autism therapy Designing & Developing QueBall, A Robotic Device for Autism Therapy. In: The 23rd IEEE International Symposium on Robot and Human Interactive Communication, 2016 (October), pp. 574–579 (2014)
40. Zheng, Z., Young, E.M., Swanson, A.R., Weitlauf, A.S., Warren, Z.E., Sarkar, N.: Robot-mediated imitation skill training for children with autism. IEEE Trans. Neural Syst. Rehabil. Eng. **24**(6), 682–691 (2016)
41. Ackovska, N., Kirandziska, V., Tanevska, A., Bozinovska, L., Bozinovski, A.: Robot - Assisted therapy for autistic children. In: Conference Proceedings - IEEE SOUTHEASTCON, pp. 1–2 (2017)
42. Kevin, C.: Moving, Speaking Robots Help Detect Autism Earlier. University of Minnesota (2018)
43. Mavadati, S.M., Feng, H., Salvador, M., Silver, S., Gutierrez, A., Mahoor, M.H.: Robot-based therapeutic protocol for training children with Autism. In: 25th IEEE International Symposium on Robot and Human Interactive Communication, RO-MAN 2016, pp. 855–860 (2016)
44. Jiménez Moreno, R., Espinosa Valcárcel, F., Amaya Hurtado, D.: Control de movimiento de un robot humanoide por medio de visión de máquina y réplica de movimientos humanos. INGE CUC **9**(2), 44–51. Recuperado a partir de https://revistascientificas.cuc.edu.co/ingecuc/article/view/5

Mobile Technology for Cognitive Training and Evaluation of People with Mild Cognitive Impairment

Panagiota Giannopoulou(✉)

Department of Informatics, Ionian University, 7 Tsirigoti Square, 49132 Corfu, Greece
c16gian@ionio.gr

Abstract. Mild cognitive impairment (MCI) affects an increasing number of the elderly. MCI is in many cases the first sign of dementia, which is one of the main reasons for disability in the elderly worldwide. In people with MCI, it is essential to regularly evaluate their cognitive status due to the uncertain course of symptoms, that is not completely achieved with traditional assessment procedures. Technological advances, especially in mobile and portable devices, have made possible the delivery of new forms of cognitive training and new methods for cognitive evaluation of healthy older adults or of individuals with MCI. Easy to use and engaging applications can serve as a new means of providing enjoyable cognitive interventions that offer the required commitment of their users. The ability of long-term, remote and autonomous monitoring of the cognitive course of individuals in combination with new technological measures, new specialized algorithms and built-in sensors in their mobile devices offer new data streams to clinicians and the possibility of timely and personalized intervention. This review presents existing cognitive interventions and evaluation studies in adults with or without cognitive impairment, that utilized mobile devices in this context. Their encouraging results provide the breeding ground for the proposal of developing new interventions on future research, that will take advantage of the potentials and prospects of mobile digital devices technology.

Keywords: Cognition · Impairment · MCI · Mobile devices · Intervention · Training · Evaluation · Long-term · Remote

1 Introduction

Mild cognitive impairment (MCI) refers to the condition that is characterized by memory impairment, learning difficulties, and decreased ability to concentrate for more than short periods of time in a task. Individuals suffering from MCI may also experience mental fatigue when performing mental tasks or difficulties in the learning process. They may also show noticeable declines in attention and memory functions as well as decay in cognitive functions such as attention, language, and reasoning. [1]. MCI based on the skills affected is categorized into Amnestic MCI (aMCI) where memory is mainly affected and Nonamnestic MCI where thinking skills and other cognitive features are

© Springer Nature Switzerland AG 2020
C. Frasson et al. (Eds.): BFAL 2020, LNAI 12462, pp. 186–192, 2020.
https://doi.org/10.1007/978-3-030-60735-7_20

primarily affected [2]. These minor changes in the cognitive abilities of individuals are perceived by relatives and friends but not by third parties and are worse than normally expected for healthy older adults in normal aging. Individuals with MCI do not present severe enough symptoms to interfere with their daily life, and to diagnose dementia [1].

The clinical syndrome of Dementia, usually of a chronic or progressive nature, is caused by several brain diseases that affect memory, cognitive abilities and behavior of individuals, compromising their ability to support daily life activities. Although it is typically caused by age-related pathophysiological processes, it is not a normal evolution of aging [3, 4]. Among the diseases that cause changes in the brain, resulting in loss of neurons and the consequent appearance of dementia [3, 5] are Alzheimer's disease, Cerebrovascular disease, Lewy body disease, and Fronto-temporal lobar degeneration (FTLD), including Pick's disease. There are also mentioned and rarer causes, such as Parkinson's disease, progressive supranuclear palsy, multiple sclerosis, and others, where there is an increased risk of developing dementia. Alzheimer's disease is the most common cause of dementia and responsible for 50% to 80% of all dementia cases [3, 5].

Although Dementia can occur at any age, it is more common in older people, introducing one of the major causes of disability and dependency among them worldwide. The pathophysiological chain of dementia begins up to 20 years before the onset of obvious clinical symptoms and affects each person in a different way. Before the onset of dementia, individuals usually develop MCI [6, 7]. There are some patients with MCI, that will turn out to have a different, often treatable, cause such as by anxiety or depression [8]. Some individuals facing MCI are possible to return to normal for their age cognitive function or remain stable, but a significant proportion of those, mainly with gradual memory loss, are expected to develop dementia, usually Alzheimer's disease [3, 7–9]. It is estimated that up to 20% of individuals at the age of 65 or above have MCI from any of the aforementioned causes [8].

Despite global research efforts that prioritize research in this area, there is still no cure for any of the irreversible causes of dementia or treatment to change the course of the disease [14]. As for Alzheimer's disease, which is the leading cause of dementia, none of the approved by the US Food and Drug Administration (FDA) pharmacological treatments can delay or stop the progression of the disease, only to temporarily improve symptoms [3].

The research community is also particularly interested in non-pharmacological treatments that target various aspects of the disease. Non-pharmacological interventions aim to maintain or improve cognitive function and the ability to perform daily activities, as well as to reduce behavioral symptoms. In these interventions and the consequent studies, participants are not only individuals with symptoms of dementia or MCI but also normal cognitive individuals who would like to prevent dementia or delay cognitive impairment [3]. This kind of interventions that aim at cognitive training and stimulation, offer benefits in various areas such as memory (episodic, semantic, working), language, attention, processing speed, visuospatial and functional abilities, anxiety and depression, daily activities, and overall quality of life, and therefore are effective in people with MCI [10]. However, these interventions, despite their benefits, also show high abandonment rates, due to the cost (money and time) and the symptoms of apathy or depression that are often present in older people, facing memory difficulties [11].

2 Technology

Diagnosis, assessment, and monitoring of cognitive function for individuals with MCI are the same as for dementia. Assessment is performed in clinical settings using interviews, standardized neuropsychological assessments, and cognitive tests [12]. These methods of assessing cognitive status are resource-demanding, and in addition the time between each monitoring can be longer than 6 to 12 months [12]. As a result, clinicians find it difficult to follow up on the patient's cognitive status, as they do not have access to data of improvement or decline in the patient's cognitive function in the interim [13]. However, individuals with MCI should be re-examined at regular intervals due to the uncertain course of cognitive impairment, which may worsen, improve, or remain at the same level. Therefore, the detection of changes in people with MCI should be immediate in order to modify, if necessary, the management of the patient in a timely manner [2].

Advances in technology and information science have led to the development of cognitive interventions that utilize computers, mobile devices, virtual reality, and interactive video games, providing improved accessibility, usability, interaction, and real-time feedback. The increase in the number of adults at the age of 65 or older using smartphones, combined with new applications and sensors applied to mobile devices, has allowed the exploitation of new data streams in order to identify sensitive indicators for monitoring cognitive impairment. In addition, applications in the form of games can provide targeted cognitive training programs leading to improvement in mobilization deficits [11]. These tools made possible for patients to screen their cognition and monitor their condition by incorporating them into their daily activities. The new methods offered unattended and personalized interventions in individuals with as much independence as they desire, in their home environment [14]. In addition, it enabled long-term monitoring by frequent or continuous evaluation of their performance variability, allowing the remote, regular and discreet collection of data.

3 Surveys with the Utilization of Mobile Devices

The potentials and prospects for the exploitation and integration of mobile and portable digital technology have increased research into the evaluation of cognitive impairment and the development of more effective non-pharmacological interventions. Many existing evaluations and cognitive training interventions have been formed in mobile-friendly versions, while new ones have been developed specifically for mobile platforms.

CogState is a brief computerized cognitive battery that requires minimal administrative oversight. CogState evaluates psychomotor speed, visual attention, learning and attention, working memory, spatial working memory, learning efficiency, and error monitoring. The system records, the reaction time, the accuracy, the average correct moves per second, and the total number of errors. Mielke and colleagues (2015) analyzed the performance of the two CogState versions for PC and iPad. The speed and accuracy of the participants were slightly better on the computer, but the participants stated that they believed their performance was better on the iPad version. In addition, data analysis revealed that older people with little PC experience and arthritis or tremor performed better in this version of CogState. The researchers also examined the performance of a lighter version of CogState both at home, using the iPad, and in a clinic, using the PC. They recruited 194 non-demented individuals aged 50 to 69 years, for a period of 6 months. The analysis showed that the participants' accuracy did not differ, but the speed at which they completed the tests was better at those utilized iPad [15].

Based on the observation, that cognitive training packages are usually repetitive and boring, Savulich and colleagues (2017) developed a memory game, the iPad gamified application Game Show. Visually appealing screens and music were used to make it fun, motivational, comprehensible and suitable for this age group. Developers tested its effect on both cognitive function and participant motivation on two separate groups of patients. The cognitive training group consisted of patients who used the game on an iPad and the control group that was following a traditional program at a clinic. Patients in the cognitive training group were found to have improved episodic memory and high levels of commitment. This, according to the researchers, demonstrates that digital cognitive training can be used to enhance memory and motivation in patients with MCI [11].

The iBeni app was developed for the Android operating system and aimed to stimulate cognition, improve cognitive functions, and slow cognitive impairment in healthy older adults or older adults with MCI. The developers of the application conducted a study in order to analyze the effect, viability, and impact of a cognitive stimulation application on mobile devices, such as the iBeni app. They divided the participants into two groups the experimental group, that used the iBeni app on a 10.1-inch Samsung Galaxy Tab 4 tablet and the control group, that followed a traditional paper and pencil training. The difficulty of the iBeni's exercises was increased automatically, based on the user's progress. Both groups increased their scores on neuropsychological assessments, however, the experimental group scored better in the evaluation, as the participants were able to perform the exercises repeatedly. This, according to the researchers suggests that more frequent and larger interventions are required [16].

DOREMI project (Decrease of cOgnitive decline, malnutRition and sedEntariness by elderly empowerment in lifestyle Management and social Inclusion) aimed to promote active aging by improving nutrition and strengthening areas such as physical activity, socialization and the cognitive function of elderly healthy individuals and individuals with MCI. In the context of the intervention, a gamified environment suitable for tablet devices was developed, implementing the four distinct promotion areas of the project (cognition, exercise, social interaction, and healthy eating). Scase and colleagues examined the adherence of individuals with MCI, to the DOREMI environment. The analysis revealed high levels of motivation among the participants, encouraged by the gamification of the environment [17].

The VSM (Virtual Super Market) is a virtual reality application, that simulates the daily activity of shopping in supermarkets, and is suitable for any Android tablet device. VSM aims at visual and verbal memory, attention, spatial navigation, and executive function, and requires the simultaneous activation of various cognitive processes. The application records and presents statistics about the user's performance, such as the number of correct and incorrect items purchased, and the total time required to complete the activity. Zygouris and colleagues examined whether a virtual reality application for cognitive training, such as VSM, could be used as an assessment tool for MCI. The analysis of the data collected from the conducted research showed a high degree of correlation and a satisfactory classification rate in the differentiation of healthy older adults and patients with MCI [18].

Also, Zygouris and colleagues, evaluated whether monitoring the long-term performance of older adults in a virtual reality application, could provide useful diagnostic information for their cognitive assessment. For this purpose, they utilized a modified version of the virtual reality application VSM, the VSM-RAR (VSM-Remote Assessment Routine) and recruited parfticipants, that were familiar with the VSM application. All the participants used the self-managed VSM-RAR application on a tablet device in their familiar home environment. The researchers conclude that remote MCI detection via virtual reality applications is possible, while specialized algorithms integrated into the software would allow it to function as an early warning for signs of cognitive decline [19].

4 Discussion and Conclusion

Early detection and intervention through cognitive evaluation, training, and rehabilitation can assist patients with MCI to maintain or even improve their cognitive function [20, 21]. The aforementioned studies indicate that mobile devices coupled with serious gaming applications, provide opportunities for the exploitation of new data streams that could help improve of health care provided to elderly patients with or without cognitive impairment.

Furthermore, the multimedia content and the gamified form of interventions provide the desired incentive to overcome the high abandonment rate of cognitive training programs by improving motivational deficits. Also, these forms of intervention have low administration costs, allow the self-administrative monitoring of participants' long-term cognitive performance, in their familiar home environment.

According to the bibliography patients with MCI may improve, remain stable, or decline cognitively over time. That is why it is recommended, for patients diagnosed with MCI, clinicians to perform serial assessments over time in order to monitor for change in their cognitive status [2]. So, if differences are identified, the diagnosis and thus management and treatment to be informed properly and immediately. Unfortunately, this is not always possible, so clinicians do not have the necessary regular data required to follow up on the patient's cognitive status [13]. Cognitive interventions that utilize mobile devices can contribute in this direction.

Of particular interest would be the effort to integrate on the technological advancement of digital devices, algorithms that will value for both the patients' performance in the corresponding applications and their medical and cognitive profile. The subsequent individualized intervention could be effective and efficient to support differentiated cognitive training. Finally, research in the field of digital mobile devices, new data streams and specialized applications could deliver greater accuracy and detailed measurements of cognitive assessment. These tools could serve as an effective instrument to support and improve the lives of people who face cognitive impairment, and the promotion of timely and optimal intervention.

Acknowledgments. This research is funded by the European Union and Greece (Partnership Agreement for the Development Framework 2014–2020) under the Regional Operational Programme Ionian Islands 2014–2020, project title: "Enhancing cognitive abilities of people with Mild Cognitive Impairment through measurable cognitive training—NEUROEDUCATION", project number: 5016113.

References

1. World Health Organization: Risk reduction of cognitive decline and dementia: WHO guidelines. In: Risk reduction of cognitive decline and dementia: WHO guidelines, pp. 401–401 (2019)
2. Petersen, R.C., et al.: Practice guideline update summary: mild cognitive impairment: report of the guideline development, dissemination, and implementation subcommittee of the American Academy of Neurology. Neurology **90**(3), 126–135 (2018)
3. Alzheimer's Association: Alzheimer's disease facts and figures. Alzheimer's Dement. **15**(3), 321–387 (2019)
4. 10 facts on dementia. http://www.who.int/features/factfiles/dementia/en/. Accessed 2 Apr 2020
5. World Health Organization: Alzheimer's disease: help for caregivers (No. WHO/MNH/MND/94.8. Unpublished). World Health Organization, Geneva (1994)
6. Albert, M.S., et al.: The diagnosis of mild cognitive impairment due to Alzheimer's disease: recommendations from the National Institute on Aging-Alzheimer's Association workgroups on diagnostic guidelines for Alzheimer's disease. Alzheimer's Dement. **7**(3), 270–279 (2011)
7. Petersen, R.C.: Mild cognitive impairment as a diagnostic entity. J. Intern. Med. **256**(3), 183–194 (2004)
8. What is mild cognitive impairment (MCI)? Fact sheet 470LP. https://www.alzheimers.org.uk/get-support/publications-factsheets/publications-dementia. Accessed 2 Apr 2020
9. Help for caregivers. https://www.who.int/mentalhealth/neurology/dementia/help_for_caregivers/en/. Accessed 2 Apr 2020
10. Li, H., Li, J., Li, N., Li, B., Wang, P., Zhou, T.: Cognitive intervention for persons with mild cognitive impairment: a meta-analysis. Ageing Res. Rev. **10**(2), 285–296 (2011)
11. Savulich, G., et al.: Cognitive training using a novel memory game on an iPad in patients with amnestic mild cognitive impairment (aMCI). Int. J. Neuropsychopharmacol. **20**(8), 624–633 (2017)
12. Petersen, R.C., Caracciolo, B., Brayne, C., Gauthier, S., Jelic, V., Fratiglioni, L.: Mild cognitive impairment: a concept in evolution. J. Intern. Med. **275**(3), 214–228 (2014)
13. Joshi, V., Wallace, B., Shaddy, A., Knoefel, F, Goubran, R, Lord, C.: Metrics to monitor performance of patients with mild cognitive impairment using computer based games. In: 2016 IEEE-EMBS International Conference on Biomedical and Health Informatics (BHI), pp. 521–524. IEEE (2016)
14. Morris, M., Intille, S.S., Beaudin, J.S.: Embedded assessment: overcoming barriers to early detection with pervasive computing. In: Gellersen, H.-W., Want, R., Schmidt, A. (eds.) Pervasive 2005. LNCS, vol. 3468, pp. 333–346. Springer, Heidelberg (2005). https://doi.org/10.1007/11428572_20
15. Mielke, M.M., et al.: Performance of the CogState computerized battery in the mayo clinic study on aging. Alzheimer's Dement. J. Alzheimer's Assoc. **11**(11), 1367–1376 (2015)
16. Martínez-Alcalá, C.I., Rosales-Lagarde, A., Hernández-Alonso, E., Melchor-Agustin, R., Rodriguez-Torres, E.E., Itzá-Ortiz, B.A.: A mobile app (iBeni) with a neuropsychological basis for cognitive stimulation for elderly adults: pilot and validation study. JMIR Res. Protoc. **7**(8), e172 (2018)

17. Scase, M., Marandure, B., Hancox, J., Kreiner, K., Hanke, S., Kropf, J.: Development of and adherence to a computer-based gamified environment designed to promote health and wellbeing in older people with mild cognitive impairment. eHealth, 348–355 (2017)
18. Zygouris, S., et al.: Can a virtual reality cognitive training application fulfill a dual role? Using the Virtual Super Market cognitive training application as a screening tool for mild cognitive impairment. J. Alzheimers Dis. **44**(4), 1333–1347 (2015)
19. Zygouris, S., et al.: A preliminary study on the feasibility of using a virtual reality cognitive training application for remote detection of mild cognitive impairment. J. Alzheimers Dis. **56**(2), 619–627 (2017)
20. Laske, C., et al.: Innovative diagnostic tools for early detection of Alzheimer's disease. Alzheimer's Dement. **11**(5), 561–578 (2015)
21. Rodakowski, J., Saghafi, E., Butters, M.A., Skidmore, E.R.: Non-pharmacological interventions for adults with mild cognitive impairment and early stage dementia: an updated scoping review. Mol. Aspects Med. **43**, 38–53 (2015)

Mathematical Problem Solving and Cognitive Enhancement

Ioannis Saridakis[1] and Spyridon Doukakis[2]([✉])

[1] Hellenic Open University, Patras, Greece
saridakisioannis@gmail.com
[2] Department of Informatics, Ionian University, 7 Tsirigoti Square, 49132 Corfu, Greece
sdoukakis@ionio.gr

Abstract. In recent years there has been a great increase in research on cognitive enhancement issues of students and adults. For this purpose, different interventions and a variety of strategies have been proposed. According to previous studies, mathematical problem solving is a related intervention, as it has been argued that frequent involvement in such process is positively related to the improvement of one's cognition. This article presents the design and the first results of an exploratory qualitative research that investigate the effect of mathematical problem solving on the cognitive enhancement of the elderly. The findings of this research confirm the aforementioned belief and implicate that a study accompanied by the appropriate neuroimaging techniques should be conducted.

Keywords: Problem solving · Cognitive enhancement · Qualitative research method

1 Introduction

One could argue that life is nothing more than a constant state of problem solving. In order to satisfy our needs from the most simple and basic ones to the most complex and elaborate, we are daily called to solve a problem [1, 2]. Having to combine data with premises in order to achieve a certain goal, a desired result is what lies in the heart of problem solving.

There are many methods, strategies and techniques of solving a problem and the science particularly dedicated to solving problems and continuously inventing or evolving already existing ways of solving problems is Mathematics. Solving problems in general and especially in mathematics is, without a doubt, a very mentally active task [3, 4]. Consequently, a question is risen: "While solving a mathematical problem, does one have a hidden, fractionally subliminal benefit, other than the obvious one of solving the problem itself?". In other words, how does one benefit from such a process and what does our brain gain, in general, from this engagement with mathematical problem solving? The neural circuits and mechanisms needed for such a mental endeavor and their interconnection with the augmentation of brain activity are subjects examined by cognitive science with the ultimate goal to provide cognitive enhancement [5–8].

C. Frasson et al. (Eds.): BFAL 2020, LNAI 12462, pp. 193–199, 2020.
https://doi.org/10.1007/978-3-030-60735-7_21

As a species, one characteristic that describes us and distinct us from other species, is that after becoming aware of our consciousness and mental capabilities we continuously seek ways to increase and enhance them [9]. This never-ending upward helix of cognitive improvement that we, as humankind, ascend, can be observed throughout history in all kinds of civilizations and societies. This urge to overcome ourselves and evolve cognitively has led us to various kinds of inventions and has been a driving force in different scientific fields. For instance, symbolic language, written language and after that the invention of printing press have helped us communicate, accumulate and exchange knowledge and information. A quick look at the progress in cognitive enhancement throughout the last decades will reveal that the scientific mindset is mostly oriented in drug induced enhancement, called pharmacological cognitive enhancement, a swift way to refine and upgrade brain capacities, but at what cost? Every drug comes with contraindications, so pharmacological brain enhancement is not suitable for everyone and additionally, it is claimed to be unethical [10]. Therefore, the trend in cognitive enhancement during the last decade has shifted towards non-pharmacological ways [10–16]. As a consequence, a relatively new emerging field of cognitive neuroscience, that of the neuroeducation, has the leading role in this approach.

What is called cognitive science could be perceived as the convergence point of a group of different scientific fields, many of which are considered unrelated to each other or at least fields with different scientific interest in general [17, 18]. This diversity and combination of many different scientific views and theories is what gives cognitive science its multidisciplinary character. The main goal of cognitive science is to study the human brain, its activities, the processes that take place during a task, such as solving a problem, in order to understand the way the human brain works and how one could improve its performance. In particular, educational neuroscience is one of the domains of cognitive science that specializes in neural mechanisms of the brain that are responsible for procedures such as acquiring information through our sensory organs, as well as embodying this information and transforming it into what we call knowledge [19, 20]. In other words, neuroeducation thoroughly studies the way our brain learns something. Among other things, neuroeducation is interested in how one can overcome learning disabilities and amplify their brain performance through a non-pharmacological interference [21, 22]. Hence, the principal aim of this paper is to study and prove that by using such means and specifically mathematical problem solving, it is possible for one to achieve the so desired cognitive enhancement.

2   Literature Review

There is a considerable amount of literature on cognitive enhancement. Most of it is dedicated in research and studies on pharmacological cognitive enhancement, that is the improvement of one's cognitive skills and brain activity using pharmaceutical means. Nevertheless, there are many other ways of non-pharmacological cognitive interventions, sometimes considered more efficacious and better suited for certain patients [14]. Such interventions may be related to nutritional and sleeping habits of a person, as well as physical and mental exercise. Studies have established that brain training in a frequent base can upgrade cognitive abilities among the elderly whether they have a mild brain degenerative disease or not [23]. Problem solving has been used as a type of cognitive training. In particular daily mental training by solving mathematical problems such as basic arithmetic problems, is capable of improving cognitive functions and is related to ameliorated scores in Frontal Assessment Battery (FAB) and Digit-symbol Substitution Tests (DST).

One should not neglect the fact that most of the studies and researches that show the association between mathematical problem solving and cognitive enhancement were conducted on children. Some of these studies have shown that word problem solving using specified cognitive strategies help children to boost certain cognitive abilities such as their working memory capacity and their controlled attention [24].

An abundance of studies mostly conducted with the help of computer-based training, have provided evidence that cognitive enhancement can be achieved with unconventional means. For example, the use of Video Games and mostly Action Video Games (AVG), is very common in these studies. Students that were assigned mathematical exercises in the form of a video game have shown improved cognitive abilities. Some of those improvements were related to the reaction time of calculating an expression or displayed an upgrade in processing speed and better hand-eye coordination [13]. Similar experiments on second grade pupils have yielded that video games assisted children in increasing their accuracy concerning mental calculations and that working memory capacity is positively linked to better skills in arithmetic and problem-solving speed [25].

There are also studies that correlate in a positive way the usefulness of action video games regarding adult cognitive enhancement. For instance, it has been proved that cognitive abilities such as multitasking performance, reasoning and working memory decline linearly across one's lifespan [26–28]. In addition, many adults have demonstrated significant improvement on standardized assessments of complex mathematics after rigorous training with action video games. Their mathematical processes relying on approximation were improved, as well as their attentional skills.

It is very clear that this extended literature has explored and continues to explore many aspects of non-pharmacological cognitive enhancement. In the present study, an attempt will be made to enrich the literature through a qualitative research approach, exploring how mathematical problem solving contributes to cognitive enhancement.

3 Research Methodology and Problem Categorization

For the purposes of this paper a qualitative approach was adopted. A diverse group of mathematical problems and riddles, as well as a questionnaire were administered to 16 adults. Given the current measures enforced by the Greek government due to the Covid-19, certain technical limitations arose regarding the means of conducting the research. In order to overcome those hindrances, the means used to conduct the research, which was initially designed to be carried out in person, were instead posted to the participants. As far as the questionnaire concerns, a few additional sections were composed. The first one was a survey which made it possible for the researchers to collect data concerning the profile of the participants.

The problems selected for this research, were chosen to be simple requiring no advanced mathematical background. The level of mathematical technicality involved was maintained at high school level, as the main purpose of the research was to study the cognitive effects of solving a problem, rather than the ability and efficiency of the participant at solving a mathematical problem. As a matter of fact, one principal claim of this study is that one could have an improvement of its brain activity merely by trying to solve a mathematical problem regardless of their provision of a solution.

Furthermore, it is worth mentioning that the problems were categorized concerning the different kinds of stimuli existing in their presentation or the potential requirement of different kinds of stimuli a participant could employ in order to reach a solution. For instance, some of the problems were simple arithmetic problems where the participant had to calculate the exact value of an expression or a simple utilization of a formula was required for the problem to be solved. An example of a problem posed is the following:

How much money would have to be invested at 0.01% interest compounded weekly to be worth 10,000€ after 10 years?

To solve this problem someone has to remember the formula of compound interest learnt in high school,

$$A = P\left(1 + \frac{r}{n}\right)^{nt}$$

where A = future value, P = Principal (initial value), r = Interest rate, t = time and n = number of times compounded in one "t", or to try to create the formula in order to solve the problem.

Another category was riddle problems focused on visual or visuospatial stimulus. In this category there were problems that included some type of visual aid in their presentation or problems that would probably lead the participants to devise their own visual aid in order to solve them. One of those problems was (Fig. 1):

Someone wants to make a dice. But only one of the following nets makes a dice. Which is the correct one?

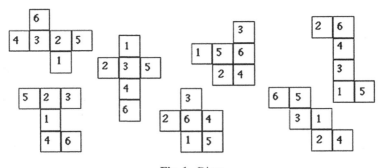

Fig. 1. Dices

An example of a problem not providing a visual aid, but most likely requires one is the following:

Suppose an analog clock whose both time and minute hands move at the same pace as a regular one but in the opposite direction. Someone wants to execute a recipe and the only available instrument of measuring time is the above-mentioned clock. This recipe requires 15 minutes of preparation and 1 hour and 30 minutes of cooking. If the execution of the recipe starts when the reading on the clock is 11:35, what time will the clock show when the food is ready to be served?

4   Research Procedure and First Findings

Sixteen adults, both male and female were selected for the research. With respect to the sampling method, the sample could be described as a combination of convenience and voluntary response sample. This sample was selected for the study because it was easy for them to participate, it was quick for the researchers to find them and the cost was low. Since it was a convenience sample, the results cannot be generalized.

The average of the participants was 46, 5 years old and the age range was from 28 to 65 years old. The participants were of different educational attainments, nonetheless not one of the participants had a solid mathematical background so as to be considered favored in comparison with the rest of the participants.

Firstly, instead of a meeting that would have been scheduled to be held in person with each participant, a preliminary section was added to the questionnaire. At this section the participant were introduced to the forthcoming procedure and the requirements they had to fulfil. In addition, they were asked to complete a brief demographic survey. After that section, each participant had to proceed to the crux of the questionnaire which consists of a set of problems. Specific orders were given related to the time span the problems should be solved and the means one could use in order to do so. Moreover, each participant was instructed (as supplementary part of the questionnaire) to compose a self-assessment report, in which they had to describe their experience and speculate about their performance. Afterwards, the questionnaire and solutions of the problems were collected by the researchers and a final set of questions had to be answered, the main purpose of which was to explore and record signs of cognitive enhancement in each participant.

The research is ongoing and after its completion, the final findings will be extracted. However, after the second meeting, it appeared that active and frequent involvement in mathematical problem solving contributes to cognitive enhancement, according to the views and self-assessment of the participants. As already mentioned, due to the conduct of the research with a convenience sample, the findings cannot be generalized, but can be confirmed through triangulation with other methods and methodologies. Therefore, a subsequent step of this study could be its confirmation using brain imaging techniques, such as functional magnetic resonance imaging (fMRI) and electroencephalography (EEG) in order to solidify and generalize its findings.

5   Conclusions

In the present study, a literature review of researches and non-pharmaceutical techniques for cognitive enhancement was initially attempted. Then, according to the literature, the importance of problem solving with the aim of cognitive enhancement emerged. Afterwards the research design that aims to examine the cognitive enhancement of adults as they are involved in a consequence of solving mathematical problems was presented. Qualitative research was chosen using a convenience sample and therefore the results cannot be generalized. According to the participants, their involvement in solving mathematical problems contributes to their cognitive enhancement.

The research is ongoing and after its completion, the final findings that will emerge are possible to contribute to the existing literature and give the opportunity for new studies that will utilize neuroimaging techniques.

Acknowledgments. This research is funded by the European Union and Greece (Partnership Agreement for the Development Framework 2014–2020) under the Regional Operational Programme Ionian Islands 2014–2020, project title: "Enhancing cognitive abilities of people with Mild Cognitive Impairment through measurable cognitive training—NEUROEDUCATION", project number: 5016113.

References

1. Stallard, P.: Thinking Good, Feeling Better: A Cognitive Behavioural Therapy Workbook for Adolescents and Young Adults. John Wiley & Sons, Hoboken (2019)
2. Nguyen, V.B., Krause, E., Chu, C.T.: Problem Solving. Comparison of Mathematics and Physics Education I. MBB, pp. 345–368. Springer, Wiesbaden (2020). https://doi.org/10.1007/978-3-658-29880-7_14
3. Hazzan, O., Lapidot, T., Ragonis, N.: Guide to Teaching Computer Science. Springer, London (2014). https://doi.org/10.1007/978-1-4471-6630-6
4. Arifin, S., Zulkardi, R.I.I.P., Hartono Y., Susanti, E.: Scaffolding in mathematical problem-solving. J. Phys. Conf. Ser. 1480 (2019)
5. Posner, M.I., Petersen, S.E., Fox, P.T., Raichle, M.E.: Localization of cognitive operations in the human brain. Science **240**(4859), 1627–1631 (1988)
6. Stanislas, D., Piazza, M., Pinel, P., Cohen, L.: Three parietal circuits for number processing. Cogn. Neuropsychol. **20**(3–6), 487–506 (2003)
7. Ayaz, H., Shewokis, P.A., İzzetoğlu, M., Çakır, M.P., Onaral, B.: Tangram solved? Prefrontal cortex activation analysis during geometric problem solving. In: Annual International Conference of the IEEE Engineering in Medicine and Biology Society, pp. 4724–4727. IEEE (2012)
8. Zhou, X., et al.: The semantic system is involved in mathematical problem solving. Neuroimage **166**, 360–370 (2018)
9. Bruehl, A., Sahakian, B.: Drugs, games, and devices for enhancing cognition: implications for work and society. Ann. N. Y. Acad. Sci. **1369**(1), 195–217 (2016)
10. Bostrom, N., Sandberg, A.: Cognitive enhancement: methods, ethics, regulatory challenges. Sci. Eng. Ethics **15**(3), 311–341 (2009)
11. Looi, C.Y., Duta, M., Brem, A.K., Huber, S., Nuerk, H.C., Kadosh, R.C.: Combining brain stimulation and video game to promote long-term transfer of learning and cognitive enhancement. Sci. Rep. **6**, 22003 (2016)
12. Oei, A.C., Patterson, M.D.: Enhancing cognition with video games: a multiple game training study. PLoS ONE **8**(3), e58546 (2013)
13. Chandra, S., Sharma, G., Salam, A.A., Jha, D., Mittal, A.P.: Playing action video games a key to cognitive enhancement. Procedia Comput. Sci. **84**, 115–122 (2016)

14. Dresler, M., et al.: Non-pharmacological cognitive enhancement. Neuropharmacology **64**, 529–543 (2013)
15. Fissler, P., Küster, O., Schlee, W., Kolassa, I.T.: Novelty interventions to enhance broad cognitive abilities and prevent dementia: synergistic approaches for the facilitation of positive plastic change. Prog. Brain Res. **207**, 403–434 (2013)
16. Hindin, S.B., Zelinski, E.M.: Extended practice and aerobic exercise interventions benefit untrained cognitive outcomes in older adults: a meta-analysis. J. Am. Geriatr. Soc. **60**(1), 136–141 (2012)
17. Ream, D., Tourgeman, I.: Cognitive Science, Encyclopedia of Evolutionary Psychological Science, pp. 1–7. Springer International Publishing, New York (2020)
18. Guggari, S., Nagendra, H., Desai, S.R., Umadevi, V.: Future of cognitive science. Cogn. Inf. Comput. Model. Cogn. Sci. 119–131 (2020)
19. Nouri, A., Mehrmohammadi, M.: Defining the boundaries for neuroeducation as a field of study. Educ. Res. J. **27**(1/2), 1 (2012)
20. Nouri, A.: The basic principles of research in neuroeducation studies. Int. J. Cogn. Res. Sci. Eng. Educ. **4**(1), 59–66 (2016)
21. De Smedt, B., Ansari, D., Grabner, R.H., Hannula-Sormunen, M., Schneider, M., Verschaffel, L.: Cognitive neuroscience meets mathematics education: it takes two to tango. Educ. Res. Rev. **6**(3), 232–237 (2011)
22. Sachdeva, A., Kumar, K., Anand, K.S.: Non pharmacological cognitive enhancers–current perspectives. J. Clin. Diagn. Res. **9**(7), VE01–VE06 (2015)
23. Willis, S.L., et al.: Long-term effects of cognitive training on everyday functional outcomes in older adults. JAMA **296**(23), 2805–2814 (2006)
24. Swanson, H.L.: Word problem solving, working memory and serious math difficulties: do cognitive strategies really make a difference? J. Appl. Res. Mem. Cogn. **5**(4), 368–383 (2016)
25. Castellar, E.N., All, A., De Marez, L., Van Looy, J.: Cognitive abilities, digital games and arithmetic performance enhancement: a study comparing the effects of a math game and paper exercises. Comput. Educ. **85**, 123–133 (2015)
26. Anguera, J.A., et al.: Video game training enhances cognitive control in older adults. Nature **501**(7465), 97–101 (2013)
27. Mishra, J., Anguera, J.A., Gazzaley, A.: Video games for neuro-cognitive optimization. Neuron **90**(2), 214–218 (2016)
28. Libertus, M.E., et al.: The impact of action video game training on mathematical abilities in adults. AERA Open **3**(4), 1–13 (2017)

Author Index